How ISLAM PLANS to CHANGE the WORLD

How ISLAM PLANS to CHANGE the WORLD

william **wagner**

Kregel
Publications

How Islam Plans to Change the World

© 2004 by William Wagner

Published by Kregel Publications, a division of Kregel, Inc., P.O. Box 2607, Grand Rapids, MI 49501.

All photos are provided by International Mission Board, Southern Baptist Convention. Used by permission.

Appendix C: "Distribution of Muslim Populations by Nation-State" is from *The Muslim Alamanc,* by Azim A. Nangi. The Gale Group Co. 1996. New York. Reprinted by permission of The Gale Group.

All English-language interpretations of the *Qur'an* are from *Al-Qur'an: A Contemporary Translation*. Translated by Ahmed Ali. Princeton, N.J.: Princeton University Press, 2001.

Unless otherwise indicated, Scripture quotations are from the *Holy Bible, New International Version®*. NIV®. © 1973, 1978, 1984 by International Bible Society. Used by permission of Zondervan Publishing House. All rights reserved.

Scripture quotations marked GNT are from the *Good News Translation, Second Edition*. Copyright © 1992 American Bible Society. Used by permission. All rights reserved.

Library of Congress Cataloging-in-Publication Data
Wagner, William.
   How Islam plans to change the world / by William Wagner.
     p. cm.
   Includes bibliographical references and index.
     1. Islam—Controversial literature. 2. Islam—Relations—Christianity. 3. Christianity and other religions—Islam.
I. Title.
BT1170.W34   2004
297.7—dc22   2004009618

ISBN 0-8254-3965-5

To my wonderful wife,
Sally,
and our two precious children,
Mark and Candice.
All have helped greatly during our thirty
years on the mission field.

Contents

Foreword

A dramatic gap in our understanding of world religions was recently exposed. Since September 11, 2001, Islam—the world's second largest religion after Christianity—has come under the spotlight of social, political, and religious scrutiny. For Western nations, gaining an understanding of this Middle Eastern religion has been an elusive pursuit. Vast worldview differences have, by and large, prevented political and religious dialogue from taking place. Instead, colonial categories were applied to interpret the clash of our cultures.

At last the obvious can be ignored no longer: *Islam is in search of world dominance* . . . a fact consistent with Islamic theology and worldview. The West, cast in the mold of its Judeo-Christian worldview, is left to conclude that it is viewed as competition for world dominance.

In this book, Dr. William Wagner gives us helpful insights into Islam, drawing from the *Qur'an* and referencing Islamic spokesmen who have taken good advantage of the new media prominence to promote their faith in the West. All are "in search of a friendly face" for Islam as it meets the West on the platform of human history. Dr. Wagner's many years of overseas experience in Europe as well as in the Middle East, along with his role as a distinguished professor, qualify him as a witness and a scholar in pursuit of understanding what is behind the clash of Muslim and Judeo-Christian based cultures and worldviews.

This book, more than any I know, speaks forthrightly to the issues that precipitated the horrors of the World Trade Center attacks, and that continue to affect world events. Exposing Islamic missionary strategies, defining *jihad* (or holy war) initiatives, addressing issues of democratic failure, speaking to global expansion realities—all are part of the discussion. For some, the phrase "the truth hurts" will take on new meaning as you read this. But ignoring the facts that have led to this historical clash and contemporary challenge would be even more painful. In this matter, too, it is correct to say, as Jesus did, "And you will know the truth, and the truth will set you free" (John 8:32).

Open marketplace discussion, with a plea for peace and love to prevail, is a worthy goal to pursue. To that end, I commend this book to you for your understanding.

—Dr. J. Ray Tallman
Director and Professor
David and Faith Kim School of Intercultural Studies
Golden Gate Baptist Theological Seminary

Preface

The "Clash of Civilizations" was an expression popularized in Samuel P. Huntington's article in the summer of 1993 in the journal *Foreign Affairs*. Since then, many have spoken about the possible coming conflict between the Christian-oriented West led by the United States and the Islamic world with its center of influence permeating from the Middle East. Interaction between these two culturally different societies could present the world with continuing conflict, which would include terrorism, suicide bombings, and even the possibility of nuclear weapons.

The attacks on September 11, 2001, seemed to testify to the fact that the official beginning of the "clash" has already occurred. Despite numerous warning signs over the past several decades, many were caught off guard and still are not sure what will come of the new world situations.

I am assuming that there is a real danger of the clash becoming more and more of a reality in the future. Coming events could radically change the relationship between these two global world blocs. My purpose is not to try to explain the problems of such an impending conflict, nor is it to explain the religion of Islam to the Western reader. Rather, the premise is simple: Islam is a world religion with a well-defined culture and a developed strategy for

11

taking control of the world. This is not meant to be a condemnation of Islam since most Christian missionaries have a similar rallying cry, "We will win the world to Christ." It is not wrong to desire to seek a world unified under one set of beliefs. However, it is necessary to understand that the expansion of Islam has a planned growth strategy and one that is well orchestrated.

I am simply presenting what is now happening in the Christian-Islamic encounter and combining the contemporary events with writings from both the secular press and Islamic writers. In doing this, it is clear that Islam's growth is not by accident but, rather, is a part of a loose strategy that is based upon the *Qur'an* and has its center in Mecca.

I use the phrase "loose strategy" because many Muslims who are actively involved in the proclamation of Islam are not aware of how they fit into the overall plan. Because Islam is growing so rapidly, there is a spontaneity to its growth that defies explanation, but when closely studied it becomes apparent that there is a strategy. The average person will not be able to find a master document that forms the basis of this strategy. Rather, there are numerous capable Islamic strategists who are articulating their faith's strategies and working toward a desired end.

Islamic leaders are well aware of Christian missiological methods and strategies, and they have borrowed what they feel will help them to achieve their ultimate aim. The best article I have read on the subject of contextualization—putting the desired message into the cultural context of the hearer—came from the *Muslim World League Journal,* published in Mecca. This article (as well as others) shows that Muslims are strategically mature in their understanding of what it takes for a religious group to grow.

In analyzing the Muslim strategy, I have come to the conclusion that they have a three-pronged plan, which is as follows: *jihad* (holy war), *Da'wah* (missions), and mosques (presence). In the writings of the many Muslim scholars and strategists, I could not find mention of their dividing up their strategy into these three methods. This trinitarian definition of methodology is mine. However, I did find that several Islamic writers explain the concept of three levels of work. Generally speaking, they could be classified as *Micro* (work with individuals and local groups), *Metta* (work with large groups and institutions), and *Macro* (work that attempts to change a whole society and its thinking). Each of these is covered in more detail throughout the book.

My intent in this book is not to condemn Muhammad or Islam as a religion, but to show how this religion plans to take over the world. Both successes and failures are listed.

It is not always easy to write a book on Islam. The difficulty is not in the writing itself but, rather, in the results that might come from the finished work. Take for example a recent book that appeared in Germany under the title *War in Our Cities*. It was written by Udo Ulfkotte, an investigative reporter for one of Germany's most respected newspapers. In the book, he identifies and explains how extreme Muslims are working in Germany to try to undermine the government. Germans bought the book, in such great quantities that it went on the top-ten best-sellers list in that country. Problems arose when the author had to contend with numerous lawsuits and certain Muslim organizations tried to get the book banned in Germany. The author also received many threats. Other authors who have written about the political side of Islam have experienced similar pseudo-persecution.

When I began this book I was well aware of the likely consequences. In the past, because of my work with Muslims in both Europe and the Middle East, unknown critics have sent me threatening letters. One, postmarked from Saudi Arabia, mentioned that the names and schools of my children were known, and if I did not cease my work with their people, all in my family would be in danger. It is important that those of us in the Western world take this clash of civilizations seriously. The Muslims certainly do.

In the June 30, 2002, issue of *Time* magazine, an article titled "Under Cover" reported about Christians who were working to proclaim Christianity in the Muslim world. At the start of the article the following statement was made: "Throughout this article, for the safety of missionaries working in potentially hostile environments or returning to them, pseudonyms are used. They will be indicated on first usage by quotation marks. Many locations will also be omitted."

The necessity of protecting people working in the Muslim world is very real. Often in this book I have given stories of real people working in real places. Generally, I have recorded the story but have not given detailed information. From an academic standpoint, this is not correct, but the topic demands that security issues be respected. As well, I have received important information in many discussions with Islamic leaders. Such persons have been quoted without any identifying documentation. Again, this is due to the sensitive nature of the topic.

Arabic words such as *jihad* and *Da'wah* form the basis of this book. These and many other Arabic words and phrases are used. Some Arabic words have such wide usage in the West that the English dictionary defines them as if they were English. Generally speaking, words that are defined in a recognized English dictionary are not italicized in this book and treated as foreign words. For the sake of simplicity, however, I have chosen to italicize all Arabic words. The glossary at the back of the book will help the reader to understand their meanings. Because of the richness of the Arabic language, it is not always easy to give short definitions to every word, but at least an attempt has been made to help the reader understand some of the basic concepts of each term.

The world is now in a period of unsettledness. The 2003 war in Iraq has given the world a good picture of the chaos and confusion that could possibly be ahead. Many are saying that it was a mistake for the United States to go into a country so far away from home, only to lose so many of our brightest and best. This war was not about oil, but as Thomas Friedman says, "This is a war over ideas and values and governance." He adds, "In short, America's opponents know just what's at stake in the postwar struggle for Iraq, which is why they flock there: Beat America's ideas in Iraq and you beat them out of the whole region; lose to America there, lose everywhere." The war is just a microcosm of the larger problem facing the world as Islam spreads around the globe. The continuing wars and acts of terrorism are a result of the unfolding conflict between Islam and the West. Many Muslim leaders feel that it is Allah's will that the whole world accept Islam. This is the seed of the problem.

An important aspect of the discussion about the "Clash of Civilizations" is the expansion not only of radical Islam, but also of Islam as a whole. If Islam were to succeed in its bid to create one global Islamic state, would it be a radical or a moderate form of this religion? This should be a concern of all who live in the West.

At the end of the book, I have tried to show possible scenarios of the final results from the "Clash of Civilizations." In playing the role of a futurist, I find that it is very difficult to be exact. As a believing Christian, however, I am convinced that the world is moving rapidly toward a final climax. I see the situation being so acute that we could easily be living in the last days. The description of exact events preceding the end must be left to others who specialize in that area of theology.

The Bible does state, "For false Christs and false prophets will appear and perform great signs and miracles to deceive even the elect—if that were possible" (Matthew 24:24). On the positive side, Jesus also said that "this gospel of the kingdom will be preached in the whole world as a testimony to all nations, and then the end will come" (Matthew 24:14).

Some might read this book and feel alarmed, but the real antidote for the problems before us is clear-cut: We should become much more active in living out our Christian faith and in proclaiming the truth as found in Jesus Christ. Together, let's dedicate our lives anew to those all-important tasks.

Acknowledgments

The preparation and writing of a book such as this entails many years of work. It could not have been written without the help and encouragement of many of my associates as well as those in my family. I want to thank Sally, my wife, and my two children, Candice and Mark, who lived with me during the eighteen years that I was associated with Muslims in Europe and the Middle East. Their support has been invaluable.

After my retirement from the mission field, I was given the wonderful opportunity of being the professor of missions at Golden Gate Baptist Theological Seminary. Many of my students helped with the research for this book while taking my courses on Islam. I am grateful to them for their help and prayers. Also, the faculty at the seminary helped to provide a working environment that allowed me to research and write this manuscript. Others have read the manuscript and given many valuable suggestions. Three people I would like to mention are Dr. Ray Tallman, my esteemed colleague; Dr. Ray Register, a former missionary to Muslims in the Middle East; and Dr. John Landers, a well-respected leader in Christian publishing. All three have been a great help.

Stephen Barclift and Jim Weaver from Kregel Publications have given me both valuable advice and encouragement during the final phases of publishing this book. Additional help was also provided by

Renée and David Sanford, Sanford Communications, Inc., Portland, Oregon.

Much of the typing and work on the format was accomplished by my longtime coworker Alice Webb. Also helping in this area was my teaching assistant Jeff Summers. Many others have made smaller contributions, but each one has added valuable content to the finished product.

chapter one

Don't Panic

Islam's Plans for World Dominance

I t was a normal summer day in Central Asia. Several of my colleagues and I were scheduled to take a flight from Alma Ata in
Kazakhstan to Moscow. The airport was crowded, the smell was sti-
fling, and confusion seemed to be the rule of the day.

Our flight was supposed to take off at 8 A.M., but, as usual, we
were informed that it would be late. After waiting for eight hours
and still not knowing when or if we would leave, we boarded the
plane. It was packed not only with people but also with various
packages and suitcases of many sizes and shapes. Most were piled in
the aisles.

As our plane rolled to the runway, we all felt that we had finally
crossed the last hurdle. The Boeing 727 of Trans-Aero Airlines began
its takeoff, but just before we rose into the air, there was a loud explosion under the wing. A tire blowout! The pilot tried to get the plane
airborne, but ten seconds later there was a second explosion as the
second tire on that same side also gave way.

As the plane was shaking terribly and swerving to and fro on the
runway, one person was heard to cry out, "Don't panic! Don't panic!"
Those instructions seemed strange at a time like that! Only in frightening situations do people ever cry out, "Don't panic!"

Thankfully, the pilot was able to get the aircraft under control and bring it to a stop. We disembarked, only to have to wait for two more days in Alma Ata.

After the horrific attacks of September 11, 2001, many were heard to say: "Don't panic! Don't panic!" Many were asking themselves how these warlike events could be happening in a peaceful, advanced society like America. As leaders tried to understand the chemistry of what had taken place, it seemed that some unknown forces were at play that made life different from the way it was the day before.

What were these forces that made the world sit up and take notice? Certain names and concepts now were on the lips of thinking people. Suddenly, average Americans were talking about Osama bin Laden, *jihad*, Muslim extremism, the Taliban, and so forth. New words and new ideas were now forming the basis of coffee table discussions.

A new day had dawned. Muslim extremism was now recognized as a more powerful force than most had imagined. It seemed like only yesterday that Christians and Muslims stood shoulder to shoulder when the Berlin Wall came down. Both saw Marx's brand of atheism as an enemy of monotheism, and both saw a brighter day ahead. Faith had won out over disbelief. Christians felt that their ideas of individualism, liberalism, constitutionalism, human rights, equality, liberty, the rule of law, democracy, free markets, and the separation of church and state were now the norm, but suddenly another force had raised its head— one that was in total opposition to their basic belief patterns.

September 11 could best be described as "the twenty-first century shot heard around the world." What happened in just one short day was the start of a new relationship between Islam and the West. "Don't panic" seemed to be the cry, not only because of the terrible events of 9/11 but also because of the realization that a clash of civilizations was now much more visible than ever before.

Many woke up to the fact that the attack was not an isolated event but part of a well-planned and highly financed movement that has a desire to dominate the world. In the year 2000, bin Laden announced the formation of the World Islamic Front for the *jihad* against Jews and Crusaders (bin Laden's term for Christians)—an umbrella group of radical movements across the Muslim world. He issued a *fatwa* stating that it is the duty of all Muslims to kill United States citizens and their allies.

Also, it has been publicized that Islam is the second largest and fastest growing religion in the world, numbering between one billion and 1.3 billion—about one-fifth of the population of the world. Many areas of the world have regional conflicts, such as Jews versus Palestinians, Hindus versus Muslims in Kashmir, and Russians versus Muslims in Chechnya. Are all of these related, or should they be seen only as separate occurrences in world history? After taking a closer look, it is apparent that there is a worldwide conspiracy for world dominance by Islam.

Understanding both the history and the dynamics of the conspiracy might help us. A simple explanation for the problem is not possible since there are political, cultural, economical, sociological, and religious implications. One writer, John Esposito, has stated that, in light of 9/11, we in the West must ask three questions:

1. Is there a clash of civilizations between Islam and the West?
2. Why do they hate us?
3. Is there a direct connection between Islam, anti-Americanism, and global terror?[1]

These questions, taken with the many facts before us, are reasons for concern. Attempts will be made to address all three in this book.

The growth of the Muslim population in the West and particularly in America has been both silent and alarming. Between 1989 and 1999, the Muslim population grew by more than 100 percent in Europe, to fourteen million (2 percent of the population), and in America by 25 percent. There are one thousand five hundred mosques in Germany, and five million Muslims in France. The number of the followers of Muhammad in the rest of the European Union is between twelve and fifteen million.[2]

Many believe that Islam will be the second largest religion in America by 2015. The number of participants in American mosques has increased by more than 75 percent during the past five years and there are now more than one thousand two hundred mosques in the United States.[3] Islam is definitely on the rise.

From a worldwide perspective, it is also interesting to note that according to a United Nations demographic report, Muslims will represent at least half of the global birthrate after the year 2055.[4] Islam's rapid growth gives us new impetus to ask, "What strategy is Islam employing to facilitate such growth?"

ISLAM'S BASIC STRATEGY

While living in Germany, I had a long discussion with a Muslim leader from that country. He stated, "Islam's race to win the world was detoured for about four hundred years, but now it is back on track to achieve our ultimate goal—the setting up of a world-wide *ummah*."[5]

One school of thought founded in 1953 by Sheik Taqiuddlin an Nabhani states, "Muslims nowadays live in *Dar-al-Kufr* (the world of infidels). To them this is intolerable, and the only solution to the problem is for Muslims to reestablish the *Khalifah* or Islamic State."[6] According to this school of thought, the Islamic state does not yet exist in the world since *Khalifah* is one large Islamic state, ruled by a single leader (called a *caliph*) without national boundaries. Just as the founders of communism felt that world conquest by Marxism was inevitable, so do many Islamic scholars and politicians feel that the depravity of the West, coupled with the dynamism of Islam, will provide for a worldwide Islamic state in the future.

One well-known strategist was Ayatollah Khomeini of Iran. During his years of exile (supposedly supported by the French government), he developed the strategy that was so successful in bringing about revolution in his homeland. Literally hundreds of thousands of his taped sermons advocating an Islamic revolution flooded the country. His overthrow of the well-established Shah has been studied by many as an example of how a religious revolution against a contemporary secular government can be accomplished. It was common knowledge in Iran that Khomeini had as his goal a five-stage plan. It was as follows:

Step 1: The overthrow of the Shah and the establishment of an Islamic Republic in Iran.

Step 2: Encouraging the creation of Islamic Republics in the surrounding Muslim countries either by revolution, war, or negotiations (thus the war against Iraq).

Step 3: The defeat of Israel.

Step 4: The Islamic takeover of Europe.

Step 5: The fall of the Great Satan (United States of America) as the last step in the creation of a worldwide Islamic *ummah.*

Khomeini was one of the more important influences in the Islamic strategy. Some have said that only the *Wahabi Sunnis* have taken a hard-line position, but Khomeini, a *Shiite,* was probably the ultimate revolutionary leader. President Jimmy Carter's ambassador to Tehran reported that Ayatollah Khomeini was a "twentieth century saint." It is said that Carter himself, being a religious man, felt that it would be possible to deal with him. History has clearly shown that this was a wrong assumption. As we look at Khomeini's plans for world dominance, it is interesting to see what he thought of the West. Here is a quote from Khomeini:

> Those who know nothing of Islam pretend that Islam counsels against war. Those who say this are witless. Islam says, "Kill all the Unbelievers" just as they would kill you. Islam says, "Kill them, put them to the sword and scatter their armies." Islam says, "Kill in the service of Allah." Whatever good there exists is thanks to the sword, and the shadow of the sword. People cannot be made obedient except by the sword. The sword is the key of Paradise, which can only be opened for Holy Warriors.[7]

In reading Khomeini's *Islamic Government,* one has a tendency to compare it to Adolph Hitler's *Mein Kampf.* Both state clearly their grand ideas of world conquest, but people today do not take such writings seriously. The key difference between the two is that Hitler was an atheist while Khomeini claimed to be a man of God.

Another so-called twentieth-century saint, the Mullah Muhammad Taqi Sabzevari, who also worked in Iran, was quoted as saying:

> Allah has promised that the day will come when the whole of mankind will live united under the banner of Islam, when the sign of the Crescent, the symbol of Muhammad, will be supreme everywhere. But the day must be hastened through our *jihad*, through our readiness to offer our lives and to shed the unclean blood of those who do not see the light brought from the heavens by Muhammad. . . . The Satanic rulers must be brought down and put to death.[8]

It is no wonder that large numbers of Muslims claim to be international revolutionaries. They form an important part of the Muslim global strategy.

In the past few years various strategies have been proposed by either Muslim clerics or organizations. Some go as far as even listing which of America's fifty states will be the first to become Islamic. On one list Michigan was given this honor. It is not so foolish as one might think, since one well-known Christian demographer, Jim Slack, the director of research for the International Mission Board of the Southern Baptist Convention, stated that in the year 2000 more than 50 percent of the population of Detroit proper was Islamic or of Islamic background. He also mentioned that Washington, D.C., and London, England, were not far behind.[9] A news report from the Voice of America stated, "Dearborn, Michigan is said to have the largest population of Muslims of any American community. Other cities with large Muslim populations are New York, Los Angeles, and Chicago."[10]

When we look at the military scene, we are appalled. Among the nine largest purchases of arms in the world since 1983, four were by Arab states: Iraq, Saudi Arabia, Libya, and Egypt.[11] Most of the Arab states have twice as many of their people in military service as Western countries have in theirs. Recently on television, Benjamin Netanyahu, the former prime minister of Israel, stated that the day would come when the West must fight against the Arab world. If it is now, it will be easier, but if we wait, it will be much more difficult since they are gaining military strength every day. Weapons of mass destruction are not far away for several Muslim states.

Some have said that 15 percent of all Muslims are sympathizers of extreme Islam. How many Muslims in America would fit into this category? What would happen if hundreds of thousands of soldiers from a foreign power invaded the United States? A great alarm would be sounded. Americans would be called upon to fight and defend the flag, our country, and our way of life. Yet, many Muslims in America *are* now politically sympathetic with the goals of the *al Qaeda* movement—yet we almost do nothing.

When did the Islamic revolution begin? What are its plans for the future? There has been contact and conflict between the Christian and Islamic worlds since the founding of Islam in A.D. 621. The Golden Age of Islam was said to be between the seventh and the fourteenth centuries. At the end of that period they began to suffer a number of defeats at the hands of Western empires. The era of colonization was then introduced, and the growth of Islam was halted. Some say Islam entered into its own "Dark Ages," similar to our Middle Ages. Their period of enlightenment first began in the twentieth century.

THE NEW DAWN FOR ISLAM (1945–1969)

A little-known fact today is that the Muslim Brotherhood grew up in Egypt in the 1920s as an imitation of European fascism, which itself was a revolt against modernity. In Italy and Germany they were known by their black or brown shirts. In Egypt they had green shirts, which symbolized the Muslim Brotherhood. Fascism failed in Europe but survived in Egypt and spread to other parts of the Islamic world.[12] The influence of this radical movement is still very powerful in Egypt. It became fiercely anti-Western in the 1940s and 1950s under the direction of Sayd Qutb, an Egyptian fundamentalist. This movement was credited with many assassinations, including that of Anwar Sadat.

It was always easy to identify those who belonged to the Brother-hood in the Middle East. In 1983, when I attended a meeting of Bap-tists in Egypt, I and two of my younger colleagues were told that we all had to shave our beards. When we asked for a reason, we were told that in Egypt the only ones who wore beards were members of the Brotherhood.

This movement planted the seeds that were to grow during what Ralph Winters calls *The Twenty-five Unbelievable Years*.[13] No matter how you look at it, the twentieth century was amazing, but no period had more change and more influence on today's problem than did the twenty-five years described by Winters. This was a period that could best be described as "the official end of political imperialism," or better, "the retreat of the West." In his book, Ralph Winters shows that before 1945, 99.5 percent of the non-Western world was under Western domination. By 1969, 99.5 percent of the same area was in-dependent.[14] Political colonialism was ended. Economic, national, and cultural imperialism, however, remained.

Among those countries that experienced this new freedom were the Arab nations that formed the cradle of Islam. Those who talk about the Arab world are talking about the citizens of the states that are members of the Arab League created in 1945. It started with seven states (Egypt, Iraq, Saudi Arabia, Syria, Lebanon, Jordan, and Yemen) and expanded its membership to twenty-two states, including latecomers such as Djibouti, Comoros, and Palestine. Also included are Algeria, Bahrain, Kuwait, Libya, Mauritania, Morocco, Qatar, Somalia, Sudan, Tunisia, and United Arab Emirates.[15] Non-Arab countries such as India, Indonesia, Malaysia, and other countries with large Muslim populations also escaped out from under the thumb of Western colonialism.

The extension of Islam into the West had many sources. Europe still had a residue of Muslims after the Moors were expelled from Spain and the Turks were defeated in the southeastern part of their continent. There continued to be some limited contact in America when Muslims were first brought over as early as 1717 during the Af-rican slave trade period. Years later, Muslims migrated voluntarily to

America in five separate waves from 1875 to 1967. Most of those coming were unskilled Arabs who found work in the larger urban areas of the Northeast and the Great Lakes regions.

During the period of time prior to Winter's closing date of *The Twenty-Five Unbelievable Years*, Muslims seemed to have little or no effect on the society. They either became a part of the "melting pot" or they hid themselves in small groups, so as not to be too conspicuous. The only exception to this was the Nation of Islam among African-Americans, but their form of Islam was so radically different that more orthodox Muslims shunned them.

After 1969, the more orthodox Muslims seemed to fall into one of two groups as described by Larry Polson. He said they were either "offensive-activists Muslims" or "defensive-pacifist Muslims." The "offensive-activist" Muslims usually come from a traditional Islamic country like Saudi Arabia and seek to

> propagate their faith and persuade Americans to abandon their current religious beliefs or secular lifestyle and convert to Islam. Their goals do not always include political conquest, but they refuse to assimilate into American society. The "defensive-pacifist" Muslims are Muslims who have come to America in search of greater economic and political freedom. They have assimilated into American culture and have played a huge role in the establishment of mosques and Islamic institutions for the purpose of helping Muslims preserve their Islamicity in the midst of "Christian" America.[16]

Jane Smith describes it differently, "Many Muslims living in the United States . . . want to assimilate as much as possible into American culture and try not to emphasize elements of their identity that would differentiate them from others."[17] She goes on to add, "Others do not want to relate too closely with the West but prefer what they refer to as the 'real Islam.'"[18] The end of colonization and the new world order now gave Muslims a new identity and a readiness to re-dream their original dream of world domination.

Muslim countries were now also free to determine their own religious future but still had to work under the constraints of cultural and economic imperialism. Radical Islam grew under these ripe conditions. The West was blamed for the lack of a better life as radicals took the moral high ground. The fact that most of the new developing countries established dictatorships actually helped fundamentalists, even when those leaders drew in the reins out of fear of a revolutionary takeover.

In Islamic thinking, the failures of the past or present can be blamed on economic oppression by the West and Christianity in general. Fatema Mernissi, a Muslim, stated, "Today few Arab heads of State would dream of a . . . [large] scale solution to the problems of unemployment and instability; their solution would more likely be to send an army into the streets or to imprison the rioters."[19]

I would add "or to declare a *jihad* against the West to divert the criticism." If the new nations did not flourish economically with their newly gained freedoms, Islam as a religion did.

As early as the 1950s, the situation in America began to change. There was an influx of a new type of Muslim. The new immigrants were better educated, and they came to live in the "land of freedom" because of the higher standard of living. Many had studied in America and grew to genuinely love their new homeland. Elisabeth Silddiqui says of this period:

> . . . There was the formation of the early Muslim communities and mosques in such places as Detroit, Ann Arbor, Gary [Indiana], Cedar Rapids [Iowa], Sacramento and the like. Visiting scholars and missionary groups from the Middle East and the Indo-Pakistan subcontinent also began to arrive. And Islam began, in a very slow manner, to gain adherents among white Americans.[20]

This was also a time when the Muslim population of America began to look for their roots. They began to have conferences, find places to worship, and create organizations that could help them live as a people in a Western world. New national Islamic groups such as the Muslim Students Association of the United States and Canada began to spring up. Even in the small town of Abique, New Mexico, there was the creation of a large training center for Islam. Many Muslims began to find their way back into the faith they had previously seen as dormant. Now a new dynamic was introduced into the community. For the first time Americans had to face the fact that the existence of Islam in their country was a reality.

Meanwhile in the home area of Islam, the newly founded countries of the Middle East began to see a growth of a more fundamental Islam—following the lead of the Egyptian Muslim Brotherhood. Other groups formed. The mixture of weak economies, oppressive governments, and frustration drove many back to their faith, one that allowed them to use might to find fulfillment, if necessary. The radical groups set up terror networks that distilled a host of economic, cultural, and political problems into a concentrated toxin of hatred aimed at Western cultures and their perceived flagship, America.

Many in the West saw this movement toward fundamentalism as only a small sect of Islam. However, in an article in *Newsweek* dated October 15, 2001, a Muslim leader, Fareed Zakaria, said, "To say that *al Qaeda* is a fringe group may be reassuring, but it is false. The problem is not that Osama bin Laden believes that this is a religious war against America. It's that millions of people across the Islamic world seem to agree."[21]

Around the globe new movements gave hope for Muslims living in poor conditions. From Indonesia to Nigeria a new enthusiasm emerged out of the former colonial, secular societies. The awakening appeared not only in the historic Islamic homelands but in all countries where the followers of Muhammad lived. The groundwork for September 11 had been laid.

THE DEATH OF THE WEST

While this new vibrancy in Muhammad's religion was growing, the Christian foundation of the West was taking a beating. Patrick

Buchanan, in his controversial book, *The Death of the West*, outlined how America and the West were losing the cultural wars. Buchanan wrote:

> The West is dying. Its nations have ceased to reproduce, and their populations have stopped growing and begun to shrink. Not since the Black Death carried off a third of Europe in the fourteenth century has there been a graver threat to the survival of Western civilization.[22]

Among the threats to our present day society are (1) secularism, (2) immigration, (3) ethnic population decline, and last but not least, (4) Islam. Buchanan gives a convincing argument for the secularism of the West. It is a secularism that tends to disapprove of the Christian heritage of the West, with the separation of church and state— once a strong Baptist issue—now being used to rid the society of all remnants of its Christian heritage. Through the courts of the land and the media, a concerted attack is being made against the very soul of the West. It was an unprecedented attack against a faith that had stood for two thousand years.

It would appear that this decline of Christianity in the West has paralleled the rise of Islam in the West. In Europe, the death of the church is much more advanced, as is the rise of Islam. In America the process is more inhibited by a lingering faith. Buchanan and others have asked the question, "Where is the sense of outrage?" As the battle unfurls, the church seems to be silent. Buchanan quotes Jim Nelson Black as writing:

> But one of the greatest reasons for the decline of American society over the past century has been the tendency of Christians who have practical solutions to abandon the forum at the first sign of resistance. Evangelicals in particular have been quick to run and slow to stand by their beliefs. In reality, most Christians have already vacated "the public square" of moral and political debate by their own free will, long before

civil libertarians and others came forth to drive us back to our churches.[23]

What is the major problem facing the West? James Kurth, in *The American Way of Victory,* contends: "The real clash of civilizations will not be between the West and one or more of the rest. It will be between the West and post-West within the West itself. This clash has already taken place within the brain of Western Civilization, the American intellectual class. It is now spreading from that brain to other body politic."[24]

While some see the major clash as being between Islam and the Christian West, I see that in reality there are three entities, each fighting against the other. The first two are already recognized as Islam and the Christian West. I dare to add a third—secularism. Christianity views this humanistic form of thought as a problem. Islam sees the resulting atheism as a residue of Western nonbelief that erodes Islamic influence with both Western Muslims as well as those in the predominately Islamic countries. Television, the Internet, radio, and international travel all seem to present a threat to their faith. The faith-based entities see humanistic secularism as a nonoption in their plans to win the world for their faith. The reason is obvious. Secularism preaches the oneness of man and the idea of pluralism but detests any group that claims to hold the true faith including Islam and Christianity. As the two largest religions of the world seek to further their own goals, they must keep a close eye on the third.

The second threat to the West is the mass migration of peoples, which has gained in intensity over the past twenty years. The world is going through a demographic change of a magnitude never before seen. People of many nations and tribes seeking a better way of life are invading the more affluent countries of North America and Europe. Uncontrolled immigration threatens to change the West at its very core. Muslims do not always desire to become a part of the new chosen land. For a variety of reasons (which we will look at later), many prefer to remain distant and distinct. I find it ironic that those from the Islamic cultures want to come to the West because of the failure of their own system, yet at the same time seek to impose their failed system upon the West.

Americans are growing more concerned about the problem. Many Americans now want immigration reduced, and others want English to be America's official language. The remainder are human secularists who see a union of people as the salvation for mankind (with a liberal agenda, of course).

Europe is in a more difficult situation. It now has immigrants trying to enter into it from the south, east, and west. Today, many of the socialist led governments (such as in Belgium, Netherlands, France, Austria, and Germany) are in danger of falling because of their unqualified support for immigration. Only recently has there been an outcry from the far right for immigration reform. These governments are now changing and demanding laws that limit the numbers that can come into the country. Immigration is changing the face of many countries, and many of the immigrants are Muslims. In France it has been said that more Muslims participate in weekly religious services than do Roman Catholics and Protestants combined.

The decline of the ethnic (European) population is also a great concern. Today, it is as difficult to find a Western nation where the native population is not declining as it is to find an Islamic nation where the native population is not exploding. Secularization and the "good life" have presented us with a new problem. A combination of an extremely high number of abortions, the desire for higher economic security, and a better standard of living often hinders the formation of large families. Muslim families are generally two, three, or four times larger than non-Muslim families in the West.

The growth of Islam and the changing immigration patterns were seen as a positive aspect of a free global society simply trying to find itself. Many uttered soothing words about the positive aspects of political and religious pluralism. On September 11, many began to wake up and notice the dangers within pluralism. All acknowledged that the West was not at war with Islam, but it seemed clear that Islam was at war with the West.

THE CLASH OF CIVILIZATIONS

In the summer of 1993, *Foreign Affairs* published an article written by the highly respected Samuel Huntington, which created a world-wide debate. It warned that a clash between Western culture and Islam would dominate global politics. Huntington followed up on the article by writing a book titled *The Clash of Civilizations and the Remaking of World Order.* He does not see much possibility of a cordial cohabitation of Islam and the West. He writes that people are trying to define themselves and find their cause to serve. He states, "Religion is a central, perhaps the central, force that motivates and mobilizes people."[25]

Huntington is aware that the fault line between Islam and the West is not the world's only major problem. He identifies eight distinctive civilizations: Islamic, Sinic (centered on the "core state" of China), Western (with the United States as its core), Orthodox (with Russia as its core), Japanese, Hindu, Latin American, and (somewhat tentatively) African. He says that divisions between each of these civilizations could be problematic. The major players in the forthcoming struggle are Islam and the Christian West. In a review of the Huntington book, A. J. Bacevich stated:

> Huntington does not attribute the West's recent difficulties with Islam to the influence of a handful of fanatics. The underlying problem for the West is not Islamic fundamentalism, it is Islam. A different civilization whose people are convinced of the superiority of their culture and are obsessed with the inferiority of their power.[26]

Have politicians and analysts defined the current crisis accurately? Some describe the struggle as between democratic and nondemocratic forms of government. In theory, Islam is an inherently political religion. As well as being the bearer of divine revelation, the prophet Muhammad founded a political state. Those who followed him were primarily political leaders and heads of governments and empires rather than pious religious leaders. It is interesting to note that few of the Muslim states in the world are truly democratic. All of the Arab states seem to have a leader for life. When Hosni Mubarak of Egypt was asked if he was ready to allow free elections in his country, he answered that he had spent his entire life preparing to serve his people and he would be letting them down by not leading.

For Huntington, the concept of religion is extremely important since it signifies "who we are" and "who we are not." Many see the fault lines of the next conflict as geographical, but neither Islam nor Christianity fits into this category. The problem today is not a clash of governments or cultures but rather of civilizations—which include governments and cultures. Increasingly, it is a clash of religions. Both Islam and Christianity now have adherents in all the countries of the world and are actively seeking to increase their numbers. Huntington refers to the global aspects of both religions as "an inter-civilizational phenomenon." Both faiths continue to be vibrant and alive. The coming conflict will be between these two world religions and their related cultures.

THE AMERICAN *Jihad*

At the beginning of this new century, most Americans felt that they were secure. Communism had been defeated, the economy was strong, and there was, after all, only one real world power—the United States of America. But when New York's twin towers fell, this security began to unravel. For the first time, many began to see Islam as a threat. Most, however, had little or no idea of what Islam was and what Muslims believed.

After that fateful day in September, many Americans from foreign countries began to bear the brunt of persecution or were looked upon with suspicion when they boarded a plane. Among them were Hindus and Sikhs. Because they wore different types of clothing or hats, they were viewed as Muslims, but they also had their own problems with Muslims.

Many assumed that the new situation would be a distraction for

Islam in its goal of converting America, but the opposite was true. When isolated instances of persecution occurred, many rushed to the side of those being threatened and harmed. This was to be expected since it is the American (and I might add, the Christian) way. What was not apparent was that the Muslims capitalized on the situation and made great gains in making their faith known to the American people. Americans were asking, "What is Islam?"

Mosques in America were put on the alert, and many of them immediately began to have open houses and public meetings so that they could explain what Islam teaches. Letters were sent to mosques telling their people how to take advantage of the events. I went to one of these meetings and was amazed to hear that Islam was a religion of love, peace, and forgiveness. The speaker distanced himself and his mosque from the evil events of destruction while promoting the positive aspects of his belief. It worked. Many mosques reported large numbers of Americans converted to Islam after 9/11.

Democratic America has been an excellent breeding ground for not only Islam as a religion but also for radical Islam. As the FBI and the CIA began to search for terrorist cells, they found numerous Muslim organizations with varying ties to radicals. In his book *American Jihad,* Steven Emerson gives a fascinating description of the various Muslim organizations now operating in America and their ties with various terrorist organizations. The political freedom afforded in this country gives a convenient cover to those who seek the establishment of a global Islamic state.

The key to understanding the link between Islam as a religion and the terrorist movement now dominating the news is to understand the *Wahabi* movement. Emerson quotes Sheik Muhammad Hisham Kabbani who spoke to an open forum at the United States State Department on January 7, 1999. Kabbani stated:

> The man who brought it to the tribes was a Muslim scholar by the name of Muhammad ibn Abd al-Wahhab. This was in the Eastern part of what we call Saudi Arabia during the seventeenth and eighteenth century. These ideas were going

forth and back. Sometimes they were put down and other times they were supported. There was a struggle with the Muslims trying to keep them down with the support of the Ottoman Empire. They were successful until the Ottoman Empire dissolved and finished in the middle of 1920 and the new regime came—it was the secular régime of Mustafa Kemal (Ataturk). They then found an opportunity in the tribes, which no longer had the support of the Ottoman Empire in that area. They had freedom to go and change the ideas and brainwash the minds of the Muslims in this area. Slowly, in the many years from 1920 until today they were very successful in establishing a new ideology in Islam that is very extremist in its point of view. It was not so militant (at first), however; it didn't take the form of militancy, but it took the form of revival or renewal of Islamic tradition.[27]

Wahabism was the religion of the al-Saud family when they unified the tribes of the Arabian Peninsula in the 1930s and seized power, establishing the kingdom of Saudi Arabia. They are very orthodox and puritanical in their theology and tend toward a form of Islamic militancy that advocates reform through the use of the sword. Some have even stated that the religion of all of Saudi Arabia is *Wahabism*. It is no wonder that Osama bin Laden considers himself an adherent of this movement. Perhaps the most disconcerting part of this is that Saudi Arabia is taking the lead in the worldwide missionary work of Islam. Together with its seemingly unlimited economic strength and its religious fervor, this is where the main threat to the West lies.

Stephen Schwartz, author of *The Two Faces of Islam*, says we should not be alarmed by the growth of Islam in the United States but by who controls it. He writes, "I would say billions of dollars have been spent in the United States to advance *Wahabism*. The *Wahabi* sect, backed by Saudi Arabia, controls 70 to 80 percent of the mosques in the United States. That means they control the teaching, the preaching, the literature that's distributed, and they control the training of the *Imams*."[28]

Dale Hurd of CBN News gives another example of this situation. He says, "American Muslim leaders have said they are not under the control of Saudi Arabia because they don't take money from the Saudi government, but only from private Saudi citizens. However, one spokesman admitted to the Associated Press that the 'money does not come free. It always comes with strings attached.'"[29]

Da'wah consists mainly of motivating Muslims to do mission work, and many Muslim missionaries are heavily financed by Saudi sources. The main missions organization is the Muslim World League, which is a worldwide Islamic organization.[30] Since the Saudis finance them, it is natural that they embrace the stricter form of *Wahabism* that is a part of the Saudi society. In his interview with the State Department in 1997, the moderate Sheikh Kabbani made two controversial assertions: "80 percent of all mosques and Muslim charitable organizations in the United States had been taken over by 'extremists' who did not represent the mainstream community; and Osama bin Laden represented an imminent threat to America."[31]

From many different sources I have heard that 80 percent of all *Imams* in the mosques in America are *Wahabis*. My own experience in speaking with many *Imams* has confirmed this assertion. Often I will take a class of students to pay a friendly visit to a mosque. In our dialogue concerning what Islam believes, I often hear words of peace, love, and forgiveness, but when I enter the political realm, I find a completely different atmosphere. Bitterness and hate take the forefront; words that claim a future world conquest for Islam are spoken. At the end of the conversation there is a reverting back to peace, forgiveness, and love. *Wahabism* has made its mark not only on individual faith communities within Islam but on all of America.

In the fall of 2001, there was a strong debate in the halls of Washington, D.C. The question was simply, "Can we trust the Saudis?" In a briefing from the Rand Corporation to a Pentagon advisory board, the briefer charged that "the Saudis are active at every level of the terror chain from planners to financiers, from cadre to foot soldiers, from ideologist to cheerleader."[32] There was an equally strong rebuttal from the Saudi ambassador. He denied that they were to be blamed for all that they were accused of doing. In a sense, both were telling the truth. Those in Washington have been taught to separate religion and politics in their thinking. In the Arab mind these two are one. Those from the Rand commission could look at the heavy financial aid given to groups in America that support terrorism as proof that they are seeking to aid the terrorists and seek the overthrow of democracy. The Saudis see it as a legitimate function of the state to support all Muslim work, no matter what form it takes.

CONCLUSION

The question must still be answered: Is Islam a threat? My experience of working with Muslims both in the Middle East and in the West has shown that the answer is a strong yes. Years before the fall of New York's twin towers, I was saying there were storm clouds ahead. The rain has now begun to fall. I could give many hundreds of examples to support my answer. People have suffered greatly under Islam; some have lost loved ones, others have been beaten or had their homes burned down, and still others have been ambushed while worshiping peacefully in their church. Almost every day in some part of the world, there are news reports of brutalities against non-Muslims by Muslims. Those suffering often tell of the loud cries of *"Allahu akbar"* ("Great is God") shouted by those who perform the evil deeds.

chapter **two**

The Quiet Revolution

Islam's Mission Strategy (Da'wah)

The story of the camel and the Arab is often recited in the Middle East. An Arab was making a long trip across the desert. During the day the heat can be scorching, but at night it can get bitter cold. On one especially cold night, the Arab was in his nice warm tent where some embers kept the environment warm. As the man began to go to sleep, he noticed a large camel nose sticking in under the tent.

"Camel," he said, "why is your nose in my tent?"

"O Master," he replied, "it's so cold out here, and if only my nose were warm, then I could have a good night's sleep."

The Arab thought it over and allowed him to keep his nose in. A little later the man awoke and saw that the camel now had his whole head in the tent. "What are you doing, Camel? You said you only wanted your nose in the tent."

"O Master, you just do not know how cold it is out here, and if my head is in the tent, then I will be satisfied."

After thinking it over, the Arab agreed and he went back to sleep. Once again he was awakened, this time to find that the camel had his head, neck, and two feet in the tent.

"Camel, this is too much. You must stop."

"O Master, now I am really comfortable. I can sleep the whole night through."

"OK," said the Arab, "but this is the last time."

Later in the night the Arab awakened to discover that the tent was now full with the whole body of the camel inside the tent, and the Arab had little room.

"Camel!" he shouted. "What are you doing?"

"Get out of my tent, you stupid Arab," was the camel's reply.

Most Americans see Islam as a threat to the West mainly through *jihad* or holy war. They are not aware that there are actually three easily definable elements in the Muslim world strategy. The three are:

1. *Da'wah*—the Islamic equivalent to Christian missions
2. *Jihad*—holy war
3. The Mosque—their physical presence

The next three chapters will study, in depth, each of these three elements. The first, *Da'wah*, is the same slow but effective method that the camel used to gain possession of the tent.

UNDERSTANDING *Da'wah*

A friend of mine who is the leader of a mosque in Europe says, "You in the West do not use the correct translations of Arabic words." This critique is generally aimed at westerners who use the word *jihad* and call it "holy war." There is some truth that a person who only speaks English has a difficult time understanding the complexities of Arabic. Several years ago a group of linguists concluded that the most difficult languages for a foreigner to learn are Navajo, Arabic, and Mandarin Chinese. Translating from a more complicated language into a simpler one can pose significant problems. This is the case when a native English speaker tries to understand Arabic. It should be added that Muslims feel that Arabic is the heavenly language, and for many years it was prohibited to translate the *Qur'an* into any other language. This prohibition is now gone, but many of the more orthodox schools have problems with the issue.

Da'wah is one of those words that has several valid meanings.

Jane I. Smith, professor of Islamic Studies at Hartford Seminary in Connecticut, in her book *Islam in America,* gives three different definitions for the word. She writes:

1. *"Da'wah* means the active business of the propagation of Islam with the end of making conversions.
2. *"Da'wah* involves the effort to bring those who have fallen away from Islam back to active involvement in the faith.
3. *"Da'wah* means the responsibility to simply live quiet lives of Muslim piety and charity, with the hope that by example they can encourage wayward coreligionists as well as others that Islam is the right and appropriate path to God."[1]

Dr. Ghassan Khalif, president of the Arab Baptist Seminary in Beirut, Lebanon, said, "The two words *ad-Da'wah* mean the invitation, the calling, and/or the vocation."[2] The word *ad* is the article "the." *Da'wah* is a feminine word. The verb form of *Da'wah* is the often used word *Dah'u,* which means to invite or to call.[3] Others have given the meaning "come" to the word. *Da'wah* is the extending of an invitation to come into a close fellowship with Allah through Islam.

Another important word is *daa'i,* which is the nearest Islamic equivalent of the Christian missionary or mission worker. *Daa'i* could be defined as a preacher or a worker for Islam. Since every Muslim is to be a witness to Islam, each member of the faith should be a *daa'i.* This, however, has taken on another significance and is used for those who have felt a definite call to be involved in the work of spreading Islam. A *daa'i* has six different responsibilities. They are:

1. To oneself
2. To one's family
3. To one's neighbors
4. To one's fellow citizens
5. To one's countrymen
6. To one's fellow human beings[4]

The doing of *da'wah* is an important part of the work of all who profess to be *daa'i*. There are large numbers of these Islamic missionaries working in both Islamic and non-Islamic countries. Recently *Time* magazine reported:

> More recently the Saudis have focused on nearby Kosovo. Half of the $1 million the Saudi Joint Relief Committee spent in the two months after the 1999 war there went to sponsor 388 religious "propagators" intent on converting Kosovars to Wahhabism.[5]

These "propagators" also carry the title of being *daa'i*. Sometimes these Islamic missionaries are fully funded, and other times they do their work on a bivocational basis. Most likely, there are more *daa'is* preaching Islam in the West than there are missionaries in the Muslim countries preaching Christianity.

COMPARISON TO CHRISTIAN MISSIONS

Both the Christian Bible and Islamic writings give the command that their followers are to be involved in the proclamation of their faith. Here are two examples:

> Go then, to all peoples everywhere and make them my disciples: baptize them in the name of the Father, the Son, and the Holy Spirit, and teach them to obey everything I have commanded you. And I will be with you always, to the end of the age. (Matthew 28:19–20 GNT)

> And thus we made you an *ummah*, a party equally balanced on a Presidential party so that you be Witness to the people (Shahid al an Naas) and the Prophet be a witness upon you. (verse 143 of *Surat-ul-Bakara*)

Both Islam and Christianity are missionary religions. Both have some of the same goals and both believe that the widespread propagation of their message is God's will. These similarities can lead to conflict. David Kerr of Selly Oaks College in England has stated: "The absolute commitment of the Christian to missions and of the Muslim to *Da'wah* has undoubtedly been one of the principal contributory factors to the tension. . . . Each feels itself to have been abused by the other."[6] Since many in the West understand missions, it might be a help to make a short comparison of the two in order to gain a better understanding of *Da'wah*.

As stated earlier, *Da'wah* is defined as "an invitation" or "to come." This was the same approach made in the Old Testament by God's people, the Israelites. To know God you needed to come to his land and his people to find him. The abode of God was the Holy of Holies located in the temple at Jerusalem. Much is the same in Islam today. To find God you must come to his people and his abode, which is the *Ka'aba* located in Mecca. Of course both religions realized that God is not limited to a single definable space, but their missions' concept was colored by their identification of the location of his presence.

Christianity broke from this concept of mission when it built its strategy for proclamation on the words of Jesus when he told his disciples to "Go into the world." The very word *missions* means "to be sent." Christianity is a "go" faith while Islam is a "come" faith. Muslims are very much aware of the different emphasis in this wordplay, and they take seriously the missionary and evangelistic visions of Christianity. One Islamic leader told me that prior to 1990 the greatest enemy to Islam was Communism, but after that date the greatest enemy became Christian missions.

Two words are on the black list of the Muslim psyche. They are the Arabic words *irsalyyaat* (missions) and *tabshir* (evangelism). These two words are not used by Muslims to describe their work of *Da'wah*. In fact, when missionary activities are taking place among Muslims, their preachers feel responsible to warn their people of Christian missions and evangelism. The very use of these two words in Arabic sends an intensely negative message. While Christian mission and Islamic *Da'wah* run parallel with each other, they are not the same. The following chart outlines the similarities of both as well as their differences.

Differences

Christian Mission	Islamic *Da'wah*
1. Christian mission has used social action as a means of showing a love that could lead to conversion.	1. Islam uses social service within their mosque as a part of the service that a believer can obtain after conversion, but most do not consider it as a part of *Da'wah*.
2. Christian mission uses large numbers of full-time missionaries who are involved in a cultural incarnation ministry.	2. Islam depends mostly on semitrained laypeople and mosque leaders in their work of expansion.
3. Christian mission emphasizes a cultural divergence that seeks to create indigenous churches within the existing social system.	3. Islam seeks to bring uniformity in law, culture, and religious practices.
4. Christian mission emphasizes going.	4. Islamic *Da'wah* emphasizes coming.
5. Christian mission invites people to become members of churches.	5. Islamic *Da'wah* invites people to become members of the *Ummah* (Community of God).
6. Christian mission engages in the establishment of schools, hospitals, and other benevolent institutions through cooperative methods.	6. Islamic *Da'wah* stresses the construction of a mosque and then establishes its ministries.
7. In Christian missions, the church is to be responsible for the propagation of the faith.	7. In Islamic *Da'wah,* the *Ummah* is responsible for the propagation of the faith.
8. Conversion through conquest is no longer considered a valid form of missions.	8. Conversion through armed conflict is considered helpful to *Da'wah*.

Similarities

1. Both have well-defined philosophies as well as fully thought-out methodologies.
2. Both see their faith as a worldwide faith, although their areas of strength are localized.
3. Both see the source of their communion as issuing from their Holy Book, which gives support to their position.
4. Both have mission organizations that have as their main purpose the furtherance of their faith.
5. Both see conversion to their belief as a positive aspect of their actions.
6. Both see the actions of the other as satanic and have some fear of the other's successes.
7. Both Christianity and Islam are "fractured religions," which have many different expressions and theologies. This plurality carries over to mission and *Da'wah*.
8. Both are aware of the paradigm shift taking place worldwide and feel there is a spiritual vacuum that they can fill.
9. Both see Eastern Europe as fertile fields for expansion.
10. Both extend a call for people to enter into a broad community of believers, Christians into the kingdom of God and Muslims into the *ummah*.

METHODS OF *Da'wah* IN THE WEST

When people think about the expansion of Islam, most are concerned about *jihad*, yet *Da'wah* is more subtle and possibly more successful. As they look upon the world in general and the West in particular, they see the circumstances as very conducive for new growth. Three reasons why Islamic scholars feel the time is right for the progress of Islam:

1. There is a great aptitude toward ungodliness. The world has not found true happiness. Because of this, the world is more

receptive than ever before. People still have an emptiness that can only be filled with Islam.

2. The world today is rational and open. Once the truth in Islam is heard, all will surely accept it.

3. In this age, many people are going back to mankind's true nature. This is at least a right direction on the path of life. People's desire to harmonize nature and mankind with God will actually bring them to Islam.[7]

Let us look at several of the ways that *Da'wah* is effectively used today.

Da'wah IN THE ACADEMIC WORLD

American universities and colleges are prime targets of Islamic propaganda. Fatema Mernissi states: "Their main goal is to promote Islamic education in both public schools (from elementary grades to the University level), as well as in the mosques and Islamic centers."[8] She goes on to add, "Strong Islamic education and knowledge is the key to both the future of Islam in this country and to attracting the interest of non-Muslims to Islam. One cannot help but notice the sense of *Da'wah* that motivates and accomplishes such practices in reality."[9] The number of Muslim students on university and college campuses is growing.

There are approximately one thousand to fifteen hundred international students from twenty-five Islamic countries in the greater Los Angeles area alone. The majority are affiliated with the Islamic Society of North America and are preparing to work for the establishment of Islamic governments. Muslim alumni who remain in this country are encouraged to establish and organize mosques wherever they live.[10]

Muslims seek to evangelize not only American students but also other international students studying at American universities. Several years ago I was invited to speak at an English class in Morocco. The room was filled with more than two hundred young, intelligent students. One of my first questions was, "Why do you want to learn English?" One student answered, "So that we can win the world to Islam." I then asked, "How many feel the same?" Every hand was raised. After class a group spoke with me and said they wanted to become *daa'is* and work in universities for Islam.

Fatema Mernissi wrote: "Some Westerners are surprised to find that today university science departments and technological and scientific institutions are the breeding grounds of [Islamic] fundamentalism; it is there that a large number of fundamentalists are recruited."[11]

One method of penetrating the university communities is by using the immense economic strength of Middle Eastern Islamic countries. Financially strapped institutions receive offers to endow a chair of Islamic studies or build a nice building to house an institute of religion. One report states that "Saudi Arabia has given tens of millions of dollars to Howard University and the University of Arkansas to fund Islamic study centers."[12] In many of the poorer countries of Africa, fundamentalist groups with the financial backing of Saudi Arabia will send a large number of professors to teach in their universities. The main aim of these projects is to promote Islam.

Recently, there was a national debate on the work of South Florida University Professor Sami Al-Arian. As a tenured professor, he could not be released without due cause. Much evidence was brought forth to show that he and his department were supporters of terrorist groups, including videotapes in which he called for "death to the Jews." The FBI named two of his associates with him as members and leaders of terrorist organizations. When the university attempted to fire him, cries of free speech and intellectual freedom rang out in his defense. While Professor Al-Arian later was indicted for his actions and fired from the university, he and many others have found that in the West educational institutions provide a safe and profitable base from which to operate.

Muslims also see possibilities for *Da'wah* in primary and secondary schools. Behind the veil of freedom of speech and pluralism, they are promoting Islamic instruction. In California one of the approved textbooks had the students' role-play such activities as wearing Muslim dress, taking Muslim names, and taking the pilgrimage to Mecca. When several school boards were challenged on this, their reply was that they were simply helping the students appreciate other cultures.

CBN News reported a more disconcerting example of this on February 8, 2002. A segment titled "Islam Taught in California Schools" featured a textbook required by all public schools for seventh grade social studies. The textbook is *Across the Centuries* and is a "world history textbook published by Houghton-Mifflin. Chapters three and four outline the origins and early growth of Islam, including a detailed account of the life of Muhammad."[13] During the study of Islam there is a "10 to 15 day simulation," the purpose of which "is to be the first group to complete a pilgrimage to Mecca. Students pretend to travel in caravans, engage in trade, dress up, and even pick a Muslim name, and even stage their own *jihad* as part of a dice game."[14] The curriculum also states "one important phase three activity is learning Islam's five pillars of faith by imitating a requirement of each pillar." This means that, at some point in the simulation, students could be asked to imitate a Muslim profession of faith, Muslim prayer, the giving of alms, a Ramadan fast, and/or a pilgrimage to Mecca.[15]

Another book that has been published by Interaction Publishers of Carlsbad, California, is intended as a curriculum manual for use by history teachers in grades six through twelve. The book *Islam: A Simulation* consists of lesson plans and handouts for a three-week program of classroom instruction in which students "will simulate becoming Muslims" and allegedly "will learn about the history and culture of Islam."[16] One reviewer of the book, William J. Bennetta, a fellow of the California Academy of Sciences and president of the Textbook League, stated, "Page for page, this is the most malignant product that I have seen as a reviewer."[17] If the same students were required to take Christian communion or to read the Bible, numerous lawsuits would immediately follow.

Dr. Ralph Winters, former professor of missions at Fuller Seminary, related his story of attending an open house at his child's high school. The whole program was planned so that each parent could attend each of his child's classes for a ten-minute lecture. In the class on American history, the teacher listed the many customs and habits that America received from its European heritage. When she finished, she asked if there were questions. Dr. Winters stood and simply asked the teacher if she had mentioned that we had also received much from Europe in relation to the Christian faith. Immediately other parents stood and complained that if he spoke about Christianity, then he needed to speak about other religions as well. His answer was, "This is true if they were a part of our European heritage, but the fact is that they were not."

Islam has taken advantage of American openness and has made great progress in *Da'wah* in our schools that are closed to Christianity. The educational institutions of the West will be a major battleground for Islam in the future.

Soon schools may be challenged to provide history courses that deal with Islamic history instead of one examining Western civilization in detail. The fact that America has been built on Judeo-Christian principles will fall into the trash heap.

A sometimes bitter debate in Europe and recently in America is the issue of Muslim girls being allowed to wear their head scarves in school. Often it goes against the dress code of the school, and even though there is not a requirement in the *Qur'an* that the younger students do such, it has become a point of testing. Generally the schools allow it again on the grounds of pluralism.

Understanding the youth culture of the West has not escaped the eyes of the strategists of Islam. One item carried by the Associated Press on January 3, 2003, was titled "Hip-hopping on Faith." It was a report of a new Muslim music group made up of African-Americans founded with the intent to educate Americans about Islam. The three friends who formed the group called "Native Deen," after the Arabic word for "religion" or "way of life," describe their beliefs as mainstream Islam. The article stated, "Their lyrics address topics including tension between Islamic and secular lifestyles, pride in Islamic culture and fulfilling religious obligations. The chorus of their signature song is 'M-U-S-L-I-M, I'm so blessed to be with them.'"[18] At present, the group's fan base is almost exclusively Muslim; although they say they would like someday to have a greater reach. Their eyes are on the $918 million in annual sales by religious performers, most of whom are Christian.

Da'wah IN THE PRISONS

An important mission field for Islam in America, particularly but not exclusively among African-Americans, is the prison system. The life of Malcolm Little was portrayed in the film *Malcolm X*. In it Malcolm is converted in prison and then becomes a model for many young desperate blacks searching for meaning. The success of Islam in the prisons is hard to specify, but Jane Smith writes: "It is estimated that more than 300,000 prisoners are converts to Islam and that the rate of conversion may be more than 30,000 each year."[19]

A recent news report stated, "Almost a third more African-American men are in jail or prison than are enrolled in colleges or universities." The study also found that in the year 2000, 791,600 black men were in jail or prison, compared to 143,000 in 1980.[20]

The appeal is simple. Islam presents African-American inmates with the possibility of not only a changed life but also a changed culture. Prisoners who accept their new faith can do so by reciting the *shahada*, or confession of faith, before several witnesses. The prisoner then takes on a new identity, which includes a new name and new habits. Personal hygiene is improved, as is the cleanliness of the cell. The new convert is then invited into the community of Muslims, which in some prisons is rather large and influential. Muslims on the outside then take on the responsibility of caring for the families of those in prison and even help the prisoner when he is released. Prison authorities say that the rate of recidivism, the return to crime and imprisonment, is lower among Muslims than other groups. In spite of the adverse conditions that befall prisoners, they have definite felt needs, and Muslims have tried to both understand and meet these felt needs.

Recently, one area director for the Prison Fellowship Ministries informed me they now face a new strategy that has been developed by Muslims in prison. When the Christian chaplain holds a Bible study that is open to all inmates, well-trained Muslim inmates will attempt to lead the discussion in a direction that is favorable to Islam. After the meeting, anyone who appears to be seeking God will be immediately confronted and Islam will be presented. This Prison Fellowship chaplain ministers to a large number of prisons and states that the consistency of the approach shows a well-planned strategy instead of isolated incidents.[21]

There are a growing number of Muslim chaplains working alongside Christian and other chaplains. At least one significant Muslim organization was actually founded in prison. This was "The Junior Association of Muslim Men" (JAMM). It was established in a Sing-Sing prison in 1994. It targets inmates under the age of thirty-five and helps them become integrated into the Muslim community. Thus for *Da'wah*, Muslims work on both sides of the prison wall enlisting more people to Islam. *Da'wah* is alive and well in the prisons of America.

Da'wah AND THE BUILDING OF COMMUNITY

Whether prisoners or students, all people have a felt need for a sense of belonging. We crave a feeling of oneness with our fellow man, as well as a belief that we are all equal in the sight of God. Islam reaches out promising to fill that void. Sometimes it appears as if they have met this need, but a closer look shows that it is just an empty promise. The Muslim community continues to live in both fear and denial.

The center of this outreach is the mosque, whose responsibility and importance will be covered later. Most outreach and acts of welfare issue from the mosque, the center for both religious and secular meetings. Much as Christian churches sponsor schools, the mosque will also house an Islamic school. Churches that do not have schools during the week usually have greatly underutilized buildings, while the mosque is a hub of activity during the whole week, partly due to the "*Salah*" or prayer five times a day. In the West the average Christian will visit his or her church only once or twice a week; a Muslim will visit a mosque as often as thirty-five times a week. The actual building is vitally important to the followers of Islam.

Muslims will first build a mosque in a city and then proceed to start other mosques in the same city. Using the mosques as a foothold, they then enter into other forms of *Da'wah*.

Other organizations that attempt to propagate their faith are connected with the mosques. Joseph Gudel states:

> The Muslim Student Association is probably the most active Islamic organization in America. Their stated objectives are . . . producing and disseminating Islamic institutions, providing daily requirements, entreating *Da'wah* (the propagation of faith), recruiting and training personnel (and) promoting and nourishing the unity of Muslims.[22]

Reaching out is nothing new. Christianity began and flourished in an urban environment. Paul the apostle sought to plant and establish churches in the megacities of his time and then to use these as stepping-stones into the surrounding areas. However, Islam started in the backwaters of the known world. Mecca and Medina were hardly world-class cites but rather towns with a rural mind-set. Over the centuries these roles have reversed. Christianity is now more a rural-suburban faith while Islam is targeting the inner cities of the world. In America today, Islam is growing rapidly in the cities. The appeal of Islam within the cities has three dimensions:

First, the faith is well presented and easy to comprehend. If you ask a Muslim to define his belief system, the answer will immediately contain the five pillars and the seven basic beliefs. All Muslims, no matter to which sect they belong, will know the basics. Ask a Christian the same questions and the answer will be like a shotgun blast, with all types of descriptions.

Second, Islam tries to portray dignity, self-discipline, and a sense of community to those living in an inner-city environment where disorder prevails. Those seeking simple answers to the complexity of urban living can better understand Islam.

Third, Muslims reach out to the minority populations that form the core of most inner cities. African-Americans and others are targeted with a message of equality, mixed and flavored with anti-Western rhetoric.

Strategically, Islam is right on target since 80.3 percent of all Americans live in metropolitan areas.[23] The government welfare reform of the late 1900s left the city dwellers looking for a unification of the social, political, and religious aspects of life. The system offered by Islam combines the three areas of life into one, offering simplistic solutions that are readily accepted but seldom delivered. The offerings come under the guise of community. At a meeting in New Mexico at the *Dar al Islam* center, according to one observer: "There was a sense that there is a certain urgency to beginning work on the next phase of Islamic work in America. The last decade was the mosque-building phase, and the focus was on communities and physical structures. We have now entered an *ummah* (community) building phase, and the focus is on relationships and linking those communities and the individuals within communities. We must begin to build bridges, find common ground and connect the various elements of the community."[24]

*Imam*s and mosque communities receive detailed instructions regarding the next step. First, they are told why Americans are suspicious of Islam. One year after 9/11 the Pew Forum on Religious and Public Life took a poll covering "American opinion of Islam." The poll stated that fully 45 percent of white evangelical Christians have an unfavorable opinion of Islam. Another 36 percent of highly committed white evangelicals told Pew pollsters that Islam is more likely to encourage violence than are other religions. Thirty-four percent of secular and white mainline Americans have an unfavorable opinion of Islam. Between one-forth and one-third have no opinion.[25]

In addressing these concerns, Dr. Jamal Badawi sees several problems faced by Muslims as they attempt to build community in the West. In answer to the question, "Why does the West distrust Islam?" Badawi says:

1. People are not receptive to change.
2. The bad image of Islam—many Muslims want to hide their faith.
3. Many people in the West have not been guided in the truth of Islam.
4. Many have been taught that Islam is not a religion but a culture.
5. Some people feel that Islam is a simplistic religion.
6. People understand this religion as opposed to rational thought.
7. Some people are instructed not to inspect other religions because they can be satanic.
8. Some are considered apathetic to religion in general.
9. Some people are governed by national pride. They see Islam as the religion of the Third World. Islam and Arabs are equated, even though only about 15 percent of Muslims are Arabs.[26]

These are expressed concerns for Muslims operating in the Western world.

The terrorist attacks on the World Trade Center in New York and the Pentagon in Washington have resulted in a two-edged attitude toward Islam in the West. First, they created a negative attitude toward Islam, thus making it more difficult for dedicated Muslims to carry out *Da'wah* in the Christian-oriented West. Second, and conversely, the attacks renewed interest in Islam as a world religion. The old political saying might apply here: all publicity, whether negative or positive, can get you elected.

Badawi suggests ten points for Muslims that could be used in successful outreach:

1. Be aware of our duties to Islam and to bringing the truth to all people.
2. We must motivate each other to offer *Da'wah*.
3. Islam spreads by *Da'wah*.

4. Just be a good example.
5. Organize functions where we can invite non-Muslims. Do not condemn others.
6. We must explore the use of mass media. This can be done in the West.
7. We should use literature. Put books in libraries and public schools.
8. Invite contacts with school boards so that Muslims can have access.
9. Create seminaries for *Da'wah*.
10. Emphasize the good ways that people see Islam.[27]

It should be noted that more and more institutions are giving better training in the Islamic world in the use of better methodology for *Da'wah*. Christian missions, at the present time, have a lead in this area, but there have been tremendous gains by Islamic strategists in the past ten years.

Da'wah AMONG MINORITIES

Unquestionably, Islam is successful with many African-Americans. Many converts have come into the more indigenous Nation of Islam, which is highly criticized by orthodox Islam. In the last ten years, however, membership in orthodox Islam has also grown among blacks.

Currently a good deal of attention has been given to the importance of making more converts from the worldwide Hispanic community, especially to those living in the United States. In their strategy planning, Muslims recall that prior to 1492 the Muslim Moors occupied Spain. In the 1990s, the government of Spain declared a new readiness to accept different religions and several villages turned back to Islam, claiming they never left that faith. Building on this historical fact, the strategists see a real possibility for quick gains with this growing segment of the American population. The Hispanic community in the United States now outnumbers African-Americans, and they, too, have a disproportionate population in the prison system. One recent issue of an Islamic mission magazine, *The Message,* was titled "Ole to Allah" and described their new emphasis. Many of the articles were devoted to work among American Latino Muslims.[28]

Several new missionary organizations have sprung up with the purpose of spreading Islam among Spanish-speaking people. One effort in New York City is PIEDAD (Propagacion Islamica para la Educacion y Devocion de Ala'el Devino), which focuses on Latinos who are married to Muslims. Another organization in California is the Asociacion Latina de Musulmones en las Americas (ALIMA). It seeks to "spread Islam among Spanish-speaking people, educating them about the contribution of Islam to their society and culture with the hopes of bringing them back to their ancestors' way of life."[29]

Native Americans have not been ignored, and some Muslims see significant commonalities between Native North American and Middle East worldviews. They point to the fact that both have a reverence for sacred sites, both have a deep awareness of the divine nature, both have a respect for nature and God's law regarding how to treat God's creation, and both are minorities in a "white Christian environment."

While the number of Muslim Native Americans at this time is small, they are a definite target. Recently when traveling through my home state of New Mexico, I passed through Gallup, which calls itself "The Indian Capital of America." On the main road now stands a large mosque. I asked if there were many Muslims in the area. The answer was, "No, but they are growing."

Jane Smith shows how Islam sees its commonality with Native Americans:

> Seminoles in Florida claim that some of their numbers are descended from African slaves who before emancipation managed to escape and mingle in their ranks, even converting some of the Seminoles to Islam. The Algonquian and Pima languages are said to contain words with Arabic roots. Cherokees claim that a number of Muslims joined their

ranks and say that the chief of the Cherokees in 1866 was a Muslim named Ramadham Ibn Wati.[30]

Islam is focusing on people groups in America and the West and is creating strategies to meet the needs of these target peoples. As of now the numbers are not large, but as Christians have learned, people who feel displaced or alienated are more open to conversion than those who have deep roots. The minorities in America fit into this category.

MICRO, INTERMEDIATE, AND MEGA MISSIONS

There is a true sense that *Da'wah* must also be done among weaker or nonpracticing Muslims as an attempt to reinforce their sense of identity and devotion, but for our purposes we will continue to concentrate more on the *Da'wah* as it relates to the non-Muslim. Kherviam Mural sees three levels at work in the creation of a global Nation of Islam. They are:

1. The macro level: the level of overall *ummah* and Muslim societies and states.
2. The intermediate level: the level of very large groups, institutions, and structures.
3. The micro level: the level of the individual person and small organizations.[31]

Mural admits that, though the goal of Islam is much broader, in the present situation most persons involved in *Da'wah* must be active on the third and possibly the second state. Their plan is to have a high enough percentage of Muslims in a democratic society to use the election process to establish an Islamic Republic.

In respect to the microlevel, Mural sees *Da'wah* as a "state of mind, a worldview, an attitude of life, indeed a kind of life."[32] This definition runs parallel to the view of Islam being more than just a religion but, rather, being a full-time life mission. They see Islam as living in total surrender to the will of God. The microlevel will include existing Islamic groups and organizations that work closely with people.

The intermediate level works more with larger groups that have broader influence. Examples might be a mosque, a business, a school, a training center, etc. It is not enough to simply exist in community, but for the sake of Islam, Muslims should enter the political scene. This can best be done by success in business. One area of great gains is in the motel and hotel business in America.

While individuals are the best suited for missions on the microlevel, finances are needed for effective intermediate and macromissions. These funds are used to influence a society. And this level has been very successful in the materialistic West. A doctor who worked many years in Saudi Arabia was speaking about the tremendous wealth of Saudi Arabia and the Gulf States. He said all you need to do is some simple math. Saudi Arabia produces approximately eight million barrels of oil every day of the year. They receive a pure profit of twenty dollars a barrel. There is immense wealth in oil revenues alone. This does not take into consideration the large investments they have in the West. Some of this wealth is used for their people (which number less than six million), but much is used in the promotion of *Wahahbi* Islam in the world. More will be said later about macrolevel *Da'wah* when we look at the building of mosques and Islamic public relations.

There are only three global religious organizations that operate successfully on all three levels at once. They are Mormons, Roman Catholics, and Muslims. Obviously the most successful of the three in the past fifty years has been Islam.

CONCLUSION

Let us end by stating an obvious but disturbing truth. What is being done among non-Muslims in the world today? In a quiet but effective way, Islam is gaining both respect and converts. It is not *jihad* that will be successful in the West but rather *Da'wah*. The importance of *Da'wah* has been stated well by Khurram Murad:

Da'wah among non-Muslims cannot, and should not, be treated as an isolated phenomenon. We will not undertake it properly unless we recognize its proper place at the center of the Islamic life that we as Muslims must live. We will not devote our energies to it as we ought to unless it forms an integral part of our total endeavor and struggle . . . *Da'wah* among non-Muslims must not be merely an appendage attached to our Islamic existence.[33]

Islam sees *Da'wah* as an important and useful tool in their search for world dominance. It is not right for Christians to condemn what is done through *Da'wah*, but it will be helpful to understand the dynamics of *Da'wah* as we seek to reach Muslims with the message of Jesus Christ.

A mosque towers over the neighboring church in Alexandria, Egypt.

chapter **three**

Jihad

Understanding the Muslim Concept

A close missionary friend in the Middle East once suggested that the movie *Khartoum* was one of the best portrayals of the Islamic-Christian conflict. Charlton Heston played General "China" Gordon, a legendary British officer who was well known as a strong Christian. Laurence Olivier played the charismatic *Mahdi,* a leader of the Muslim forces in Sudan. Khartoum was in danger of being overtaken by rebellious forces led by the self-proclaimed *Mahdi,* who many felt was the "chosen one." Gordon, who had previously served as governor of Sudan for Great Britain, returned to Sudan to bring a solution to the crisis.

Agreement was hard to achieve despite the deep religious convictions of both. The *Mahdi* was driven by the conviction that he was ordained to unite the Arab nations, and even the world, under himself, the promised chosen one. Gordon, a Westerner, felt it was possible to reach a compromise.

In the end both lost. As the true history unfurled, Khartoum was defeated, Gordon was killed in the battle, and the *Mahdi* died not long after that, failing to secure for himself a place in world history. Some see the "Clash of Civilizations" in the same light—a continuous conflict with no winners but with great losses for civilization.

Through the centuries, most religions have been involved in wars and conflict. But sharp contrasts exist between the teachings and practices of Jesus and Muhammad, and between the New Testament and the *Qur'an* when it comes to war and violence. It can be said that Islam is the only major faith that can truly be defined as political.

Generally, when a discussion on *jihad* begins, someone will immediately bring up the Crusades to show that both faiths have their violent history and nature. The best starting point, however, is not history but rather the holy books that form the foundation for belief—the Bible for Christians and the *Qur'an* for Muslims.

Again, I refer to my many conversations with adherents of both faiths. When we speak about religion being the basis of violence, many will point to the Old Testament and say that it forms an important basis for the Christians' belief system. In it we find examples of tremendous violence, especially in the book of Joshua, as the children of Israel were commanded to take the land. Some see this as proof that Christianity is just as violent as some make Islam out to be. However, most Christian theologians see the Old Testament as a book of progressive revelations—God slowly revealed his will for humanity in the people of God, the priests of God, and the prophets of God. This revelation was continuous until the coming of Jesus Christ, the Son of God. It is in him that mankind received the full revelation of God.

When comparisons are made between Islam and Christianity concerning the issue of war and violence, they must be made between the two founders, Muhammad and Jesus Christ, and between the *Qur'an* and the New Testament. It is here that we see tremendous differences.

The use of violence was never commanded or even suggested in the New Testament. When Peter took up the sword to protect Jesus, he was rebuked: "Jesus commanded Peter, 'Put your sword away! Shall I not drink of the cup the Father has given me?'" (John 18:11). In the development of the early church as recorded in the book of Acts, not once were people influenced to become Christians by use of the sword. The use of war, conflict, and violence is totally foreign to the New Testament. This is not the case in Islam. Most Islamic authorities will admit that Muhammad was both a political and military leader later in life. Descriptions of his battles with Jews and others form an important part of the history of Islam.

To understand what Islam teaches about holy war, it is necessary to understand the meaning of the word *jihad*. While Christians see *jihad* as meaning holy war, Muslims generally want to have a much broader interpretation of the word. What does *jihad* really mean?

THE MEANING OF *Jihad*

What significance does *jihad* play in the life of a Muslim? This is a complex question about a complex word. Most people from the non-Islamic world consider *jihad* an excuse for terrorist behavior from an extremely volatile part of the world—the Middle East.

The term *jihad* has, as its root meaning, "struggle" or "striving." *The Muslim Almanac* defines *jihad* as "striving." This is a *Qur'anic* concept that encompasses the idea of a just war as well as other forms of striving by which individuals or the community extends the practice of Islam and safety for Muslims.[1]

In Islamic textbooks the concept of *jihad* is often mentioned as the sixth pillar of Islam. The reason for this is that all the other pillars—prayer, giving of alms, fasting, faith, and the pilgrimage—are considered struggles in one's attempt to walk the path to God. For a Muslim, *jihad* is a system of related ideas to help the struggle against all forms of temptations and difficulties that one must face as he attempts to live for Allah. This struggle can be both spiritual and military.

It is written that Muhammad, upon having returned from fighting a battle with some of his enemies, said, "We have returned from the lesser *jihad* to the greater *jihad*." When the people heard him, they said, "O Messenger of God, what *jihad* could be greater than struggling against unbelievers with the sword?" He replied, "Struggling against the enemy in your own breast."[2] Thus, Muslims define this greater *jihad* as a warfare against sin and all that is against Allah and his teachings. It is the struggle in one's own heart to follow the will of Allah and is an internal battle for righteousness.

The lesser *jihad* is what we know as the traditional holy war that is declared in the name of Allah and is used to spread his will. While all Muslims must undertake the greater *jihad*, not all are required to participate in the lesser *jihad*, but they must support it when it does occur.

Many Muslim teachers state that a lesser *jihad* is allowed in only two circumstances. The first is in defense. *Jihad*, according to Muslims, is never an offensive war but only a defensive war. Only after the Muslims have been attacked in some way are they permitted to fight back, or if in some way their freedom, peace, or justice have been taken away. Some of this takes place only in theory and not in actuality. Muslims claim that *jihad* is to be implemented as a last resort, only under extraordinary circumstances. Aggression from either side is not to be tolerated. Yet a study of history shows this is not the case. Muslims have engaged in many wars with aggression as the root cause, often so they can gain territory or wealth.

Today when reading news accounts of violence between Muslims and others, Muslims will often state that what they are doing is in retaliation for what was originally done to Islam. If there is no recent reason, they will cite the need to defend Islam against the imperialistic designs of the West. Often the person issuing the call for *jihad* will list the Crusades as a reason for attacking Christians. In one *Fatwah,* Osama bin Laden mentioned that the West had robbed the Arab people of its oil; thus, the West needed to pay every Muslim in the world $30,000. If this was not paid, then there was justification for *jihad*.[3]

The second reason for the lesser *jihad* is "to right a wrong." Some say that this is also a Christian argument for a just war. An example is the Gulf War of 1991, when the allies fought to repel the invasion of Iraq into Kuwait. History has shown that in many cases Christian countries could call a war just if it fit into their plans; thus the second reason given for lesser *jihad* does have an equal in Christian countries.

Roland Armour, professor emeritus at Mercer University, gives an example of Islam's second reason for *jihad* when he writes: "The expansion of Islam in the seventh century would also be an example of righting a wrong, the idea being that it was wrong for the Middle East and North Africa not to be exposed directly to Islam and ruled by

Islamic Law."[4] With this line of reasoning, lesser *jihad* could be used in all parts of the world in order to usher in a utopian society under *Shariah* law. Precisely this argument is used by many of the more extreme Muslims in the world.

Muslims explain that *jihad* is implemented to proclaim the religion of Islam to all the nations. It was their desire to spread Islam to all the peoples who surrounded them, to take them out of a state of "ignorance" of Allah and into a state of following his will. We cannot be sure whether people converted out of a true change of heart, fear of death, or the desire to not have to pay the tax that would be imposed on non-Muslims. It may have been a mixture of all these reasons, but we know historically that Islam has often spread by means of *jihad*.

THE RULES OF *Jihad*

A *jihad* must observe several rules in order to be considered a true *jihad*. For most people, it is difficult to perceive that a religious war could have well-established rules. However, the sole purpose of a *jihad* derives from Allah, and therefore the "warring actions" must abide by his rules.

Although "outsiders" have considered some wars as *jihad*, they cannot technically be referred to in that manner because of specific actions taken during the event. On the other hand, if Muslims were attacked first, they would be justified in entering into war. For example, when Rome sanctioned war against Islam, the Muslims could not be denied the full right to fight back on any battleground.[5] As mentioned before, *jihad's* primary purpose is to spread the message of Allah. Any action that causes the message of Allah to expand is a justifiable *jihad*.

Finally, *jihad* can be used as a means to terminate or eliminate oppression. The *jihad* must not be used for selfish or economic gain. Ultimately, *jihad* must be performed with a motive that is Allah-centered and can further the expansion of Islam and its people.

There are definite benefits for those who engage in *jihad*. Those who are not killed in the battle and return home are allowed to take the spoils from their conquests. A man killed while fighting is automatically guaranteed entrance into paradise, and his family will receive an honorable name because of his great heroism. About this, *Hadith* 1:352 states:

> To the person who carries out *jihad* for His cause and nothing compelled him to go out but the *jihad* in His cause, and belief in His words, Allah guarantees that he will either admit him into Paradise or return him with the reward or the booty he has earned to his residence from where he went out.[6]

Much has been made of the fact that Islam promises paradise to those killed in *jihad*. One cleric stated to me that only when a person is killed in *jihad* is there the uncompromising guarantee of paradise. Since women were not encouraged to go to war (and in some cases forbidden), a false theory was started that said that in Islam women could not go to heaven. This is untrue, but it is clear that the path to paradise for a woman is a difficult one. It is implied in one of the *Hadiths* that many women are in hellfire because ingratitude toward their husbands is also ingratitude toward God. The *Hadith* states, "The prophet said: 'I was shown the Hell-fire and that the majority of the dwellers were women who were ungrateful.'"[7]

When an Islamic state does go to war, Muslims observe certain rules for killing. There are different rules, however, for fighting a war against non-Muslims *(harb al-kuffar)* than fighting a war against Muslims *(harb al-bughal)*. The author El Fadl Khaled describes some of the rules:

> If Muslims fight against one another, the fugitive and wounded may not be dispatched. Muslim prisoners may not be executed or enslaved, and women and children may not be intentionally killed or imprisoned. Imprisoned male Muslims must be released once the fighting, or the danger of continued fighting ends. Furthermore, the property of Muslims

may not be taken as spoils and any property taken must be returned after the cessation of fighting. Even . . . means of mass destruction such as mangonels, flamethrowers or flooding may not be used unless absolutely necessary.[8]

Since Khaled is a contemporary writer, it is of interest to read between the lines and see what will be allowed in a modern-day conflict between the West and Islam.

THE TWO FACES OF *Jihad*

Westerners are often confused when they hear two entirely different explanations of *jihad*. Americans are faced with two differing views, one saying Islam is a religion of peace, love, and forgiveness, while the other says that Islam promotes and rewards war. Which of these two options is correct? The answer is simple. There is a dichotomy in the faith that allows for both views to be held at the same time. Again it is necessary to return to the *Qur'an* to understand how two vastly differing opinions could be accepted without major problems by the worldwide fellowship of Muslims.

The *Qur'an* was written in two cities and at different times in the life of Muhammad. Of the total, ninety-two Surras were written at the beginning of his ministry, and the last twenty-four were written in Medina during the later years of his life. Muslim theologians understand that the *Qur'an* has two distinct parts. Early in his career, while in Mecca, Muhammad recited verses that were kind to non-Muslims. He called Christians and Jews "People of the Book" and gave them respect and honor. Muslims claim that this was the period when he was politically weak and was striving to gain support. Thus, he turned to the monotheists, thinking that they would support him. Two verses found in the Meccan *Qur'an* are as follows:

Those who believe [in the *Qur'an*], and those who follow the Jewish [Scriptures], and the Christians and the Sabians,— any who believe in Allah and the Last Day, and work righteousness, shall have their reward with them or on them shall be no fear, nor shall they grieve. (*Qur'an* 2:62)

Let there be no compulsion in religion: truth stands out clear from error; whoever rejects Tagut and believes in Allah hath grasped the most trustworthy hand-hold, that never breaks. And Allah heareth and knoweth all things. (*Qur'an* 2:256)

These verses and others from the early writings of Muhammad can easily be understood to say such things as:

1. Anyone who believes in one God (Allah) should be respected and left alone.
2. There should not be an attempt to force people (especially Christians and Jews) to convert to Islam.
3. Christians and Jews have nothing to fear from Islam.

Muslims quote these and similar verses to Westerners to show that Islam is a religion of love, peace, and forgiveness.

However, the second part of the story is that a section of the *Qur'an* was written in Medina. By the time Muhammad arrived in Medina, he was accepted as both a political leader and a military general with great talents in leading men. In Medina he fought many battles, including several against Jewish tribes where it is reported that all the men were killed and their possessions taken by the victors. At this stage in his life, he no longer needed the Christians and the Jews who actually did not have much military strength (though the Jewish tribes were rather wealthy). His dreams of an influential movement were now being recognized. Now he turned on those he had been courting and began to write such words as:

Then fight and slay the Pagans wherever ye find them, and seize them, beleaguer them, and lie in wait for them in every stratagem [of war]. (*Qur'an* 9:5)

If anyone desires a religion other than Islam, never will it be accepted of him; and in the hereafter he will be in the ranks of those who have lost. (*Qur'an* 3:85)

O Prophet! Strive hard against the unbelievers and hypocrites, and be firm against them. (*Qur'an* 66:9)

Those that make war against Allah and his apostle and spread disorders in the land shall be put to death or crucified or have their hands and feet cut off on alternate sides, or be banished from the country. (*Qur'an* 5:33)

It is not for any prophet to have prisoners until he has made wide slaughter in the land. (*Qur'an* 8:68)

Muhammad's language had changed. His last words commanded harm to non-Muslims. Only those non-Muslims who converted to Islam and practiced his required religious duties would escape the horror of his wrath. No matter how Muslims try to explain away the second set of verses, terrorists use them, saying that the end justifies the means. It is verses like these that form the basis of a fundamentalist's definition of *jihad*.

According to *Qur'anic* statements, Islam's ultimate goal is to enforce worldwide submission to the *Qur'an*—whatever the cost. Those that the West labels as terrorists are often people seeking to obey the *Qur'an*. What makes things more complicated is that Muslims in the world today are either ignorant of or hide their knowledge of the teachings of the whole *Qur'an*.

Four Important Questions

Since the definition of *jihad* is so germane to our understanding of how Islam plans to change the world, it is important for us to look at four important questions that need to be answered. Each has to do with relations between Islam and the West, and each shows the immense difference in worldview.

Question 1: Is *jihad* defined the same by Muslims in different parts of the world?

Often geography has much to do with one's theology. Good examples are the way Western Christian nations look at the Bible compared to how those living in underdeveloped nations look at it. Christian missions have often been accused of cultural imperialism by trying to force their values upon those living in other parts of the world. The same can be said of Islam. The world of Islam consists of forty-six countries where more than one-half of the population is Muslim. The majority of these countries use Arabic as either the main or the second language. An understanding of what is being said in various parts of the world is important in answering the above question.

For years, many in the West were at a loss to explain how Israel could accuse Yasser Arafat of being a terrorist. This was the man who had been awarded the Nobel Peace prize and who frequently and publicly condemned the use of violence. Only recently has the West begun to understand that he would say one thing in English to the media and something entirely different to his own people in Arabic. The lack of good Western interpreters meant that we had to depend on translations provided by Arafat's own people. For years this worked, but only recently has the world begun to hear what Israel has been saying for a long time. Arafat says two different things to different audiences.

The same problem exists in our understanding of *jihad.* In looking at the difference between the Meccan and the Medinan *Qur'an,* we can see that different parts of the *Qur'an* are used in different areas of the world. In the West, the Meccan *Qur'an,* which teaches tolerance and acceptance, is used. In the Islamic world, the Median *Qur'an* has a strong presence. Both are *Qur'anic* but two different messages are sent out. Both are true to the *Qur'an,* but it's essential to understand the very important Islamic doctrine of abrogation. Abrogation states that a later revelation from God abrogates an earlier one. In this way, Muslims can say that they accept earlier scriptures such as the books of Moses *(Tawrat)*, Psalms *(Zabur)*, and the Gospel *(Injil)*, as being divinely inspired, yet they view these writings as inferior to the *Qur'an* because they came earlier. It is even possible that changes made by Muhammad or other writers must be accepted since they came later and God revealed the changes. This explains why Muslims can easily say that their differing *Qur'anic* account of the crucifixion and death of Jesus is superior to that of the Bible.

In looking at the two parts of the *Qur'an*, we are told that the earlier verses are inferior to the later verses. Therefore, both ideas of *jihad* are *Qur'anic*; but when it comes to a final interpretation, those verses advocating violence are more important because they abrogate the earlier, moderate statements. According to this well-known Islamic doctrine, when God replaces a verse, the latter version is a better and improved one, and may even contain opposite instructions. For example, *Qur'an* 2:106 says: "None of our revelations do we abrogate or cause to be forgotten, but we substitute something better or similar: knowest thou not that Allah hath power over all things?"

Furthermore, man is not to allow this teaching of abrogation to cast doubt upon the reliability of Muhammad. *Qur'an* 16:101 declares: "When we substitute one revelation for another, and Allah knows best what He reveals, they say 'Thou [Muhammad] art but a forger': but most of them understood not." Thus authentication for the truth of Muhammad's claims is not required.

Geography is a determining factor in one's understanding of *jihad*. I submit that Muslims living in the West will attempt to give a less militant interpretation based upon language and on the fact that they are living in an area where Islam is weak. Those in countries where Islam is strong can and do use the more acceptable interpretation of *jihad* that calls for a more violent holy war. Newspapers and media outlets in Islamic countries condemn the West and its religion in fluent Arabic while those in the West sound a song of tolerance.

A good example of this occurred when Dr. Jerry Falwell, a well-known Christian evangelist and pastor, made a statement calling

Muhammad a terrorist. Newspapers in the Middle East reported that clerics were calling for the death of Falwell. The Iranian cleric Mohsen Mojtahed Shkabestari, in addressing his weekly Friday prayers in the northwestern town of Tabriz, said Falwell was a mercenary and "must be killed. The death of that man is a religious duty." Another cleric, Grand Ayatollah Mohammed Hussein Fadhallah, with an eye to the Western media, cautioned against resorting to physical violence against Falwell, saying Islam "is a religion of mercy and love."[9] There are many such examples of world events being reported completely differently in the Middle East media and the Western media.

Question 2: Is Islam prepared to offer equal rights to others and is it prepared to exist side by side with other ideologies?

In numerous conferences with Muslims, I have asked the question, "Why does Islam not allow Christians and other religions to build churches and religious buildings and to have a presence in their countries?" This question is never answered. Instead, it is countered by a question from the Islamic side, "Why do you Christians use the giving of aid to our people as a means to try to convert them?"

But the question remains, "Why are Muslims allowed to establish mosques and Islamic centers in the Western world when the same privilege is not granted to Christians in many Muslim countries?" For example, there is not a single church in Saudi Arabia. Christians there gather either in embassies or associated cultural centers or military bases. However, in the United States there are three thousand five hundred mosques, and they are growing at the rate of four to five a week! Wherever Islam spreads it has closed the doors behind it.[10]

If Islam is really a religion of peace, love, and forgiveness, then it should allow for the basic rights of others to have freedom of worship. That is not the case. Once while working in a strongly Muslim country, I visited one of the main cities. On a Friday morning, every one of the known Christians in that country—hundreds of them—were put into prison. One of our missionaries living in that country and myself had determined that our United States ambassador was a strong Christian.

So we went to him and asked for help. He said if we could provide him with names and places, he would see what he could do. He then arranged an appointment for us with one of the top officials in the Department of Internal Affairs. We presented him with the details and asked that the Christians be released. He refused to help.

At that point, I reminded the official that his country was a signatory to the United Nations declaration that guaranteed freedom of religion for its citizens. I shall never forget his reply. He said, "That was the Department of Foreign Affairs that signed the document. The Department of Internal Affairs makes its own rules." They were not subject to such agreements. It was clear that there are two different ways at looking at all matters.

Question 3: Are Islam and democracy opposed to each other, or can Islam exist in a democracy?

Why is there no democracy in the Arab world that ensures action and not simply words concerning human rights? Contrary to what Islamic leaders declare to the West, the voices of Arab Christians and other non-Muslim groups in their countries are not heard. They are persecuted and not given rights on an equal par with Muslims. Even Muslims themselves are not allowed to question or criticize their religion but are threatened with severe persecution and death for leaving the Muslim faith. Muslims who have converted to Christianity remain hidden out of fear. Today there is not a single visible church of Muslim converts in any Arab country.[11]

This lack of true democracy removes any common ground for dialogue or constructive cooperation between Muslims and non-Muslims as they face political, social, economic, and religious challenges. Some have even stated that the reason that countries like Saudi Arabia were not supportive of the war in Iraq had less to do with the fact that Iraq was a Muslim country than with the fear of the creation of a democratic country in the heart of the area. In dictatorship countries there is more emphasis on a holy war interpretation of *jihad*.

Malise Ruthven is sympathetic to Islam but expresses deep concerns about the political status of Islamic counties. She writes:

> Most Muslim states are ruled by bloody and repressive dictatorships that, far from satisfying the imperative of social justice exemplified by the prophet's career, seem to be incapable of granting even the most basic human rights to their citizens. Official murders, arbitrary imprisonment in all forms can be found in Muslim states from Morocco to Malaysia.[12]

Certain human rights that are recognized and respected in democratic countries are missing in Muslim countries. If Islam is truly a religion of peace, love, and forgiveness, why is there so little positive fruit in places where it has power?

Question 4: Is Islam ready to publicly condemn acts of violence done in the name of *jihad*?

After the attack on the World Trade Center in New York, there was a worldwide outcry against the use of violence—except in Muslim countries where people not only celebrated the attack but also praised those who committed the infamous deed.

The Western world awaited Muslim condemnations, but they received only condolences for those who had died. Why was the Islamic world so silent? Possibly because this was viewed as a part of the *jihad* against the West and thus should not be condemned.

Many have asked Muslim clerics: Are those who committed this crime in paradise since they did it in the name of *jihad*? The clerics' silence has been deafening.

THE FOUR Cs OF CHRISTIAN-MUSLIM ENGAGEMENT

There has been engagement between Islam and Christianity since Muhammad's flight to Medina from Mecca in A.D. 622. These two great religions have continually had conflict and war. Each blames the other and sees themselves as the victims. There is no reason to see a cessation of this conflict in the near future.

First C: Increased Contact

As Islam began its explosive growth soon after the death of its founder, the areas that fell first to the sword of Islam were Christian. Within a hundred years, Islam had taken control of an area that covered the Arabian Peninsula and extended all the way to the gates of Constantinople. Their conquests covered much of previously Christian North Africa. Wars have continued between Christians and Muslims from that time up to the present. *Jihad* has been a dominant theme from A.D. 622 to the present. Over the centuries, Muslims saw that it was their Allah-given duty to destroy the Christian empires and establish Islamic rule.

Before the fifteenth century, countries and empires fought against each other, but, with time, both Christianity and Islam began to be diffused into the various populations of the world. In the past century, globalization gave rise to a new form of multiculturalism with large minority people groups living in modern countries. Freedom of religion and human rights have each helped give an identity to minority religious groups in most countries of the world. Thus, Christianity and Islam are now living side by side in many parts of the world. This has not brought peace and understanding, only new and different problems.

Both Islam and Christianity are seen as world religions, each claiming over one billion adherents, and both have followers in almost all countries of the world. Contact on a local level is now inevitable.

Civil libertarians will preach community and understanding. Both ideas are wonderful goals and should be the goal of humanity. But the reality is that this close proximity has brought more problems than solutions. In my research I have discovered that when a minority in a country reaches approximately 12 percent of the population, problems appear as the minority group seeks more recognition and power. While this is natural in most situations, it is intensified with Islam because of the strong doctrine of the establishment of an *ummah*, or Community of God. Coupled with the strong emphasis on Arabic as the language of both heaven and the Middle Eastern culture, separation and resentment escalates in most parts of the world. Muslims see that their obligation to Allah is to help others accept Allah's mercy, whether they want to or not.

Contact need not be negative. Different cultures can learn much from each other while enriching different lifestyles. This is especially true when genuine dialogue takes place. Nevertheless, contact more often affords opportunity for conflict and problems.

Second C: Increased Conflict

Most children in the Western world have heard the classic closing sentence of many well-known fairy tales: "and they lived happily ever after." It would be nice if the history of the Islam-Christian encounter could end in this way. Many believe this possibility still exists, but they are an ever-decreasing minority. Today it seems that contact with Islam inevitably leads to conflict. In the past three decades there have been many conflicts between nations, people groups, and individuals. But leading the pack are conflicts between Muslims and their neighbors. Of the many defined conflicts in the world today, most involve Muslims who often declare *jihad* as a basis for their actions. Here is a list of some recent conflicts between Muslims and others:

Country	Opponent	Results
Israel	Jewish Israel	A continuous conflict marked by the suicide bombings of men, women, and children
Chechnya	Russia	Formation of a terrorist movement that has engaged in bombing of apartments and taking hostages in theaters and other public places

Country	Opponent	Results
Philippines	Philippine Government	Terrorist movement has bombed civilian areas and taken foreign hostages
Nigeria	Protestant Churches	Burning of protestant churches and killing of Christians, including pastors in the north
Bosnia	Orthodox Christians	Burning of churches and killing of Christians
Indonesia	Christians	Terrorism against tourists from the West, the killing of Christians in many of the islands, and bombing of churches all over the country
Pakistan	Christians	Terrorist attacks on Christian schools and churches
China	Chinese Government	Terrorist attacks in the western part of China
India	Hindus	Attacks on a train loaded with Hindus, killing most on the train; terrorist attacks in various parts of the country
Kashmir	India	Constant terrorist attacks against the Indian forces in their part of Kashmir
Sudan	Christians	Genocide against the Christians and animists in the south, including bombing of hospitals and schools; more than two million Christians have been killed
Egypt	Tourists	Terrorist attacks on tourists
Algeria	Moderate Muslims	Killing of more than thirty thousand citizens who do not agree with the establishment of an Islamic Republic
United States	Civilians	Terrorist attack on the World Trade Center and the Pentagon, killing nearly three thousand civilians

In all parts of the world, contact with Islam has led to violence. Many in the Muslim world blame others for the conflict, saying they are only trying to defend their rights or territory. However, it would appear to the educated person that the number and scope of these conflicts points to a well thought-out plan for world dominance, which includes conflict under the theological protection of *jihad.*

One would think that, after a war in which an Islamic country is defeated, others would be discouraged from continuing their *jihad* against the conquerors, but the opposite seems to be true. Roland Armour states, "For non-Muslims to take over land sacred to Islam is a violation of fundamental Islamic belief and tradition and one of the classical justifications for Islamic *jihad.*"[13] Defeat of a *jihad* only breeds other *jihads.*

Third C: Increased Conquest

The history of Islam in its first thousand years is a history of conquest, of Arab holy warriors sweeping into surrounding areas brandishing the sword against those who would resist. Many different explanations have been given for the rapid success of the Arabic hordes. Perhaps the cruelty of the attacking Arab legions threw their foes into panic. Some say that internal fighting had weakened the surrounding Christian empires. Others say that Christians had taken seriously the teachings of Jesus Christ against using the sword, even in defense. The fact remains that during this period, Islam continued its conquests to the north, east, and west with startling successes.

Ahkmed Rashid said of this expansion: "Since the seventh century, followers of the prophet Muhammad have fanned out to spread his message throughout the known world." The author continues with this evaluation:

> The conquerors would transform the vanquished empire, but in time their empires would change and become urbanized, until each was in its turn conquered by new nomadic Muslim tribes. The changes the conquerors wrought—religious,

political, social—have often been driven by the concept of *jihad*.[14]

With time, most Muslims ignored the greater *jihad* advocated by the prophet and adopted the lesser *jihad* as a complete political and social philosophy.

Rashid goes on to say that now "this perversion of *jihad*—as a justification to slaughter the innocent in part defines the new fundamentalism of today's most extreme Islamic movements."[15] It is impossible in this short space to review the history of the expansion of Islam, but there are several overall statements concerning their conquests:

1. Most of the areas now controlled by Islam were conquered by the sword.
2. Soon after Islam took over an area, a majority of the peoples converted to Islam.
3. No major areas of the world today have reconverted to their previous religion after being forced to accept Islam.

Forth C: Increased Condescension

An article in the *Muslim World League Journal* written by Hussein K. al-Hussein titled, "Islamic *Jihad*: 'Some Misconceptions,'" stated:

Jihad is not a defensive war only; but a war waged against unjust regimes. It should be pointed out that the war in this case is waged against the leaders and their forces and not against the people ruled by such regimes. People should be freed from the unjust regimes and their influences so that they can freely believe in Allah. Not only in peace but also in war Islam prohibits murder, terrorism, kidnapping, and hijacking when carried out against civilians. Whoever commits such violations is considered a murderer in Islam, and is to be punished by the Islamic state. Islam did not spread by the sword, as it is taught in the west. The state may have spread by the sword, which is always the case, but the people freely accepted Islam.[16]

The author is trying to show that, in reality, most people want to live under Islam, and *jihad* simply affords them the opportunity to achieve this goal. Understandably the Muslims think they are right, thus all people truly desire this religion. It is hard for them to see that many are not interested in being liberated, especially as defined by Islam.

Al-Hussein made an obvious error in stating that Islamic faith did not spread by the sword. There were two categories of vanquished peoples. The first were the Christians and Jews who still were considered to be the people of the Book, and the second were the animists and others who did not accept monotheism. History states that those people who were conquered by the forces of Islam had a choice to make. Roland Armour states, "The Islamic practice of permitting Christians and Jews (the people of the Book) and others to continue in their own religion, if under restrictions, has been a striking feature of the Islamic faith. Islamic law viewed idol worshipers differently and allowed them only two choices, conversion or death."[17]

The treatment of the Christians and the Jews who had been conquered was determined very early. The *Pact of Omar,* which is discussed later in this book, spelled out how they were to be treated. Among the restrictions was a yearly tax based on population of the land. The vanquished could not try to convert Muslims to their faith and were simply tolerated. In some countries they took on slave status, as we see in Sudan today.

CONCLUSION

Many different definitions of *jihad* are used today. Beyond the normal academic definitions, one fact remains. A large number of Muslims in the world today see *jihad* as not only permissible but as necessary in order to create a worldwide *ummah*. *Jihad* is thus an essential part of the Islamic faith. Muslims must admit that *jihad*, as practiced by the extremists, violates several fundamental principles.

Christians must understand that the explanation of *jihad* as only an inner struggle is no longer valid. Christians must take into account that the violent form of *jihad* is very much alive. *Jihad* forms an important part of Islam's search for world dominance.

Mosques are placed in highly visible areas in many cities worldwide.

chapter four

If You Build It, They Will Come

The Importance of the Mosque in Islam

The first time I entered North Africa, I crossed the Straits of Gibraltar from Spain and headed for the Moroccan city of Tangier. The outline of the city from the boat is spectacular. A long train of hills forms a backdrop for the city. Toward the elevated western part of the city, the two spires of an old Roman Catholic cathedral reach into the heavens. Not far to the east looms an even more spectacular edifice: a new mosque with its minarets towering over both the mosque and the city.

After my friends met me, I mentioned the two very beautiful buildings that gave a magnificent backdrop for Tangier. One of my friends then proceeded to tell me the story of these two houses of God on the hill. The church was built by the French during the time of its colonial occupation of Morocco. A wealthy man from Saudi Arabia came to visit Tangier and saw that the tallest building in town was the church. He promised to give the money needed to build a mosque next to the church—but the new mosque not only was to be bigger than the church, but its minarets needed to be higher than the spires of the church.

I chuckled at the story and the human foolishness it revealed. Only later I learned that, far from being simply a humorous story, it was a serious display of an important part of Islam's strategy.

THE IMPORTANCE OF THE PHYSICAL STRUCTURE

In Christian missiology, the "presence" philosophy emphasizes the importance of having at least one believing person in a given area so that Christianity has a presence. The next step is to build a building, so all could see that it is not just a few believers but a building that would outlive any who came to worship there.

The greatest missionaries in the history of the Christian faith were the Celts who brought Christianity to northern and central Europe as well as to many other areas. One of their favorite methods was to locate the important river in the area, and to begin at the mouth of the river and build a church, and often a monastery with it. After the area around the church became Christian, they would sail up the river to an area not yet covered and then build a church and a monastery. This continued for many years until most of northern and central Europe converted to Christendom. Tourists who take a Rhine cruise in Germany are met with churches and monasteries at intervals on the river. This is proof of the success of the Celtic strategy.

Recently Christian missions has changed its philosophy and now sees the church building as more of a liability than an asset. The emphasis is more on house churches that can be mobile and much less expensive. Thus it is difficult for the Westerner to understand why Muslims put so much value on the building of new and beautiful mosques all around the world. The typical Western attitude is that these excesses are being carried out by wealthy oil sheiks playing out fantasies by leaving a physical memorial to their lives. Nothing could be further from the truth. Islam has incorporated the building of mosques into their intentional megastrategy.

A NEW PARADIGM OF ISLAMIC MISSIONS

As a background for this idea, let us compare the historical development of Islam and Christianity. MARC, which is the research arm of World Vision, has organized the history of Christian missions into six paradigms of thinking. Recently, while teaching about the historical development of the Christian church, I became interested in the third period. This period can be described as follows:

Period of time: A.D. 600 to A.D. 1400
Scriptural basis: Compel them to come in (Luke 14:23)
Goal of missions: The expansion of Christendom
Who did missions: Monks and conquistadors
Purpose of the church: To promote the centrality of church, state, and culture
Identity of church: Church as a powerful institution[1]

As I studied this paradigm, it became evident that this is the developmental period Islam is at today. Interestingly, according to the Islamic calendar, we have just passed the year 1380. Islam is now going through the same developmental stage that Christianity went through up until six hundred years ago. Not surprisingly, *Da'wah* has been described as a "come" philosophy (while today Christianity is a "going" religion). Also, Islam does not separate politics and culture from religion.

The construction of many of Christianity's most valued cathedrals and church buildings took place during the third period. When a religious movement seeks to be powerful politically, one of the important attributes contributing to these phenomena is the building of a physical presence. This is where Islam is today.

THE FUNCTIONS OF THE MOSQUE

Although Muslims pride themselves on being multicultural and having a presence in most countries of the world, they are still rapidly identified by their Middle Eastern heritage. They are trying to address this problem by what they term the "Built Environment of Muslims."[2] The look of new mosques often is anything but Middle Eastern. As the Islamic faith expands into new areas of the world, there are those who seek to impose foreign imports of models of architecture. However, an article on the subject states, "A reading of the

Qur'an or a study of the *sunna* will not give instructions on how to design a house in Morocco or Indonesia. Those who have tried to derive specific examples from these sources are doing both themselves and the sources a disservice."[3]

While there are no *Qur'anic* dictates that prescribe the architecture used, Islam's urban ethos does encourage designers to create public spaces that promote social interaction between individuals.[4]

As the mosque became the center of society, it began to take on many different functions, the basic and foremost function being a house of prayer. With time it became a social center, a marketplace, and the political center of the local area. Jane Smith writes:

> Mosques throughout the world, such as the *Umayyad* Mosque in Damascus and the magnificent mosques of old Cairo and Tehran, are often adjoined by magnificent bazaars. Traders and businessmen were among the most successful sectors in society and were responsible for the spread of their faith.[5]

Just as Islam prohibits the separation of the political, social, and religious aspects of life, the mosque physically brings the same elements together as glue for the society.

THE HISTORY OF THE DEVELOPMENT OF MOSQUES

To better understand the place of the mosque in Islam, it will help to look at the history of its development. Martin Frishman, in *Islam and the Form of the Mosque*, argues, "From the beginnings, the monotheistic religions were opposed to the use of buildings specifically designed to house the faithful at prayer." This opposition was based on "both a desire for humility in the presence of the divine and a fear of 'idolatrous worship of the edifice itself.'" He goes on to suggest that the need for converts drives the religious establishment to build facilities that became more elaborate and impressive as the status of the religion grows.[6]

In the early years of Islam, little importance was placed on the mechanics of worship. The mosque existed wherever the worshiper prayed—a similar idea to the Christian concept suggested by Matthew 18:20: "For where two or three come together in my name, there am I with them."

The first "mosque" was the home of the prophet in Medina. Built in the standard Arabic fashion, the home featured a large walled courtyard, with living accommodations forming two walls of the structure. A large portico constructed out of palm leaves formed the *zulla,* which was a "place of deliberation for community affairs,"[7] in addition to being a comfortable place of worship in hot or inclement weather. This combination of courtyard and sanctuary, the *zulla* and *harem,* became the model for later mosques.

Some basics in mosque design have remained the same since the earliest periods of Islam. The prayer hall of any mosque should have one wall facing Mecca. Shortly after the time of the prophet, the place where Muhammad preached in his mosque was marked with a stone called the *qiba.* While initially referring to the stone itself, the *qiba* came to refer to the direction of prayer. Thus, even to this day, the wall aligned with the direction of prayer is called the *qiba* wall and is marked by the *mihrab,* a niche directly in the center of the wall, often elaborately decorated, which serves as the visual focus for prayer.

Another mosque architectural feature that can be traced back to Muhammad is the development of the *minbar,* a pulpit used for Friday prayers. Initially the prophet addressed the congregation while leaning against a pillar. However, as the crowds of worshipers grew, a rising pulpit with steps was developed to enable the followers to better hear the prophet. The *minbar* soon became an essential part of larger mosques, always positioned to the right of the *mirah. Minbars* have also developed into ornate works of art. The original three steps of the prophet have been extended into grand staircases, often capped with a covered platform. Traditionally, the *Imam* delivering the Friday prayers will stand one step below the platform, leaving that space reserved for the prophet.

Local officials have used the *minbars* as a pulpit for preaching, as well as a place of government pronouncements. Unlike Protestant Christianity's division between church and state, the mosque and state do not operate in separate realms.

Many larger mosques also feature a *dikka*, a wooden platform aligned with the *mirab*, allowing one respondent or *qadi* to lead the congregation in following the positions of the *Imam*. Frishman suggests that the role of the *Imam* is not unlike that of the cantor of the Greek Orthodox tradition. Next to the *dikka* is the *kursi*, a large lectern on which the *Qur'an* is placed for recitation during the service.

Another common pattern in mosque architecture is a pool that includes fountains and can be used for the ritual washing of religious participants, or sometimes for purely decorative purposes.

Perhaps the most universally recognized symbol of the mosque is the *minaret*. These large towers serve as commanding local landmarks in indicating the presence of Islam and a place from which the daily calls to prayer are issued. It is important to note that the adoption of the *minaret* was a slow process. The call to prayer during the prophet's lifetime was given from the roof of his home in Medina. It wasn't until the fourteenth and fifteenth centuries that *minarets* became an obligatory part of mosque design.

Architecturally speaking, the use of towers was common throughout the Near East. Frishman suggests that *minaret* adoption could have been based on a variety of traditions from "Zoroastrian symbolic fire-towers to Roman watchtowers, coastal lighthouses or church towers."[8] Dogan Kluman suggests that since the first minarets were used at the mosque of *Amr al Fustat* in Egypt, the form was most likely influenced by the many Syrian church towers of the area. Additional evidence for this view may be found in Damascus, where Muslims were using an old pagan temple prior to the construction of their own mosque. This building had four corner towers dating to the Christian period.

In time, the architectural development of the mosque began to take on regional traits. Outside the Middle East some beautiful examples of architecture are found in Africa, India, and Central Asia. As Ismail Serageldiln explains it, "Societal specificities are defined by local geographic, climatic and morphological features and social practices that give a sense of place to particular locations and character to an environment."[9]

Today there is a debate going on in architectural circles concerning the design of newer mosques. Some advocate newer and more modern design while others seek to return to the basic design of yesteryear. Those who purpose innovative additions to the traditional design appear to be the winners. However, most new mosques will immediately be recognized as mosques due to the basic design.

THE DESTRUCTION OF CHRISTIAN CHURCHES

A trip through the beautiful countryside of modern day Turkey made me remember my studies of the journeys of the apostle Paul two thousand years earlier. It was Paul and his coworkers who started churches that flourished and formed the foundation for the Holy Roman Empire. In looking for churches, I spotted numerous ruins of churches, but no churches actually being used. One guide stated that most of those I saw were Armenian churches. Since most of the Armenians had left, their churches were left to deteriorate. I accepted this explanation.

Later, I decided to look into this further to see if it would be possible for modern-day Christians to buy the ruins and rebuild the churches. In doing so, I discovered that there had been a war of genocide against the Armenians in which almost two million Armenians were slaughtered. Turkey has repeatedly denied that this genocide took place, but many Western historians accept it as fact.

During the actual battles many Christian churches were destroyed. It became forbidden to remove the ruins or rebuild the churches as a sign to later generations that Christianity was a dead religion. Today, the ruins remain as a reminder that Islam rules in Turkey, and that Christianity, with its rich history in that part of the world, is no longer welcome.

This is not an isolated instance. Not only do Muslims seek to build mosques, but they also seek the destruction of Christian churches in most parts of the world. On one of my trips to a Middle Eastern country, I was invited to preach in a large Protestant church in the capital city. The building had been built during the British rule in the 1930s. The building was large and well built, but it was sadly in need of many renovations. Some windows were broken, parts of the floor needed to be replaced, doors were broken, and an overall paint job was greatly needed. I suggested to the pastor that it would be simple to organize a team of Christian laypeople who would be happy to come and renovate the church free of charge. He thanked me for the offer but told me that the law of that country considers it a crime to repair a church without permission, and this permission could only come from the leader of the country. It was really impossible to get permission to fix up the church.

This same pastor told me of another church in the city whose large cross on the top of the church blew down in a windstorm. In its fall it broke a large hole through the roof. The hole remains today because they cannot get permission to do any repairs on the building. Several streets away stands a new magnificent mosque just recently completed.

Later in the week, I visited a small church in the countryside. Again, the church building was built about the same time as the one in the capital city. Again it was run-down, and I noticed a large hole in the front of the church. The pastor told me that previously there had been a window there but that the wood frame had deteriorated, and he wanted to put a coat of paint on the frame to prevent any more damage. After he painted the frame, the authorities came and torn out the window as punishment for not getting permission to paint the frame. Today the church still has a hole in the front.

Journeys into most of the Middle East Christian countries will show either a lack of Christian church buildings or ruins where they once stood. In Port Said, Egypt, a trip around the old town will show several previously large and beautiful churches still in ruins. The plan seems to be to show that Christianity is a dying religion while Islam is alive and growing. In the Middle East, especially, those advocating the destruction of churches are having success with this strategy.

A student of the present-day Muslim-Christian encounter will see an interesting pattern. The news will report that there are conflicts between Christians and Muslims, and as a part of this conflict, churches were burned. These reports are abundant from many areas of the world but come especially from Nigeria, the Philippines, and Indonesia. One example comes from Indonesia, where there was a change in the political leadership. The president of the country, a conservative Muslim, was being ousted by his vice president, Mrs. Megawati, who is also a Muslim but somewhat more moderate. When the changeover took place, the police were in the streets to help avoid violent demonstrations against the government. To the surprise of many, the changeover was quiet, except for the bombing of two Christian churches in Jakarta. In asking why churches were being bombed because of such a change in government, I was told that the more radical Muslims are always looking for a good excuse to destroy churches, therefore, "why not?"

An older and lesser-used system is confiscating churches in conquered areas and then turning the churches into mosques. Anyone who visits Istanbul, Turkey, must go and see the magnificent Haghia Sophia Mosque. The guide will tell you that it was originally built as the Saint Sophia Church but had been turned into a mosque.

A visit to Damascus will bring about the same results. I was told that the fourth holiest location in Islam after Mecca, Medina, and Jerusalem is the mosque in Damascus. A look at the conglomerate of sections will show that some of it was built earlier than the beginning of Islam. Again, we are told that some of it used to be a church. On the south side of the mosque, on the upper beam of a little-used but magnificent doorway, is an inscription in Greek, which reads: "Thy Kingdom, O Christ, is an everlasting Kingdom."[10] Three lofty towers and a multitude of graceful smaller minarets surround the mosque itself. One of the taller minarets is called the "Minaret of Jesus," for Muslim tradition says that Jesus will return to this minaret and preach about Muhammad.

There seems to be a definite philosophy within Islam concerning the existence of churches in Islamic countries. In a few countries the building of churches is tolerated, while in most others, such as Saudi

Arabia and Egypt, it is forbidden. Before the Taliban takeover in Afghanistan, permission was given to build a church in Kabul. It was a forty-nine-foot-high, A-frame, contemporary structure built to attract the international community of that city. It was dedicated in the spring of 1970 after endless negotiations with the government and much prayer and planning. After three years, government forces came in and completely demolished the building. J. Christy Wilson, the founding pastor of the congregation, writes:

> Government leadership was split into two factions. There were the hard-core Muslims who determined to keep the country pure of non-Islamic influences. A second faction saw the value of close relations with Westerners. . . . Sometimes the government would say one thing and then do another and visa versa. We were never quite sure what would happen.[11]

It should be noted that shrines and buildings of other religions have also been desecrated or destroyed. A good example was the recent destruction of large Buddhist statues by the Taliban.

THE LOCATION OF MOSQUES

As already stated, the construction and location of mosques are an important part of the overall Islamic strategy. Islam focuses the construction of mosques first in the major cities of the world. Expansion of Islam into the West is predominately in the urban areas. Much of their major growth is among refugees, who go to the cities where jobs and accommodations are more plentiful. After establishing themselves, these Muslims come together and rent a building for a mosque. With time, numerous mosques are founded in the urban area. In speaking with a leading Muslim convert to Christianity, he told me, "If Islam is to win the West to their faith, they first must win Western Europe. If they are to win Western Europe, they first must win England. If they are to win England to Islam, they first must win

London." In 1960 there was only one mosque in London and today there are more than six hundred.

In most of the major cities in Europe, you will find a rather new beautiful mosque located on a prime piece of property, sometimes even in a major park. Officials often will say that oil-producing countries pressured them to allow them to use land that could never be used for anything else. One of their arguments is that in the name of brotherhood it is right to allow another religion entrance into the historical old centers of the previously Christian cities. The spirit of Christianity is such that many church leaders bend over backward to help the Muslim community when they are seeking to locate a mosque.

As Anglican churches in England die due to nonattendance, their buildings are put up for sale. In a few cases, when evangelicals or another Christian group offers to purchase them or rent them, the request is met with hostility, though the building is given or sold for a reduced price to Muslims for a mosque.

In the West, Muslims will often buy the property under a false name for fear that the owners will not sell to Muslims. Such is the case in Mill Valley, California. A small Baptist church disbanded and their property was put up for sale. A local businessman wanted to purchase the building to be used as a warehouse. After the sale it was made into a mosque. It was in this mosque, located in a very trendy village of Mill Valley, that John Walker Lindh, the *American Taliban*, was converted to Islam and began his journey to *extreme* Islam.

The process of establishing mosques also follows the old Celts method of missions. In Africa there are many examples of Muslims building mosques on a road that leads to an area they desire to win. For example, northern Nigeria is Muslim while the southern part of the country is mostly Christian. Beginning in the north and going southward, the Muslims are building a mosque every mile along the main highway. They build in the direction of the south as a symbol of their strategy to bring Islam into the south. I have heard of this being done in many other countries of Africa.

Of course, Muslims are encouraged to build a mosque wherever there is a group of Muslims gathered together and have a need of a place of worship. This is a natural and spontaneous expansion of their faith. It is when a mosque is built in an area where there *are* no Muslims that it falls into the idea of a strategy. Far from all mosques being needed and used, many are built and stand empty, in hopes they will be used later. Generally, the financial costs involved in the upkeep of an empty building do not seem be a problem for those who are ready to spend the money to build the building in the first place.

THE FINANCING OF MOSQUES

The main reason Christian missionaries do not build more churches where they are working is a lack of financing, especially in the cities. The high cost of land and construction make it impossible and impracticable to build. This has been the number one reason for the change of strategy among missionaries leading to an advocacy of house churches. This does not seem to be a problem with Islam. New, beautiful, and costly mosques are being built all over the world. The financing of these is coming primarily from Saudi Arabia and other oil-producing states in the Middle East. One report from Nigeria states, "The Saudi government has been directly involved in the construction of several large and elaborate mosques in the country."[12]

A physician friend who had worked for five years in Saudi Arabia stated that all one needed to do was a little mathematics to see the enormous wealth that countries like Saudi Arabia have. He stated that there is a minimum of eight million barrels of oil a day produced by Saudi Arabia. They receive at least twenty dollars a barrel for their oil. This goes on every day of the year with the revenues flowing into a country with only six million citizens.

The exact amount spent for the building of mosques and for their overall mission work is kept secret. One author, Marsha Haney, stated, "The Saudis donated most of the $8.5 million to build a mosque for south-central Los Angeles, and five other major mosques across the country."[13]

Paul Johnson wrote in *Forbes Magazine,* "They [Saudis' royal family] use their vast financial resources to back subversive Islamic movements of all kinds as one way of protecting their family empire. They are currently, for example, paying for the building of what is rumored to be 400 new mosques in Bosnia."[14]

Another proof of the Saudi Arabia involvement in the financing of mosques was given in a recent *Time* magazine article on that country. The article stated:

> In March 2002, *Ain al-Yaueen,* an official Saudi magazine, wrote that the royal family wholly or partly funded some 210 Islamic centers, 1,500 mosques, 202 colleges and 2,000 schools in countries without Muslim majorities.[15]

The same article reported, "According to a Western intelligence report, the Saudis are spending 11 million a year in Tanzania to build new mosques and buy influence with the ruling Chama Cha Mapinduzi Party."[16] If there were a complete accounting of the total funds that have flowed from the Arab states to the building of mosques, the amount would be staggering.

As mentioned before, many have estimated that the *Wahabi* movement, centered in Saudi Arabia, influences approximately 80 percent of all mosques in the United States. The Saudis are willing to financially help mosques in the United States if they agree to accept the basic beliefs of the *Wahabis.*

MOSQUES IN THE UNITED STATES

On April 26, 2001, a national Islamic advocacy group released the results of a major study of the Muslim community in the United States. This organization issued a report titled "The Mosque in America: A National Report" and stated that mosques in America are becoming dynamic centers for social and political mobilization. Nihad Awad, the executive director of the Council on American-Islamic Relations, the organization that commissioned the report, said that "Mosques are not only centers for spirituality, they are now bases for political and social mobilization."[17]

Muslims have made a study of the number of mosques and their activation in the United States. Dr. Ihsan Bagby, the report's primary researcher, said, "One of the most significant findings in this survey is that mosques are quite ethnically diverse." Bagby noted that more than one ethnic group attends 93 percent of all mosques.[18]

During a news conference at the National Press Club in Washington, D.C., the council outlined some major findings in the survey. Some of them are as follows:

- There is tremendous growth both in the number of mosques and in the number of those who take part in mosque activities. On the average, there are more than 1,625 Muslims associated in some way with the religious life of a mosque.

- The average attendance at Friday prayer is 292 worshipers. Some two million American Muslims are associated with a mosque.

- Report findings support conservative estimates of a total American Muslim population of seven million.

- The number of participants has increased at more than 75 percent of mosques during the past five years. Growth is across the board, but suburban mosques have experienced the greatest increase.

- Conversion rates are steady. On average nearly 30 percent of mosque participants are converts. The average mosque has sixteen conversions per year.

- Mosques are relatively young: 30 percent of all mosques were established in the 1990s, and 32 percent were founded in the 1980s.

- Four-fifths of mosques are located in a metropolitan area, most often a city neighborhood.

- At the average mosque, 33 percent of members are of South Asian origin (India, Pakistan, Bangladesh, etc.); 30 percent are African American; and 25 percent are from the Arabic-speaking world.

- Most mosques are involved in some outreach activities. During the past twelve months, a majority of mosques have done each of the following activities: visited a school or a church to present Islam, contacted the media, contacted a political leader, and participated in an interfaith dialogue.
- Almost 70 percent of mosques provide some type of assistance for the needy.
- More than 20 percent of the mosques have a full-time school.
- More than 90 percent of respondents agree that Muslims should be involved in American institutions and should participate in the political process.
- In general, mosque leadership does not appear to be highly formalized or bureaucratic.
- At the majority of mosques, the leader is a volunteer, works part-time, and is employed outside the mosque.
- In a majority of mosques, final decision-making authority rests not with the leader but with a *Majlis Ash-Shura* (executive committee or board of directors).
- In most mosques with a board, women are allowed to serve as members.[19]

This appears to be the most complete study made in the United States. It must be kept in mind, however, that those involved in the study could have a hidden agenda. They desire to show Islam in the most favorable light possible. However, the report does show that there is a growing presence of mosques in America and that they are gaining power. The building and use of the mosque in the United States have proven to be a very effective strategy, indeed.

An important question that needs to be asked is this: "Is there a tendency for a community of Muslims and their mosque to change to a more conservative position after they attempt to blend in to the Western society?" The answer to the question seems to be yes. An example of this would be the *Dix* mosque in Dearborn, a suburb of Detroit. Nabeel Abraham's ethnographic study of this community reveals a tension between the culturally assimilated Arab-Americans and more recent immigrants. Abraham relates that one Friday in 1976 a group of Muslim immigrants gathered at the mosque for prayer. When they found the door locked, they simply forced the door open and performed their midday rites. Traditionally the mosque was opened only on Sunday, in an effort to fit in with the predominant culture, but this was scandalous in the eyes of the more conservative immigrants.

This tension culminated two years later with a divisive court battle in which the immigrants wrestled control of the mosque away from the more established community. They immediately began to "reform" the mosque, disallowing weddings, dancing, and other social activities within the structure. The position of women was also dramatically altered. Previously, women were allowed free use of the mosque without restrictions. However, the newcomers believed that women ritually polluted the sacred space, and they sought to "replicate in Dearborn the public forms of female segregation and subordination they were accustomed to in their countries of origin."[20]

IMPORTANT MOSQUES WORLDWIDE

1. The Grand Mosque in Mecca

This mosque is one of the largest buildings in the world and the largest mosque in the world. In the center courtyard is the *Ka'aba* of the large black rock that is contained in a square building. It is this spot that Muslims believe was both the Garden of Eden and the place where Abraham was ready to sacrifice Ishmael.

2. The Islamic Center of Washington, D.C.

By 1957, it was determined that there needed to be a mosque in the capital city of the United States. The incentive came from a group of ambassadors stationed in the capital. Through diplomacy they obtained a favorable piece of land located in the prominent heart of the embassy quarter on Massachusetts Avenue. Finances for the mosque came from a number of Muslim countries, with considerable help from Egypt and Turkey. A 160-foot Mamluk-inspired minaret overshadows the whole structure. The actual prayer hall was designed for eight hundred persons and is square and covered by a large dome. At the time of the center's construction, the question of whether to admit women to prayer was in question, but today a small curtained space is provided for female worshipers in the southeastern corner of the prayer hall.[21]

3. The Mosque in Rome, Italy

For many years Islam desired to build a large mosque in the city that was considered the center of Christianity as a statement of their expansion. There was strong opposition from the Vatican, especially since some of the builders wanted it to be larger than St. Peter's. In 1963 the Vatican Council agreed that it would allow the building of a mosque in Rome, on condition that it not be in sight of St. Peter's Basilica and that its minaret be no taller than St. Peter's dome. A committee of thirteen ambassadors sponsored the project, and funding came from twenty-four Muslim countries. The building is on six acres of land, and the building itself covers most of this area. It was designed to accommodate twenty-five hundred men worshipers. A gallery covering about 10 percent of the prayer area is designated for the women.

4. The Mosque in Cordoba, Spain

Here is an example of a mosque being turned into a church. When the Moors were driven out of Spain in 1492, most of the mosques were converted into churches. The most dominant of those was the Cordoba Mosque, which became a cathedral. There are continued attempts by Muslims to retake the building. Recently an Islamic news organization reported an incident where fifteen Muslims entered the cathedral and prostrated themselves on the floor. When the guards surrounded them, the Muslims shouted, "Allahu Akbar" ("God is the greatest") and started reading aloud Suret Al-Fatiha (the first chapter of the Holy *Qur'an*). Such attempts to retake buildings that were previously mosques are more frequent today, especially in Spain.[22]

5. The Central Mosque in London

In 1940 the first attempt to build a mosque in London was made by the Egyptian ambassador to England. By 1974 construction began on the Central Mosque of London that was built for $4.5 million, the bulk of which was provided by the Mosque Trust, which receives funding from a number of Muslim governments. The site, provided by the British government, is in the city's much-beloved Regents Park. An Islamic culture center stands alongside the mosque. The prayer hall was designed to hold approximately one thousand people.

6. The Nazareth Mosque

At one of the holiest locations on earth for Christians, there is a growing debate over the construction of a new huge mosque. Nazareth has several mosques, but when plans were unveiled to build a plaza in front of the historic Christian basilica, a group of Islamic militants claimed that the land was Muslim property and announced that they would build a large mosque on the site. The plan to build the mosque has divided the city. Many see the building of the mosque as an attempt to drive the Christians from Palestine. The percentage of Christians has significantly dropped from 10 percent to 3 percent in the last fifty years. (Like Nazareth, where 35 percent of the sixty thousand inhabitants are Christians, Bethlehem has lost a large number of Christians. A mere thirty years ago there was only one mosque in Bethlehem; today there are eighty-nine.[23])

The issue of permission to build the mosque in Nazareth has engaged the Christian population, the Muslim population, and the Israeli government. Once again it is apparent that Muslims desire to use the mosque as a way of graphically showing Islam's superiority to Christianity.

7. The Mosque in Abique, New Mexico

In the early 1980s Muslims built a mosque and a training center in the isolated village of Abique in northern New Mexico. The mosque became the headquarters of Dar-al-Islam, "an organization dedicated to the betterment of our society and strives to achieve its purposes through education in the broader sense . . . and through programs that benefit both Muslims and non-Muslims of North America."[24] The mosque itself was built using an Indian pueblo form of architecture. I attempted to visit the adobe-style mosque but could not due to the "No Trespassing" sign. In talking with the local people, I asked why they had such a big mosque in such a small village. I was told it was to school the children of Muslims. Later, I learned that it contains a major training center.

CONCLUSION

A well-known statement says, "Man molds the buildings and the buildings mold the man." Apparently it is very difficult to divorce Islam from the mosque. Far from being a simple relationship, the mosque is also an important part of Islam's search for world dominance. In summary, several observations can be made:

- The mosque in Islam is more than just a building; it is the center of community and has many uses.
- The physical presence represented by the mosque is very important to those who are planning the strategies for Islam's growth.
- Large amounts of money are being invested in the building of mosques, not only in Muslim countries but also in Western areas.
- The burning of churches and the building of mosques go hand in hand within the overall Muslim strategy.
- New mosques reflect the architecture of the host country but still retain the traditional forms from the Middle East.

The *Qur'an* is taken very literally by most Muslims.

chapter **five**

It's the Law

The Social Implications of Islamic Law (Shariah)

In reading the story of the Arab and the camel, one assumes that the camel did not belong in the tent, but one could also ask, "Why not?" The answer is clear: The size of the camel was such that the Arab would lose freedom of movement and will within his own tent. Once the camel was in, the Arab had no control over what went on in the tent— or even whether he was allowed to stay! There is a fear in the Western world that the same thing would happen if Islam were to be successful in dominating the world. The camel would be in the tent and nothing could be done about it.

Shariah law could be compared to the camel. A recent poll taken among Ivy League students in the United States asked this simple question: Do you believe that your lifestyle would change if the United States became Islamic? More than 70 percent of those asked replied "no." They couldn't foresee any change in their lifestyle. This shows a real ignorance among most Americans concerning the social implications of an Islamic takeover. One of the most observable results of such a change would be the implementation of *Shariah* law.

For Muslims, *Shariah* law is not considered as an option but rather an obligation. If a country becomes an Islamic Republic, then this Muslim legal system becomes the law of the land. All living in the country, Muslim and non-Muslim alike, are under its rules and

103

regulations. Again, even if the Arab did not want the camel in the tent, once it was in he had to live with its realities. If Islam takes over a country and it becomes an Islamic Republic, its inhabitants must live with *Shariah* law since it is a crucial element of the whole Islamic way of life. In this chapter we will try to better understand *Shariah* and its implications where it is practiced in contemporary societies.

DEFINITION OF *Shariah*

The literal definition of the term *Shariah* is "a path or way to a water hole in the desert." For the early Muslims it was seen as a utopian way of life that was given to prepare men for the heavenly society. The term defines what Muslims believe is the divine and eternal law and the perfect way humanity should live. But since perfection is not possible, the Muslims have another term that relates more closely to the way that this divine law is practiced here on earth. This second term is called *fiqh*. Despite these delineations, the term *Shariah* is used to refer to the Islamic law as practiced by Muslims.

Another explanation is given by Ghulam Sarwar in his book *Islam, Beliefs and Teachings*. This book is used in England to teach Muslim schoolchildren the basics of their belief. Sarwar writes:

> *Shariah* is the code of law for the Islamic way of life which Allah has revealed for mankind and commanded us to follow. . . . *Shariah* or Islamic law consists of the code of conduct for Muslims and is based on two main sources: The *Qur'an* and the *Sunnah* of the prophet. It aims towards the success and welfare of mankind both in this life and life after death.[1]

Muslims like to see their *Shariah* law as having come down to humanity from God while they see all other legal systems as being "man-made laws." They claim that it is a complete and perfect system and guarantees them success, welfare, and peace in this life on earth as well as life after death. In understanding how Muslims compare

Shariah to other legal systems, let us return to Sarwar and see what he wrote to those trying to understand the basics of their Islamic faith. He compares the two in the following chart:

Man-made Law	*Shariah* or Allah's Law
1. Men make laws when they feel the need. These laws start from a few and then grow in number over the years.	1. Islamic Law is complete, perfect and includes all aspects of human life.
2. Man-made laws are not permanent; they can be changed according to the time and circumstances. For example, in a particular country at a particular time, drinking alcohol may be banned; but this can change when public pressure grows. The American government once banned alcoholic drink but removed the ban after a time because it could not be applied.	2. *Shariah* is permanent for all people all the time. It does not change with time and conditions. For, example, drinking wine and gambling are not allowed under Islamic law. And no one can change this; it is a law that is valid for all time and for all places.
3. Man does not have knowledge of the future. Hence, man-made laws cannot stand the test of time.	3. Allah is All-knowing and All-powerful; he is the most Wise and his laws are the best and are complete.
4. Man is a created being. His laws are the creation of the created.	4. Allah is the Creator and his laws are for man, his creation.
5. Man-made laws may be suitable for a particular nation or country. They cannot be universal.	5. Allah's laws are for all nations, all countries, and for all time. They are universal.
6. Men make laws to suit their own needs. Suppose members of parliament want to decrease the rate of tax on the rich, they would do so, even if the majority of the people suffered and there was high unemployment in the country.	6. Allah is above all needs. He is not dependent on anything, so his laws are for the good of all people and not for a few selfish people.[2]

Muslims feel their legal system is far superior to that of the West, thus it is understandable that they would do all possible to seek to institute *Shariah* as the one universally accepted system. In other words, within an Islamic state the law is equal to *Shariah*.

THE FIVE MAIN SCHOOLS OF JURISPRUDENCE

In understanding *Shariah*, it should be noted there is not universal agreement on the details. Over the one thousand four hundred years of the existence of Islam, five definable schools of *Shariah* have developed. They all agree on the *Qur'anic* basis for their legal system, but they differ in their interpretations.

One example would be in determining the time for the start of Ramadan. *Shariah* defines this event as beginning at the start of the new moon. The problem is, who determines when the new moon becomes visible? In the early days this could be accomplished by looking at the sky; when a small sliver of the moon could be seen, then the start of Ramadan was declared. But what do you do if the sky is cloudy or the *Imam* has poor eyesight or if one person claims they can see the moon while others disagree?

Each of the legal systems has defined exactly how to determine when the first sightings of the moon are acceptable. One system says that if three men see the new moon, this is sufficient. Others say that since the testimony of two women equals that of a man, the combined testimony of men and women (with two women being equal to one man) is acceptable. Another system states that it must be the leader of the community that makes the determination. There are differences in the details, but the fact remains that the Muslims must adhere to the month of fasting or be in danger of punishment.

The five main schools of Islamic interpretation of *Shariah* are:

Hanafi School: Created by Abu Hanafi, considered the most tolerant of differences of opinion. Most influential in Turkey, the Balkans, Central Asia, Chinese Turkmenistan, Afghanistan, Pakistan, and India.

Malikis:	Centered on customary and legal practice in Medina. Mostly in Spain, North and West Africa, where it remains the most important legal school.
Shafi'is:	Use of *Hadith* and analogy. Observed in Egypt and Arab states in the Middle East, as well as by the Kurds and Muslims in the Indian Ocean and Southeast Asia. Founder was a student of Ibn Anas.
Hanbalis:	Based on the use of authentic *Hadith* in preference to analogy. Dominate in the Arabian Peninsula. Associated with Islamic Fundamentalist Ahmad Ibn Hanbal.
Jaf'aris:	Followed by most Shii'as.[3]

THE PACT OF UMAR

The Pact of Umar (sometimes called the Code of Umar or the Covenant of Umar) was an agreement with the Christians of Jerusalem that concluded on the occasion of the conquest of that city by the Muslims. During this time Umar rescinded the Roman decrees that had banished Jews from Jerusalem and accorded Jews all the rights granted Christians. Umar supposedly saw both the Christians and the Jews as people of the Book and desired to treat them the same. It is claimed that the pact allowed "The People of the Book" who had been conquered by the Muslims to be treated equally.

Historically, Muslims have claimed that this pact shows how tolerant Islam was in dealing with non-Muslims in newly invaded territories. Contrary to this claim, both Jews and Christians have been severely oppressed and made second-class citizens of their own countries. Christians living under Islamic rule today expect to be treated the same as those of earlier periods. In fact, millions of Christians who currently live in Muslim countries live as second- or third-class citizens.

The Pact of Umar was made by the Caliph Umar Ibn Khatib soon after the death of Muhammad in A.D. 638. It was purportedly written by the conquered Christians themselves since most statements begin with the statement "We shall . . . ," but the pact was forced upon them by the Muslim conquerors. In exchange for agreeing with the pact's conditions, the non-Muslims were allowed to live in the country where they had the benefit of limited protections. Among the laws restricting non-Muslims were:

- Non-Muslim males to pay a poll tax plus a land tax
- Non-Muslims not allowed to be engaged in military service
- No new churches or synagogues to be built; existing ones can only be renovated with permission
- No display of crosses and no religious processions
- A Christian's house could not be built taller than those of Muslim neighbors
- Clothes must be different from those worn by Muslims
- Non-Muslims forbidden to ride on horses and had to ride on mules or donkeys or walk if Muslims were walking
- Non-Muslims had to show respect to Muslims, i.e., by giving up their seats to them
- The testimony of a Christian or Jew could not be accepted against a Muslim in a court of law

DHIMMA STATUS

The Arab word *dhimmi* means "protected people" and is directly related to the Pact of Umar. Those under a *dhimmi* status refer to the Christians and Jews living in a covenant relationship with their Muslim conquerors. This status is open to many different interpretations and is often ambiguous or contradictory. This status does not define the rights of the person living in this status and also does not always define the penalties for those who break the covenant.

Down through history different rulers have interpreted these *dhimmi* laws differently. Leaders from Islam will point with pride when the Muslim leaders have treated the conquered people with dignity. They have a short memory, however, when the people have been treated harshly. Often the conquered believers had only the same choice as that afforded to nonpeople of the Book: conversion or death.

One author has stated that *dhimmi* status is based on two important concepts:

> First, that Muslims are superior to any other religious group ("Ye are the best community that has been raised up for mankind" 3:110), and secondly, that Christians and Jews who had not accepted Islam should be conquered, humiliated, and subjected to the payment of the tribute poll tax, the *jizya*, not payable by Muslims ("fight against those who have been given the scripture and . . . follow not the religion of truth until they pay the tribute readily, being brought down" 4:29).[4]

While unification of all mankind seems to be one of Islam's most dominant propaganda themes, when the religion is studied closely a great deal of separation exists between various groups. People are placed in boxes, each afforded its own definition and rights or lack thereof.

ISLAMIC LAW AND RADICAL ISLAM

The social implications of the establishment of a global Islamic state together with the institution of *Shariah* law are frightening, but this is the aim of many Muslims. Dr. Kalim Siddique, director of the London Muslim Institute, called upon Muslims to murder Salman Rushdie, author of *The Satanic Verses*. He states clearly that the goal of the contemporary Muslim movement is "to eliminate all authority other than Allah and his prophet; to eliminate nationalism in all its shapes and forms, in particular, the nation-state; to unite all Islamic movements into a single global Islamic movement to establish the Islamic State; to reestablish a dominant and global Islamic civilization based on the concept of *tawheed* (the unity of Allah)."[5]

The *Wall Street Journal* on April 15, 2003, published an article titled "In Law Seminars, A Saudi Group Spreads Extremism." The article began by saying, "In late February, more than 300 young men from across

Europe gathered for a weekend seminar on Islamic Law put on by the Al-Waqf al-Islaami Foundation."[6] The article went on to explain that the most famous graduates from the seminar were half a dozen members of the group of young men from Hamburg, Germany, who plotted the September 11 attacks. The language of the seminar was Dutch, but "the message was imported from Saudi Arabia, via Saudi books and lecturers who taught a strict orthodox interpretation of Islam."[7] One of those who attended was quoted as saying, "I don't want a separation of state and religion. I want *Shariah* (Islamic Law) here and now."[8]

Financing for this and similar conferences comes from the *Wahabi*-dominated World Muslim League. The leader of the conferences, Mohammed Cheppih, spokesman for the Al-Fruqaan Mosque and Al-Waqf Foundation, stated that he does not know how much money the Al-Waqf Foundation spends on its programs in the Netherlands. He does say, "The local branch of the Muslim World League (which he represents) spends $50,000 a year to offer courses on Islamic Law and beliefs in Rotterdam and Amsterdam, among other activities in the Netherlands."[9]

Time magazine, in an article on Saudi Arabia titled "Saudi Arabia: Inside the Kingdom," stated: "Apart from channeling money to foundations that have assisted terrorist groups, Saudis have for years supported institutions abroad that propagate Wahhabism."[10]

Historically, the teaching of *Shariah* and radical Islam have been closely related. Al-Waqf and other Muslim organizations have helped to create a world where there is a division between Muslims and non-Muslims. The next step is the separation of governments of the world into two groups: those who have *Shariah* and those who do not. There will be constant pressure on the non-Islamic states to conform to the Muslim idea of the *ummah*.

Shariah AND THE FAILURE OF THE ISLAMIC STATE

"Almost the entire Muslim world is affected by poverty and tyranny."[11] This statement comes from the pen of Bernard Lewis, the respected professor of Near Eastern Studies at Princeton University. In his chapter titled "The Failure of Modernity," he speaks about the failure of the Muslim states to keep up with the rest of the world. In statistic after statistic, Islamic countries lag behind. The countries that practice *Shariah* as the law of the land, such as Iran, Afghanistan, and Sudan, rank close to the bottom in most categories. Lewis says, "In the listing of economics by Gross Domestic Product, the highest ranking Muslim majority country is Turkey with 64 million inhabitants, in twenty-third place between Austria and Denmark with about five million each. The next is Indonesia, with 212 million, in twenty-eighth place, following Norway with 4.5 million and followed by Saudi Arabia with 21 million."[12]

In other categories, such as "purchasing power, living standards, industrial output, manufacturing output, life expectance, and ownership of computers the Islamic countries are far behind."[13] A report on Arab Human Development in 2002 prepared by a committee of Arab intellectuals working with the United Nations reveals some more interesting facts. Lewis quotes, "The Arab world translates about 330 books annually, one-fifth the number that Greece translates. The accumulative total of translated books since the Caliph Maa'moun's [*sic*] time (the ninth century) is about 100,000, almost the average that Spain translates in one year."[14]

Lewis goes on to comment on the economic situation, which is no better, stating, "The GDP in all Arab countries combined stood at $531.2 billion in 1999—less than that of a single European country, Spain ($595.5 billion)."[15]

The more astute students of Islam realize that, in the mind of the average Muslim, Islam is much more than just a religion—it is a complete way of life. Because politics, economics, and social actions are fused together, the condition of Islamic dominated societies is telling.

Quoting Lewis again, we learn that "Most [Muslims] would agree that God is concerned with politics, and this belief is confirmed and sustained by the *Shariah*, the Holy law, which deals extensively with the acquisition and exercise of power, the nature of legitimacy and authority, the duties of ruler and subject, in a word, with what we in the West would call constitutional law and political philosophy."[16]

Extreme Islam has its eye on the West with the attitude that the utopian society can be created if Western wealth could be under the control of an Islamic republic. They fail to look at the possibility that life under *Shariah* has led to the miserable conditions in which many people in their countries live.

Social Implications of *Shariah* Law in Central Asia

Much of Central Asia had been predominately Muslim prior to the culmination of the U.S.S.R. and its communist form of government. There was some limited freedom afforded to the Muslims in such countries as Kazakhstan, Uzbekistan, Kyrgyzstan, and Tajikistan.

Prior to the early 1900s, these areas were not radically Islamic as we define them today. With the imposition of atheism, some began to search for their own identity and began to recruit dissidents from all of Central Asia's major ethnic groups. Ahmed Rashid stated: "[They had] little to offer except the deposition of the current regimes and the institution of *Shariah*. . . . Support flowed in from across the region, and funding comes from as far away as Saudi Arabia—as well as from the narcotics and weapons trade out of Afghanistan."[17]

The rallying cry from many of the radical groups, some of whom are aligned with *al Qaeda*, seems to be the establishment of *Shariah*. They do not need or attempt to define the types of reform that they plan nor how they will run the government. They just want to establish *Shariah*. This was also the case in Afghanistan, where we have already seen the tragic results of that experiment under the Taliban.

Social Implications of *Shariah* Law in Saudi Arabia

Saudi Arabia is the home of the *Wahabi* movement and is considered one of the strictest Muslim countries. It is here that *Shariah* law is practiced in its strictest form. Because this society had little outside influence for several centuries, it has stood the test of time. In a report in *Parade Magazine*, David Wallechinsky described life in Saudi Arabia. He wrote:

In Saudi Arabia, one must not criticize the royal family. Trials often are held in secret. Adultery and abandoning Islam are crimes punishable by beheading, and people given the death penalty often are not told their sentence until the execution itself. Lesser crimes are punishable by flogging: Using a cell phone on an airplane earns 20 lashes. Floggings often are given in shopping malls and announced on the public-address system.[18]

In describing the effects of *Shariah* on the women of the country, he writes:

Saudi women may not drive. If they walk alone in the street, they risk being stopped, beaten or detained as suspected moral offenders. Last March, at a girl's school in Mecca, 15 students died in a fire. Witnesses said the religious police prevented the girls from escaping because they hadn't put on their headdresses and denied male rescuers access because they are not allowed to mix with females.[19]

There are no Christian meetings or churches allowed even among the expatriates. Islam is the only religion allowed to be practiced; thus freedom of religion is an unknown concept. Saudi Arabia is one of the world's most closed societies, both because they do not desire outsiders to influence their people and because few desire to travel to the country for fear of their harsh legal system. *Shariah* law in this country is one of the best examples of what would probably become universal if a global *ummah* were established.

Social Implications of *Shariah* Law in Iran

After the revolution in Iran in 1979, the social consequences of an Islamic republic were severe. They included a government constitution that invested final authority in the *fiqih* to the supreme religious-political leader of the state. He is the final interpreter of Islamic law and appoints the Council of Guardians, the heads of the military and judiciary, and the revolutionary guards. He also acts as a check on the president, prime minister, and parliament, and has the right to over-rule each. John Esposito reports, "neither criticism of Khomeini nor of the ideological foundation were tolerated. Opposition newspapers were banned, censorship occurred, and Islamic programming was introduced to promote their beliefs and values."[20]

Esposito continues to show how the revolution changed the state. The Office for the Propagation of Virtue and the Prevention of Sin addressed moral ills of society by banning music and dancing in public. Drugs, prostitution, gambling, alcohol, homosexuality, and pornography were banned. Nightclubs and bars were closed. Prostitution and drug trafficking were made subject to capital punishment. Thousands of teachers were purged, textbooks revised, and coed institutions were transformed into single-sex schools. Islamic associations were formed on campuses and are used to monitor un-Islamic behavior. Women who wore makeup or did not dress modestly or Islamically were punished.[21]

Christiane Bird, in her book *Neither East Nor West*, describes how "every Iranian lives in two worlds—the public and the private. The public is for wearing dark colors, obeying the laws of the Islamic society, and generally presenting a serious and pious face to the world. The private is for enjoying forbidden music and literature, watching banned videos and TV shows, wearing miniskirts and halter tops, drinking alcohol and doing drugs, and criticizing the Islamic government."[22]

Iran remains the clearest example of what could happen if Islam extremists were to take control of a Western country.

CONCLUSION

Democracy is a form of government best defined by being ruled by the people. With its doctrine of *Shariah,* Islam could be best defined by being ruled by God (theocracy). Is it possible for the two to co-exist? There is in Islam itself a debate on this very subject. Muslim states that have signed the United Nations Universal Declaration of Human Rights find themselves ruled by two contradictory laws. One law gives citizens the freedom of thought, while the *Shariah*, in its official interpretation based on *ta'a* (obedience), condemns it.

Some argue that not only is it possible for *Shariah* and democracy to coexist but that it is being practiced in a limited way in the United States today. The only way the two possibly could be brought together, however, is for a more moderate form of Islam to win the debate. History has shown us that the more fundamental forms of Islam have not been ready to accept any form of government other than its own form of theocracy with its own definition of *Shariah*. Some say that Islam will be mollified in today's global village, but the past twenty years have seemed to show that when Islam takes over a state or country, the institution of *Shariah* is not far behind. I doubt that democracy and Islam can live and function on a long-term basis without intense conflict.

Shariah not only limits religious and political freedom, making second-class citizens of both non-Muslims and the "people of the Book," but Islamic law also robs societies of freedom of speech, dress, and behavior. Islamic law is clearly designed to advance Islamic religion and stop Christian growth and missions as illustrated by the mandates of capital punishment for those who convert out of Islam.

Shariah law has proven itself to be both a burden for Muslims and a threat to the rest of the world.

A large mosque filled with worshipers.

chapter six

The Whole Truth and Nothing but the Truth

The Role of Truth and Fear in Islam

I first met Ali in Frankfurt at a conference for Christian missionaries from around Europe. He was a very impressive man and brought several copies of his new book with him. The book told the hair-raising story of his life as an officer in the Shah's air force in Iran and the persecution that he experienced after becoming a Christian. The stories were vivid and intriguing, showing how Ali had suffered for his newfound faith. I was so impressed with him that I convinced our area director that Ali would be a great person to lead our Muslim awareness group in Europe. The director agreed. So Ali and his new wife of only six months, a talented young woman from Texas, came to work with me in Europe.

Everything went well until Ali had his first opportunity to speak before a church. I was taken back by his bitterness and harshness toward just about everyone. This continued for about a year. At the end of the year, his wife announced that she was going to divorce Ali.

This turn of events put us into a difficult position because of our board's policy on divorce; thus I had to tell Ali that he had only six more months of employment with us. Several days later I visited Ali and he told me that he had been badly beaten up by some Muslims as he was witnessing to them and that he had hurt his back. Of course, I was sympathetic with his condition. Previously, we had played tennis together. I bemoaned the fact that we could not play tennis for a while. He assured me that he could try but would quit if the pain were too intensive. We played for an hour and a half and he did great. We played several more times, but off the tennis court he still complained that his back hurt him greatly.

When the six months were up, Ali left for the States. He soon filed a five million dollar lawsuit against the Foreign Mission Board claiming that we had put him into a dangerous situation without warning him of the dangers. The lawsuit was later thrown out for lack of evidence.

During the time that Ali was working with me, some of my co-workers and I began receiving threatening letters from the Middle East telling us that unless we ceased our work with Muslims our lives were in danger. They even gave the names and ages of our children and said that they also were in danger. About a year later, we learned that Ali was probably an agent sent to discover what we were doing in our missions work with Muslims.

After this experience, I began to question what Muslims considered truth. I discovered that truth has different meanings for different religions.

TRUTH IN ISLAM

Is it possible for us to accept Islam as a truthful religion? It is always difficult when a writer accuses a person, especially a world religion, of not telling the truth. We must seek to have a complete understanding of what Islam teaches concerning truth and how it is practiced in the proclamation of their faith.

Islam teaches that there is absolute truth as well as relative truth. Absolute truth never changes despite changes in time and place, while relative truth is dependent on time, people, and conditions. Since both of these types of truth exist in Islam, how does one determine if truth is absolute or relative?

Millions of people all across the globe profess faith in Islam and try to live their daily lives in obedience to its proclaimed truth. Many who seek converts to Islam promote Islam is the one and only true religion and the only valid truth. There is tension in Islam, however, between absolute and relative truth as they seek to make Islam the world's only religion. This inner conflict has been a problem for Muslim peoples throughout history and continues to manifest itself today.

Absolute Truth

Every Muslim will state that truth is a very important section of the foundation of Islam. One author has stated, "The *Qur'an* has promised that if a person is honest in his search for the truth and is completely willing to surrender and submit to it, God shall Himself guide him to His absolute truth and open His ways for him."[1]

All absolute truth, from the perspective of Islam, is related to God and His existence as the one and only true God. God's essence, names, and works remain true and unchanging throughout time. Other areas of absolute truth are principles of faith that include the concept of divine justice, with its dimensions of unity, predestination, forgiveness, and mercy.

Another area of absolute truth are the divine books; however, the *Qur'an* is seen as the only divine book that has remained pure and unaltered by man, and therefore, the only divine book of absolute truth. Other books that they see as coming from God such as the *Tawrah, Zabur,* and the *Injil* are inferior to the last and greatest revelation of God, the *Qur'an;* thus, they do not contain absolute truth.

With their high view of Allah, Muslims believe that absolute truth never begins with man but comes only from revelation, that is, revelation from God through a prophet. It is necessary to have religion in order to know absolute truth.[2]

Since Muhammad is believed by Muslims to be the last of God's prophets, his revelations are the source for absolute, universal truth. It is believed that Christians and Jews did not carefully protect the revelation given to them by God from impurities and human alterations. Therefore, where there are differences in beliefs between the three monotheistic religions, they claim Islam has the correct belief and is the source of absolute truth.

Relative Truth

Relative truth, as previously stated, is dependent on time, individuals, or conditions. One Muslim writer states: "Examples of relative truth include color, tone, and character."[3] For instance, the appearance of color changes when the intensity of light that illuminates it changes. A person's character may be admired or disdained depending on the location and time in which his character qualities are displayed.

An example can be the fact that most people in most situations admire honest character. A family may uphold honesty in their children and urge them to always tell the truth. Yet, if the family were hiding fellow Palestinians from the Israeli military, they would likely instruct their children to lie to the Israeli authorities if questioned— and in lying they would be admired.

So how does a Muslim arrive at truth in such a situation? It is here that Islam arrives at an understanding not unlike the Christian view of situational ethics that says that the situations in which people find themselves determine what is truth.

An example may help to explain the differences in the Islamic understanding of relative truth. From the perspective of Islam, the number of relative truths is much greater than the number of absolute truths. They appear in all areas of life from the common concept of relative truth in color and tone to more controversial areas such as ethics, violence, justice, and legal matters. Even the interpretation of truth from the *Qur'an* may be left up to the reader.

One writer on Islamic truth states, "As long as there is no conflict with the literal meaning of a word and the root of the word is studied and the results of the Arabic language are not violated, the understanding of every reader of every verse in the *Qur'an* can be listened to with respect."⁴ From this reasoning, it can be understood how each Muslim has a certain right to interpret the *Qur'an* as they feel it should be understood. Understanding can change in respect to time; thus, one meaning of the *Qur'an* can change to another in a different epoch of history.

An important theme from the *Qur'an* is doing good deeds. This is one of the highest virtues of the Islamic faith, encouraged numerous times throughout the *Qur'an*. However, virtues under certain conditions may not be considered virtuous in others. For instance, one's boss at work may be frank and curt, which can be considered quite appropriate in an office atmosphere. Yet, this same action to young children at home could be considered as impatient and unloving.

Al-Ghazzali (1058–1111), one of the greatest Muslim theologians, wrote: "Know that a lie is not wrong in itself. If a lie is the only way of obtaining a good result it is permissible. We must lie when truth leads to unpleasant results."⁵

Islam differs greatly in its admonition against or encouragement of violence depending on the situation. Islam professes to be a religion of peace, love, and forgiveness especially between Muslims. The *Qur'an* states, "Whoever kills a person, unless it be for manslaughter or for mischief in the land, it is as though he had killed entire humanity. And whoever saves a life, it is as though he had saved lives of all men" (*Surah* 5:32).

Concerning violence in Islamic ethics, one Muslim writes, "Islam is basically a non-violent religion, it does not approve of violence at all."⁶ This appears to be a statement of absolute truth, ending the negative statement with an emphatic "at all." However, in the same paragraph of this essay, the author clarifies the "absolute" statement by saying: "But Islam approves of violence (in a highly controlled sense, of course) only to remove *zulm*—the structures of oppression."⁷

We know from history that Muslims did not hesitate to conquer other peoples using violence; but in these numerous cases it was not the Muslims being oppressed but rather the opposite. The *Qur'an* itself has many verses that sanction and encourage violence and killing, but such verses are usually within the context of establishing justice for Muslims, and after peaceful men's attempts have resulted in no change. After that, a Muslim appears to have instruction to inflict violence if he or she is feeling oppressed or is being treated unfairly. Therefore, the act of violence is a relative truth in Islam, dependent on the conditions and beliefs of those inflicting violence.

COMPARISON OF ABSOLUTE TRUTH TO RELATIVE TRUTH

One Muslim author gave the following example of the comparison of the two different types of truth. He said that the relationship of absolute truth and relative truth could best be explained by using the illustration of a flashlight beam pointed at a circle painted on a wall. The center of that beam of light is the brightest, while the area around the circle of light is not quite as sharp or clear. However, the area surrounding the circle of light is still illuminated; in fact, the light is being reflected to the circle's circumference. Each ray of light on the circumference of the circle, representing relative truth, is connected back to its source, the center of the beam of light, which symbolizes truth.

The article continues, "What gives relative truth its particular dimensions and properties, its relevance, is the nature of the receiving point, its own properties, time, and conditions."[8] In Islam this would mean that their understanding of God as the ultimate truth is the center; the farther you get away from the center, the weaker the light, but it is all a part of "the light."

In this way, Muslims can take more freedoms in the areas of relative truth and still call a falsehood a truth. As stated previously, Islam sees no problem in showing two different faces when it comes to presenting the truth. With this understanding, it is easy to see how Muslims can say one thing and live another. To them, it is not a lie—just a different perspective.

RELATIVE TRUTH, JUSTICE, AND ISLAMIC LAW

Islam prides itself on the fact that it is a religion of "justice." However, the sphere of justice within a community also has multiple shades of relativism. In its highest form, justice should serve both the individual and the community, but a disturbance of the peace can prevent the protection of either. It has been stated, "During such times, relative justice, which sacrifices the individuals rights for the sake of the public good, becomes necessary and application of it becomes absolutely mandatory."[9] This might sound acceptable to the Western mind but it also allows the government to strip an individual of his rights for the sake of the "public good." It is this line of reasoning that allows a country like Saudi Arabia to forbid Christians to worship within the country because to do so has the potential of leading good devout Muslims astray and thus damaging the public good.

Often a Muslim will tell a lie instead of telling the truth because of a concern for the community and how he or she understands law and order. Characteristics of Allah and certain principles of faith are proclaimed as absolute truth by Muslims; yet conflicting evidence suggests that Allah's character and principles of faith are more relative than absolute. For example, in Islam the task of obtaining salvation is relative to the person. One Muslim author writes, "Pious deeds of righteous people are the sins of those near to God. . . . An act that is a single merit for one person can earn a million merits for another."[10]

Not only is salvation in Islam extremely relative according to an individual and his personal deeds, but also God himself is shown to be relative and arbitrary toward the salvation of his creation. The *Qur'an* states, "He punishes whom He will, and pardons whom He pleases, for God has the power over all things" (*Surah* 5:40). Concerning the law given by God to man, Caesar Farah states, "Allah may vary His ordinances at pleasure, prescribing one set of laws for the Jews, another for the Christians, and still another for Muslims."[11]

Christians see God as one who is "the same yesterday, today, and forever" while, in Islam, God is one who changes his mandates and expectations for different people groups of the world. This means that a Muslim who says that Islam is the only real religion may not actually have any assurance of salvation.

Concerning faith in Allah the *Qur'an* states, "There is no compulsion in religion . . ." (*Surah* 2:256). Muslim leaders will often claim that there is religious freedom in Islam and use the above verse from the *Qur'an* to support that idea. Many say, "Muslims are absolutely forbidden to force faith on others; this negates the very idea of free will and choice."[12] Yet this idea of religious freedom has been contradicted by Muslims and Islamic governments throughout history and continues to be contradicted today in countries where religions other than Islam are greatly restricted or even forbidden.

How can it be said that one is under no "compulsion" in Islam when essentially no other religious choices or freedoms are given? This is the same concept as when other countries claim to be democratic by offering "people's choice" elections but have only one name on the ballot. This was the case recently when Saddam Hussein received 100 percent of the votes in an election in Iraq. Clearly religious freedom is another of the "truths" that is relative in Islam.

WHEN LYING IS PERMITTED IN ISLAM

There are two categories of lies that are not tolerated in Islam. The first category is a lie against Allah. The basis for this is:

> Who can be more wicked than one who inventeth a lie against Allah, or saith, "I have received inspiration," when he hath received none, or (again) who saith, "I can reveal the like of what Allah hath revealed"? If thou couldst but see how the wicked (do fare) in the flood of confusion at death!—The angels stretch forth their hands (saying) "Yield up your souls: this day shall ye receive your reward,—a penalty of shame, for that ye used to tell lies against Allah, and scornfully to reject of His Signs!" (*Surah* 6:93)

The second category of a forbidden lie is one against Muhammad:

Narrated Al-Mughira: "I heard the Prophet saying, ascribing false things to me is not like ascribing false things to anyone else. Whosoever tells a lie against me intentionally then surely let him occupy his seat in Hell-Fire." (*sahih al-Bukhari* 2.378 cf. 1.106–108)[13]

One of the most interesting moral dilemmas for Islam are the cases in which lying is permitted. The traditions tell us that there are instances where deception can be acceptable. Ibn Shihab stated that "a liar is not one who tries to bring reconciliation amongst people and speaks good (in order to avert dispute), or he conveys good." He goes on to say that he had not heard of any exemption granted in any situation when the people spoke a lie with the exception of three cases: in battle, for bringing reconciliation amongst persons; the narration of the words of the husband to his wife; the narration of the words of a wife to her husband (between them).[14]

This and other areas of written history show us a common Muslim belief is that it is allowable to tell a falsehood on four occasions:

1. To save one's life,
2. To affect a peace or reconciliation,
3. To persuade a woman, and
4. When taking a trip (business transaction)[15]

A fifth could be added to this from other sources:

5. In winning someone to Islam

It could be argued that in each of these cases we are dealing with relative truth and many Muslims will not define this as lying. At least this is the Islamic view of the problem while Christians would see it differently. Christians hold to a much higher understanding of truth. In fact, Jesus himself said that he "is the truth" (John 14:6).

When a Muslim tries to win someone to the Islamic faith, the use of the truth is not always the best way to proceed. If a praiseworthy aim is attainable through the telling of a lie, then this is allowed. There is no more praiseworthy aim than that of bringing someone to an acceptance of Islam.

Many who have carried out business transactions with Muslims have been surprised to see that the deal has been built on deceit. The grounds given for such is that lying is permitted when on a journey, and the journeys during the time of Muhammad were almost always business trips. Therefore, in business, the truth may not always be accepted when the common good is to be achieved. The question comes not in the ethics of lying but in what is the common good. The person telling the lie generally defines the common good.

Often when I have taken part in dialogue sessions with Christians and Muslims, I come away with the distinct feeling that the two sides have never really met on the same plane. Differences of the understanding of truth makes its difficult for the two to have a real understanding and a true meeting of the minds.

UNDERSTANDING FEAR IN ISLAM

Many writers on Islam have tried to find one word that will best describe Islam. In my reading I have found different authors using a number of different words such as *justice, sacrifice, submission,* and *community.* It is now apparent to me that the one word that best describes Islam is "fear." While many will disagree with my evaluation on this subject, there are specific reasons why I have come to this conclusion.

One Morocccan scholar, Fatema Mernissi, used fear as her main theme when writing her book, *Islam and Democracy: Fear of the Modern World.* She bases seven of her ten chapter titles on the different types of fear now faced by the modern Muslim:

- **Chapter One:** "Fear of the Foreign West"
- **Chapter Two:** "Fear of the *Imam*"

- **Chapter Three:** "Fear of Democracy"
- **Chapter Six:** "Fear of Freedom of Thought"
- **Chapter Seven:** "Fear of Individualism"
- **Chapter Eight:** "Fear of the Past"
- **Chapter Nine:** "Fear of the Present"[16]

It needs to be noted that Dr. Mernissi not only concentrates on the fear factor within Islam, but she herself also used fear as the basis for her arguments in answer to the provocative questions about the possibilities for democracy and human rights in the Islam world.

The Fear of Allah

Western civilization is built upon the idea of looking forward to the possibilities for mankind. It is dynamic and filled with hope for the future. Islam, on the other hand, is completely Allah-centric and has a tendency to be dominated by an intense fear of Allah. This fear colors how a Muslim sees the past, the present, and the future. A common phrase in Arabic is *insha-Allah* or "as God wills." Another phrase is "so it is written." There is a strong predestinarian concept of life that motivates the life of the individual believer.

The *Qur'an* stipulates: "O Believers, do not be hasty and forward in Allah and His Messenger's presence but instead fear Allah: for verily, Allah is Hearer and Knower."[17] This verse has two teachings: the first being the respect for Allah's prophet, Muhammad, and the second being the fear of God. Several Muslim writers wrote an article on the signs of fear of Allah. They listed just some of these fears:

- The fear of death before repenting
- The fear of not living up to one's repentance and breaking one's promise
- The fear of not being able to fulfill Allah's obligations
- The fear of losing one's softness in the heart and its hardening
- The fear of losing consistency
- The fear of allowing temptations to dominate

- The fear of Allah making one's self responsible for doing good deeds because of conceit
- The fear of becoming arrogant and egotistical due to the abundance of bounties
- The fear of being distracted from Allah by other creation
- The fear of being led to an evil ending through excessive bounties
- The fear of being punished early (i.e., in the world)
- The fear of being disgraced at the time of death
- The fear of being beguiled by the glitter of this world
- The fear of Allah revealing one's secret in one's state of oblivion
- The fear of being stamped with a bad death at the time of death
- The fear of the questions of Monkar and Nakeen in the grave[18]
- The fear of the punishment of the grave
- The fear of the horrors of the horizon (at the time of resurrection)
- The fear of the Awe during the presentation in front of Allah
- The fear and shame of being naked (at the time of the resurrection)
- The fear of being questioned about every little thing in life
- The fear of the bridge (over hell and its sharpness, the fear of the fire, its chains and its torment)
- The fear of being deprived of Paradise, the eternal and ever-lasting kingdom and abode, and
- The fear of being deprived of seeing Allah's tremendous visage.[19]

Fear of Eternal Damnation

Islam is a works religion. That means that the individual must do good works in order to earn their way to heaven. Both the glories of paradise and the agonies of hell are very dominant teachings in Islam. Most westerners (even those who know very little of the basic teachings of Islam) are aware that a person who is killed in *jihad* has the promise of eternity in paradise and will be ministered to by seventy-two virgins. Although the teaching of an eternal bliss is a dominant theme, there is little that guarantees a person's entry into this paradise outside of dying in a *jihad*. This leaves most average Muslims living in fear of eternal damnation.

Allah has prepared paradise for his devoted friends and hell for his enemies. The explanation of judgment day sounds very similar to that of Christians until Allah brings forth his book of judgment with all the records of people's deeds in them. So it seems that although Allah forgives, he still writes the deeds of a person, good or bad, in a book.

Al-jisr is the bridge that will be laid over hell, which everyone must pass in order to enter paradise. The disbelievers and those whose bad deeds outweighed their good deeds will then fall into hell. Only the disbelievers, however, will be kept in the consuming fire of hell for eternity. The unbeliever's eye of his heart will then be opened to the "last life" and different periods of visualizing the past for eternity.[20]

Paradise also contains *al-Houdh*—the pool that will appear with cups near to it to quench people's thirst. But those who are allowed to drink will be few.

What then is the motive of a believer for doing good deeds? Will it be because of faith that they are moved to goodness or will it be out of fear for crossing *al-jisr* with too many bad deeds and being driven into hell?

According to the *Qur'an*, Allah has created man in a form of original character and temperament. In other words, by nature man knows what is good and how to be appreciative, but it is coming to know true religion that this nature or character is fully developed. The *Qur'an* commends those whose character of goodness has become strong, and it condemns those whose nature has become dull.[21] It is stated that a Muslim who does good will inherit the life of delight hereafter, but those who do not do good will suffer all kinds of punishment.

K. M. Islam in his book, *The Spectacle of Death*, vividly describes the circumstances of hell that he gleaned from the verses of the holy *Qur'an* and the *Hadith* of the holy prophet:[22]

The fire of Hell is 70 degrees hotter than the worldly fire. It has seven levels, and each level has a big entrance. The first level of hell is reserved for those Muslim sinners and [the second level is for] idolaters who were polytheists, [the third level is for] worshippers of fire, [the fourth level for] atheists, [the fifth level for] Jews, [the sixth level for] Christians and [the seventh level for] hypocrites respectively. These levels of Hell are known as (1) Jaheem, (2) Jahannam, (3) Sa'ir, (4) Saqar, (5) Nata, (6) Haviya, and (7) *Hutama*. Every one of these extensive levels is replete with incalculable pains, tortures and torments, and multifarious houses. For instance, there is a house *Ghayy*, the severity of its torments is such that the denizens of [the] other six levels pray 400 times daily for salvation from its tortures. . . . There is a pond, *Aab-l-hamilm*, with water so hot that the moment a sinner drinks it, his upper lip swells to such an extent that it covers his nose and eyes; the lower, his chest. As this water passes down the throat, his tongue burns, mouth contracts, and ultimately this boiling water tears apart the human lungs, stomach and intestines.[23]

The vivid descriptions of hell are long and gruesome. It is understandable why the average Muslim fears that they will not make it over the bridge but rather fall into hell for all eternity.

While it is true that Christianity also has a belief in an eternal hell, the Christian finds security in the words of the Bible that promise that "Everyone who calls on the name of the Lord will be saved" (Romans 10:13). Through a living relationship with Jesus Christ, we have peace, guidance, and an assurance of our eternal salvation. For the Muslim, salvation basically comprises three conditions or beliefs: repentance, faith, and good works. Thus, salvation consists of the declaration of faith, abiding in the five pillars of Islam, and doing good deeds to outweigh the bad ones.[24] However, in Islam it depends on the whim of Allah as to who will find salvation and who will not. Tragically, the average Muslim lives a life of not knowing if Allah will allow them to enter paradise.

Fear of Apostasy

Apostasy is the unbelief of a Muslim who was born into a Muslim family or who has previously publicly confessed faith in Islam. Apostasy can occur through an overt questioning of the substance of God or the value of the *Qur'an*, burning the *Qur'an* out of disrespect, or soiling it, for instance, by turning the pages with fingers that have been licked. It also includes defiling the names of Allah or the prophets or the wearing of a belt that is a custom assigned to unbelievers. Other acts of unbelief for a Muslim are entering a church, worshiping an idol, or practicing magic. Muslims are considered to have lost their faith when they say that the earth has existed since eternity, thus denying the Creator.

The basis for a charge of apostasy is the determination of two or more witnesses coming forth and giving account of a person's actions. When four *Imams* agree that one who falls from Islam must be killed, then their blood should be spilled without hesitation or reluctance, in accordance to the Islamic law.[25]

These risks of apostasy produce fear in the life of a Muslim when they come into contact with a non-Muslim. They often see the danger of pressures that might cause them to commit the sin of apostasy. Any Muslim considering conversion from Islam to Christianity, for example, at best can expect to be ostracized by their community and disowned by their family. At worst they can be put to death. The *Hadith* stated that Muhammad demanded the death penalty for anyone who turns his or her back on Islam. The *Qur'an* states, "Anyone who, after accepting Faith in God, utters unbelief, except under compulsion, his heart remaining in faith—but such as open their breast to unbelief, on them is wrath from God, and theirs will be a dreadful penalty" (*Surah* 16.106).

In Islamic republics that have adopted *Shariah*, there is a common fear that enemies will accuse a person of apostasy for personal or financial gain. Several modern-day examples of the results of apostasy are as follows.

1. In Iran, Rchullah Rowhani, age fifty-two, was executed in 1998 for converting to the Baha'i faith from Islam. Others have been sentenced to death in that country for the same reason.
2. In Tehran, Reverend Mehdi Dibaj had converted from Islam to Christianity and was sentenced to death in 1993 forty-five years after his conversion with charges of apostasy. There was an outcry from the international community and he was released in 1994 after an appeal. He was killed soon thereafter. The same happened to two other pastors in the same year.
3. In Cairo, a couple was forced to separate on the grounds that the husband wrote that Islamic teachings should evolve with the changes in society; he was declared a heretic for such thoughts. Since a Muslim woman must not be married to a heretic, there was a call for separation. The couple has appealed the verdict and is now waiting for a final decision. They still face the risks of losing their jobs and being killed by fanatics for living together in sin as adulterers or apostates.

The average Muslim is very much aware of these and many other examples. Thus, they live in fear that they might transgress the law and also be condemned to physical pain or death, or even worse, the torments of hell for eternity.

The Fear of the West

Fatema Mersissi sheds some light on this topic by showing us how fundamentally different people from the Middle East view those from the West. She writes:

> *Gharb,* the Arabic word for the West, is also the place of darkness and the incomprehensible, always frightening. *Gharb* is the territory of the strange, the foreign *(gharib).* Everything that we don't understand is frightening. "Foreignness" in Arabic has a very strong spatial connotation, for *gharb* is the place where the sun sets and where darkness awaits. It is in

the West that the night snaps up the sun and swallows it. . . . It is there that *gharaba* (strangeness) has taken up its abode.[26]

I remember visiting in the home of a North African Muslim family who was then living in Brussels. I was taken back when they asked if all Muslims who went to America were killed or just some of them. I tried to assure them that this was not the case, but I left the family unconvinced. Since Islam sees no separation between the religious and the political, this is carried over in the Muslims' attitude toward the Christian West. They cannot differentiate between Western political entities and Christianity.

In many discussions with Muslims both in the West and in the Middle East, I have come to understand the underlying basis of their concerns:

1. They have been taught to fear the Christian church. Often they will point to historical events such as the Crusades or present events such as the Western world's attitude toward Iraq to prove that Christians have a desire to destroy Muslims.
2. The breakup of families, low morals, and a lack of basic values in Western society all point to a decadent Christian church and a system that should be avoided.
3. They see Christianity as a dying religion in contrast to theirs, which they feel is alive and vibrant.
4. They see a lack of community in the Western social pattern.
5. They see Christians as having no belief system. They cannot understand why Christians do not pray openly five times a day or perform others acts as do the Muslims.

Politically, the average Muslim sees the world in only two colors—black-and-white. They put the entire West into the black column and fail to see any good. It is much easier for people to simply put all aspects of the West into one large basket and then fear the basket because of its size.

Fear of Democracy

Once again we quote Merissi: "We don't have an Arabic word for democracy; we use the Greek word, *dimuqratiyya*. Two Arabs talking about democracy speak to each other in Greek, all the while remembering that Greek heritage has been forbidden to them on the pretext that it is foreign."[27]

It is every bit as difficult to convince Muslims of the value of democracy as it is to convince an American of the value of a dictatorship. Both peoples have grown up within the system and tend to say that their system is the best. One must remember that the ultimate goal of Islam is to set up a worldwide *ummah* or Islamic system that will be headed by only one *caliph*. Since this is the ideal, it would be incorrect to embrace a democratic system.

It is important to note that there are no functioning democracies in the Middle East, although some will argue that there are Muslim countries such as Indonesia and Pakistan that have adopted the democratic system. A closer study, however, will show that, even in these countries, there is a drift to a more theocratic form of government that makes up the Islamic republic. Muslims who do not live in democratic nations see our form of government as foreign and thus they fear that which comes from outside of Islam.

In the days leading up to the 2003 war on Iraq, some commentators stated that those Muslim countries that opposed the war did so more because of their fear of the creation of an Iraqi democracy in their midst than because of a fear of the Western presence. Most of the surrounding countries did not like Saddam Hussein, but they also did not like democracy.

THE FEARS OF THE IMMIGRANT COMMUNITY

As many Muslims come to the West seeking a better life, they bring with them some of the previously mentioned fears and may accumulate more during the journey. In my position as the coordinator of Baptist missions to Muslims in Europe for the European Baptist Federation, I had the opportunity of visiting many individual Muslims and meeting with numerous Muslim groups. We met to dialogue and find ways that we could render aid. After we gained their confidence, they would share their feelings about living in the West. I have tried to categorize their fears as follows:

- **Fear concerning the situation in their home countries.** Most Muslims come from countries that are living in periods of political upheavals. Muslims from such places as Libya, Iraq, Algeria, and Lebanon all fear for their families and friends. They continue to keep posted on the latest piece of news. They are constantly concerned with the possibility of a change of government or an assassination. Each of these events could cause a radical change in their personal life.
- **Fear of the new culture.** It is difficult to be an outsider in a strange culture. There is always the possibility that they will be sent out of the country or be forced to move. Some Muslims fear that if one country such as Germany could eliminate 6.5 million Jews, could they do the same to the 5.5 million Muslims living in Western Europe?
- **Fear of Islam.** As Islam grows in strength, radical groups such as the Muslim Brotherhood and Al-Queda become more active. The European Muslims also may become radicalized. Coupled together with their fear of apostasy and eternal damnation leaves many in a state of fear of their own religion.
- **Fear from within.** Many Muslims living in Western countries face major identity crises. This is particularly true with the second generation. Are they German or Turk, French or Algerian? They are not sure what their real language is or where they belong. These inner conflicts can turn into fear if no one helps them find their identity.
- **Fear of losing their children.** The second and third generations are growing up in another culture, and their parents fear that they will take on the ways of the world and leave Islam. This is one of the reasons why there is a renewal movement

among Muslims living in the West. They want their children
to keep the traditions and culture of their background.

- **Fear from September 11.** Stories abound about how many
Muslims have been beaten, persecuted, and killed because of
the events of September 11. Even when they are presented
with facts that the number of such incidents is minimal, they
retain their fear of possible retaliation. One Muslim girl, who
had heard about an attack on a Christian school in Pakistan,
during which several children were killed, said to me, "I was
afraid it was a Muslim fanatic and now my fears are that
Christians will do the same to us."

CONCLUSION

Christianity and Islam are different in many aspects including social philosophies, theology, and culture. In this chapter it becomes
apparent that there are also great differences in other areas such as
values (truth) and emotions (fear). It is at the last two levels that the
differences take on the greatest challenge for those who seek to find a
way for both to live side by side. Values form the rock-bottom foundation for a person's character and personality; emotions are where
the human being has the least amount of control.

In the search for world dominance, Islam will use truth as they
understand it even if it conflicts with the Christian understanding of
the term. They will use the emotion of fear as a tool to keep their
people within the fences of their faith and to mobilize people against
a common enemy. Both the concepts of truth and fear have proven to
be helpful in the overall Islamic strategy.

chapter **seven**

Power Shortage

*The Power Encounter
Between Islam and Christianity*

W orld Cup, Davis Cup, Super Bowl—these terms are well
known in the contemporary world. There is a craze for sport-
ing events that pit one team against another and even one country
against another. Two Central American countries war over a football
match. This need for competition, where there is a winner and loser,
spills over into the area of religion.

In 1971 an Australian missiologist, Alan Tippet, coined the term
"power encounter" to label what he saw as contests between peoples
in the South Pacific who were sure of the power of their beliefs, in
contrast to the new message of Jesus Christ. Either by design or accident, events took place that pitted one belief against the other. It became clear that the God of Jesus Christ was able to wield more power
than their gods. Consequently, many converted to Christianity. Just
as it was for the ancient Hebrews, many of today's peoples look to evi-
dences of spiritual power as the clearest way to show the superiority
of one faith over the other.

Muslims, Jews, and Christians alike recognize the encounters between Moses and Pharaoh (Exodus 5–12). They also honor Elijah for
his challenge to the prophets of Baal on Mt. Carmel (1 Kings 18). The
ministry of Jesus was filled with power encounters as he took on the

forces of Satan and defeated them through healings, miracles, and deliverances. Charles Kraft, one of America's authorities on global power encounters, notes: "Unfortunately, the majority of Christian witness coming from the West has neglected the advocacy of power encounters in the presentation of the Gospel."[1] Muslims, however, have taken this concept and made it an important part of their overall strategy, particularly as an important component of *Da'wah.*

HISTORICAL ENCOUNTERS

Since the beginning of Islam in 622, there have been continuous encounters and conflicts between Islam and Christianity. The power that both sides depended upon was their ability to make war by use of the sword alone. The rapid growth of Islam in the seventh, eighth, and ninth centuries came at the expense of the Christian areas of what is now called North Africa and the Middle East.

With the solidification of the Christian West and the rapid expansion growth of the new religion Islam, the conflicts came to a head in the Crusades, a historical clash of the two ideologies. Battles continued to rage between the two sides for about three hundred years, each side claiming to be both victims and victors at the same time. Even now the Muslims will refer back to the atrocities that the crusaders committed on their forefathers as reasons for defending Islam today. Osama bin Laden and others refuse to say that their battle is against the Christians and the Jews but rather use the terms "the crusaders" and "the Zionists." This is a direct reference to the conflicts of the Middle Ages and in some small way connects the power encounters of the Crusades with those in the contemporary period.

After the Crusades ended, there were continuous conflicts between the two civilizations. By the beginning of the Napoleonic era colonization, the world began to see the power of the empires that would become Western Europe. In the two hundred years prior to the Second World War, the Christian West subdued Islam's political influence.

One *Imam* that I spoke with stated, "For many hundreds of years the strategy of Islam has been derailed, but now we are back on track and soon the world will be Muslim." The new independence experienced by the Islamic countries brought with it the possibility of new conflicts. These conflicts take on two personalities. One would be actual physical conflict such as that experienced in Lebanon, Afghanistan, and Palestine. The other would be a more subtle form of conflict leading to power encounters between Islam and Christianity on the local levels. Both of these are in operation today.

Concerning the more physical conflicts, James R. Woosly, former director of the Central Intelligence Agency, adopted the formulation of Eliot Cohen, distinguished professor at John Hopkins School for Advanced International Studies. Cohen said that we are now in "World War IV with World War III having been the Cold War."[2] He continues by saying that there are three enemies of the West in this war. They are (1) The Islamist Shia, which includes the Iranian Shiite Clerics and the Hezbollah; (2) The Baathist parties of Iraq and Syria whom he calls fascists; and (3) The Islamist Sunnis, which includes the *Wahabi* movement. The third group entered the war in 1994.[3] These battles will continue as a part of both the *jihad* strategy and power encounters.

About the same time that "World War IV" began, the more missionary-minded Muslims began to study Christian missionary methods and to formalize a strategy that included spiritual power encounters that they felt they could win. The leadership of this movement fell to the World Muslim League, a Wahabi organization located in Mecca, because they held both the money and the expertise. They are still active today.

PRESENT-DAY EXAMPLES OF POWER ENCOUNTERS

Dialogue

One branch of Christianity has long urged using dialogue as the primary method of communication between Christianity and Islam. Many still feel that a multitude of problems can be overcome if the two sides can meet and have an honest exchange of philosophies and thoughts.

Over the past forty years, I have had the opportunity to participate in many Muslim-Christian discussions. During this period of time, I have become less enthusiastic about this method.

At a large European Baptist conference held in Germany over the topic of Islam, one of the main speakers had as his title "Dialogue: An Important Tool for Communicating with Muslims." When the speaker stood to speak, I noticed that a small group attending the conference stood and left. I rushed out to ask them why. In strong terms, they said they would not listen to anyone who advocated dialogue with Islam.

Later I realized why they had such strong feelings. Dialogue, by its very definition, is a discussion of two equal parties to share and discuss ideas. The group that left told me that too much is given away in dialogue since we must recognize Islam as an equal party and they must see us as equals, something they seldom will concede.

During many dialogue sessions with Muslims, I was amazed at the hard positions they took. They would be very courteous at the beginning, of course, but when we began to discuss ways of accepting each other, they would not budge on their position.

Often during these discussions, the Christians would bring up the question, "Why does Islam not allow Christians to worship or build churches in Muslim countries?" The question would never be answered. Instead, the Muslims would ask, "Why is it that Christians will misuse the suffering of the poor and needy Muslims by giving them welfare and thus seeking to convert them to Christianity?"

These dialogue conferences would generally end with a standoff but with an expressed desire to meet again. After many such conferences, I became aware that such dialogue was more of a power encounter between the two sides. Islam was not ready to cede anything to the Christians and the more conservative Christians had the same response.

Only the liberal Christians and the more moderate Muslims still see dialogue as both positive and productive, and they seek an honest exchange with a continued search for a common ground. Thus, dialogue continues to be a prevalent, if flawed, method.

Debate

In the last two decades, Islam has begun to replace dialogue with another form of contact, one that fits more with their expressed purposes of victory over the opposition. This is debate. There are two forms. The first is a high-profile debate held with much publicity in a large hall.

The leading proponent of this approach was the popular Muslim cleric Ahmed Deedat from South Africa. This capable man had spent much time learning about Christianity. He knew the different schools of theology and was especially up on any Christian leaders who questioned the validity of the Bible or who held liberal positions on the person of Jesus Christ. He prepared himself well for such meetings with Christian leaders. He chose his opponents carefully, but he was open for challenge from others.

On one occasion, Deedat challenged the American evangelist Rev. Jimmy Swaggart to a public debate. Swaggart was well versed on the Bible but knew little or nothing about Islam and was not aware of Deedat's abilities. At the end of the debate, unbiased persons determined that Swaggart was defeated.

Part of the Muslim strategy was to have the audience openly show their feelings during the debate. At the beginning the rules were laid down, which stated that there would be no applause or crowd response until the end. Yet the crowd would boo and hiss when Swaggart would make a point and then applaud when Deedat spoke. The longer the debate lasted, the louder the audience's responses were. More than half the crowd were Muslims. The idea was to intimidate the opposition while giving support to their man. They were sure that they had the equivalent of the home field advantage as understood in American sports. The intimidation worked. By the end of the debate the Muslims could say they had won. Thus, in their own mind at least, they proved the superiority of Islam over Christianity. This is a power encounter in its rawest form.

Today you can go into most English-speaking Islamic bookstores and find a tape of this debate titled "The Great Debate Between

Ahmed Deedat and the Well-known American Evangelist Jimmy Swaggart." They have received a great deal of mileage out of this encounter. (To make matters worse, Jimmy Swaggart later was found with a prostitute and pornographic literature in his car.)

On another occasion, Deedat held two debates with a Palestinian Christian, Dr. Anis Shorrosh. The first was held in the Royal Albert Hall in London on December 15, 1985. The Muslim used the same tactics, only this time his opponent was not only a Bible scholar but one who understood Islam, having grown up in the Middle East. The results were that, in spite of the intimidation tactics, most observers felt like it was a standoff.

During a second debate, Dr. Shorrosh was winning but the crowd became so noisy and unsettled that they rushed the podium before the debate was over. The security police had to sneak Dr. Shorrosh out a side door in order to protect him. One man was stabbed in the uproar. The Muslims again claimed themselves the winner in another power encounter.

In my attempt to buy some tapes of these debates online from a Muslim bookstore, I was not surprised to see that the tapes of the debates by Deedat carried a disclaimer saying that those buying the tapes should use them with care in a Western context. When ordering these videos from www.islamicbookstores.com, the buyer is cautioned by the following warning:

> A word of caution is in order, however. His [Deedat's] militancy and no holds barred approach to Christian apologists, heartening to many a staunch Muslim, also render many of his videos too acrid to be shown to Christians. Those apologetic of Muslims in Western countries would probably have a heart attack watching an Ahmed Deedat video. Nonetheless, there are many masterpieces among his videos too. His debate with Jimmy Swaggart shows Deedat at his best, most generous behavior, simply a gem of an item for Christians to view.[4]

On the contrary, the abuses were so blatant that anyone from the West would be turned off by what happened. Deedat recently died, but I suspect that others will arise and take his place in similar well-publicized meetings.

Local debate is also an effective Muslim strategy. A pastor first receives a letter or a telephone call and is asked to participate in a debate (often called a dialogue since Christians are more familiar with this term). A neutral place is chosen such as a park or an open area. A time is set, and in some cases, an agenda. When the two groups come together, the meeting runs somewhat along the same form as the larger debates. Each has time to give their views with both sides answering.

The Muslims will make certain that they have a much larger group than the Christians. They take such meetings seriously, something Christians seldom do. Again taunts and jeers come from the Islamic side. There is little or no attempt by their leaders to quiet them. They become louder and physically move in on the smaller number of Christians. At the end of the meeting, the Christians go home with their tail between their legs and the Muslims mark it up as another victory.

I have seen the local debates used in England and Germany, but as of now, this form does not appear to be used in the United States. I rather expect that this method will be used sometimes in the future in North and South America.

There are numerous reports of a new strategy that is gaining favor in the United States with the Muslim community as they encounter Christianity. They monitor the newspapers to see when a church is having a special program on Islam. A small delegation from the local mosque will attend. If the program is pro-Islam, then they will remain silent and seek to have fellowship with those attending after the meeting. If the speaker seems to be negative toward their faith, they will either wait until the opportunity for questions or they will demand time to reply to the speaker. Those from the mosque will not address the speaker but rather turn (generally from the front row) and address the crowd. From the time they begin to speak, they will seek to lead and control the meeting, often with success. They have a twofold purpose.

The first is to blunt any criticism of Islam; the second, to use the opportunity to help bring new converts to Islam.

Naturally, some will say that Christians and others will also try to gain the edge in debates, dialogue, and open meetings. What is being done in the name of Islam does not seem out of bounds. The problem is that westerners show good will as a general practice because of America's strong belief in freedom of speech, but they fail to understand that this methodology is not just a diplomatic exercise but an important part of their overall strategy for world dominance. Many Christians will not see such meetings as power encounters and will fail to take the engagement seriously, as their Muslim counterparts do.

Spiritual Power Encounter

I prefer to reserve the term "power encounter" for confrontation that takes place between two religions such as Islam and Christianity. Spiritual power encounters are inevitable since both see their position as being correct and both are convinced that God and truth are on their side.

Much of Islam is really "folk Islam," which puts a spiritual meaning on important life events such as birth, initiation rites, marriages, funerals, and other life-changing transitions. In their belief system they have many varieties of spirits such as *garina, jinn, dews, als,* and *pari;* each having a definite influence on the lives of the people. Islam does not separate the spiritual from the political, economical, or academic aspects of life. Many Christians also have a strong belief in spiritual warfare wherein evil spiritual forces are at war with those from God.

These beliefs set the stage for spiritual power encounters that pit the Creator God against Satan. The worldview of both religions allow for such an encounter. Islam, which has not been nearly so influenced by secularism, has a much stronger belief in these unseen forces, and as a result, many of their power encounters are understood as a part of this spiritual warfare. They see Christians (many of whom have long ceased to have a high view of spiritual warfare) as being weak in

Worshipers in Mecca gathered around the Kaa'ba during the Hajj.

A new mosque: The architecture of mosques
is now taking on more cultural elements.

A mosque built out of mud in Central Africa.

Mosques are used both for worship and for study of the *Qur'an*.

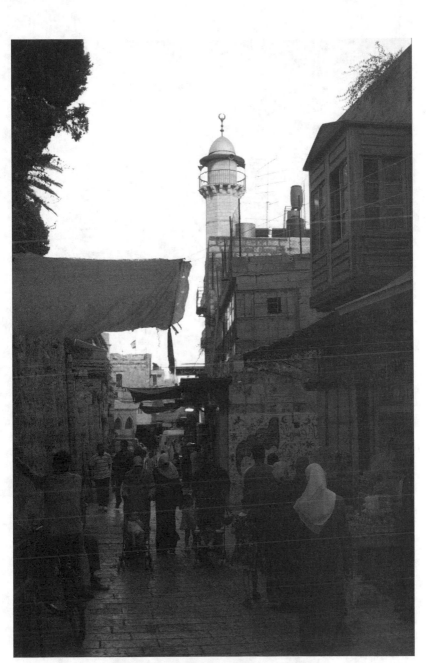

Mosques are often in the center of Muslim
cities and relate to all aspects of Muslim life.

Muslims pray fives times a day wherever they are.

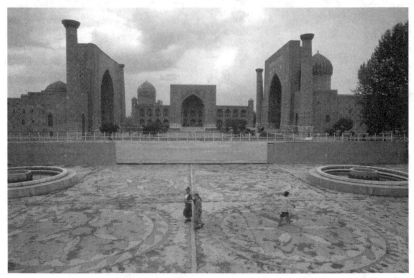

Islamic architecture is very impressive
and often influences the culture of a people.

Women are often in the shadows in Islam. They are seldom allowed to worship together with the men in a mosque.

Ritual foot washing is required before being allowed to worship in a mosque.

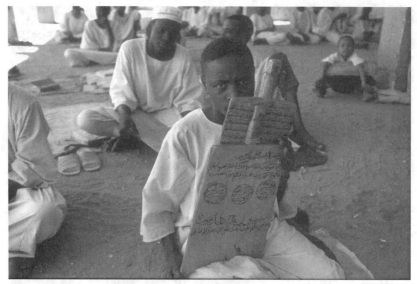

Students learning from the *Qur'an* in an Islamic school.

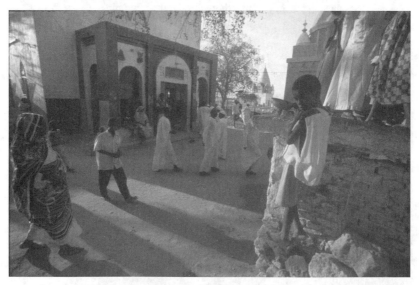

In many Islamic cities the market stands are right beside the mosque.

any encounter where the power of God is expected to intercede. The problem for the West is that the Muslims are probably correct.

The following are three different forms of encounters between the two faiths:

1. Encounters between religious structures
2. Encounters over theology
3. Spiritual and conversion encounters

Dialogue and debates generally address the first two, but the third is the one that affects the common person. I have had the opportunity of meeting with over one hundred Muslims that have converted from Islam to Christianity. During my discussions, I have tried to understand the reasons for their conversion. I originally thought it would be because of an intellectual conviction of the truths of Christianity or that the person was attracted to the religious structures and traditions of our faith.

I was surprised to discover that in all but a few cases the person who converted had either a (1) a vision of Christ, (2) a dream where Jesus appeared to them, or (3) they heard the voice of God or an angel telling them what to do. At first some of them were reluctant to talk about it for fear that they would not be believed. However, assured that I accept such revelations, they shared their experiences. This could well be the area that the conflict between Islam and Christianity will be fought in the future.

One example of this spiritual encounter occurred in a Muslim section of Black Africa. Ralph Bethea, an American Southern Baptist missionary, began work among Muslims in a large city. His love and compassion for the people was apparent to all, and in a short time he gained the friendship and respect of many Muslims in the city.

One day Bethea received a telephone call from the eighty-year-old main leader of a mosque who asked if he would "come to our mosque and bless our people in the name of Jesus." At the meeting, the *Imam* asked the missionary to pray for his people, and after praying for some in the mosque, a distinguished looking man stood up and brought his eight-year-old daughter to the front, asking Bethea to pray that God would heal her withered legs. The father said that he had heard "there is power in the name of Jesus."

After the prayer, the condition of the girl remained unchanged. The father thanked the missionary and returned to the back of the mosque. The girl struggled in her father's arms until he put her down and she stood on her legs for the first time in her life.[5]

After this power encounter, many Muslims believed and were converted to Christianity, not because of an intellectual change but because of a real spiritual power encounter.

Intimidation and Terrorism

The question must be asked: Is terrorism the result of a small number of abused persons using whatever means they can to combat what they see as the Great Satan threatening to destroy them, their culture, and their religion, or is it a part of a well-planned strategy?

I contend that when looking at the whole picture one sees that terrorism has its birth in the *Qur'an* and is being carried out as a part of the means that Islam is using to subject the world to its beliefs. Some of the leading theologians from within Islam seem to agree. In an article titled "Egypt's Al-Azhar Clerics: We declare war on America," it was written:

> Terrorism is a modern term. In Islam, the meaning of terrorism is intimidation, not all intimidation is forbidden by religious law. . . . In the modern age, when (different) kinds of oppression and persecution emerged, some ethnic groups in almost every society were stripped of their rights. When they insisted on their rights, and when the despotic regimes rejected them, the oppressed and persecuted found no way to express themselves but by means of (various) kinds of rebellion.[6]

It should be noted that Al-Azhar is considered by most to be the top theological school in all of Islam. The writer, Dr. Abd Al-Azim

Al-Mut'ani, a university lecturer, went on to write, "The most recent examples of the so-called terrorism are the recent attacks against America. Whatever the interpretations may be, no one disagrees that America is the one who killed and was killed. It is America that killed itself with its distorted policy."[7]

Another man, Dr. Abd Al-Sabour Shahin, from the same university, discussed the differences between terrorism and *jihad*. He wrote:

> The truth is that the way Islam uses the word *terrorism* is honorable, as Allah said "Make ready for them whatever you can of armed strength and of mounted pickets at the frontier, whereby you may daunt the enemy of Allah and your enemy." The terrorism mentioned in this verse refers to intimidation or threat, not necessarily to damage.[8]

It is clear that both of these scholars see terrorism as a means to both destroy and intimidate the West.

Webster's New English Dictionary defines *intimidation* as follows:

> (1) To make afraid; to make timid; daunt. (2) To force or deter with threats of violence; cow.[9]

President George W. Bush has declared war on terrorism. He continually states that we are not at war with Islam—but those who really know the Islamic world add, "But Islam is at war with the West." The success of the ongoing war on terrorism is debatable, and one's opinion is directly related to one's political philosophy. Yes, many terrorist cells have been eliminated or badly damaged, but the terrorists have gained a gigantic victory through intimidation. It is no longer possible for an American to go to a football game or fly on a commercial airliner without having a fear of terrorism. Even the structure of the government was changed with the creation of a Department of Homeland Security established to combat terrorism. Intimidation is working very well.

When anyone in the West tries to defame or critique Islam, they unleash tremendous forces that are intended to intimidate. When the

British author Salman Ruskdie wrote a book that included passages making fun of the prophet Muhammad, Muslims in England took a copy of the book, put it on a stake, and set it on fire. The media covered the story, and soon the Ayatollah Khomeini called for the author to be executed. He did not stop there but added "all of those involved in its publication and who were aware of its content."

Ruskdie was immediately taken into hiding as the debate grew about the condemnation of a Western author using his freedom of speech. While the debate continued, "The translators of *The Satanic Verses* were stabbed and seriously injured in Norway and Italy and, in Japan, murdered. In Turkey, another translator escaped when a fire set in his hotel failed to kill him, but 37 others died in the blaze."[10] Khomeini's supporters succeeded in showing the world that those who would speak out against Islam would bear the consequences.

After the defeat of Saddam Hussein, many began looking forward to a new democratic Iraq, never realizing that the Christian church in that country remains under great pressure. In the northern city of Mosul, known now as a *wahabi* stronghold, local Christians have reported growing harassment of their clergy and church communities. It was reported, "Some 15 Christians were wounded . . . when Islamist zealots stoned them coming out of church."[11] The article adds, "Bishops and leading Christian families in the northern city have received letters telling them to convert to Islam, sometimes with accompanying threats, other times offering them cash rewards."[12]

Another example concerned the 2002 Miss World Pageant. The organizers wanted to have this widely accepted program located in one of the developing countries and chose to hold it in Muslim-controlled northern Nigeria. A fashion writer from the area, Isioma Daniel, wrote that she felt Muhammad would support such a pageant. Daniel's article was seen as insulting to the prophet Muhammad, and the Information Minister of Zamfara State, Umar Dangaladima, endorsed a "*fatwa*" or religious decree calling for the Christian woman's death. The article led to widespread rioting that resulted in more than 215 deaths and the burning of Christian churches. Agence France-Presse reported that Zamfara's deputy governor, Mamuda Aliyu Shinkafi, said in a speech to religious leaders later broadcast on state radio, "Like Salman Ruskdie, the blood of Isioma Daniel can be shed."[13]

Intimidation and Christian Missions

Several years ago one *Imam* told me that, prior to 1990, the greatest enemy to Islam was Communism but now it is Christian missions. They see that many of their own are being influenced to become more tolerant of Christianity or even to convert to that faith. There are few missionaries who have labored for more than ten years in Muslim countries who have not had to attend the funeral of one of their converts or have been involved in hiding a convert so as to protect them from death. The intimidation at this level is certainly great, but there are other methods that they use as well.

Once when I was in Morocco, I was shown a popular magazine displaying photos of many of my friends who were working in North Africa. Their names and, in some cases, their addresses were also given. I was told that the article did not threaten the workers but warned all Muslims to be aware of their devious methods. One colleague from another Muslim country was home on furlough when a magazine from his country did the same thing. This time there were threats against the safety of the missionary and his family.

On May 8, 2003, it was reported that a Jordanian convert to Christianity had been killed by a bomb planted outside the home of a missionary couple in Tripoli, north Lebanon. The Dutch missionary Gerritt Griffioen, fifty-two, realized that there was an intruder in his garden. He called Jamil Ahmad al-Rifai, twenty-eight, his next-door neighbor to come help. They found a two-kilogram bomb in the garden. The missionary went to remove his family from the house. When he returned to the garden, the bomb detonated when al-Rafai was either trying to diffuse or move it. The blast made the body almost unidentifiable.[14] Griffioen is a widely known and well-respected Christian leader. He and his family have lived in Lebanon for over twenty years.

These intimidation tactics have forced many Western missionaries

societies to take on a new philosophy of missions. They are going un-
derground. They no longer seek visas using the word missionaries but
rather now have business platforms to gain visas so as to live in their
target country. This approach has been somewhat successful in allowing workers to stay in the country, but it has also led to the church becoming silent. The missionaries do all they can to not be associated
with Christians or to be known as Christian workers. Thus, they and
those they work with have been intimated into silence.

I spoke with a young Arab man concerning this new method. At one
time he had been one of the leaders in the Muslim Brotherhood but
had converted to Christianity. He spent time in jail and even feared for
his life because some accused him of apostasy. He told me that the mission societies were very naive in following these practices. First, he said
that missionaries did not appreciate the efficiency of the secret services
of the countries where they were serving. He said that the governments
were well aware of all that was going on with these westerners. Second,
he said that the authorities were happy that they had taken this approach since it had quieted them to the place that the missionaries were
no longer a threat to Islam. They could stay if they did nothing. This is
another example of the success of intimidation.

As previously stated, physical presence takes on great significance
in Islam. This results in every effort to stop the construction of new
church buildings or even the use of existing buildings to reach or help
Muslims in any way.

I was in a large German city where several members of an evangelical church desired to minister to the large Muslim community
nearby. After several months about ten citizens from a predominately
Muslim country were coming to a Bible study in a local Baptist
church. After they had been meeting for several months, I received a
call from the leader of the Baptist church. He informed me that he
had received a letter saying that the church building would be burned
down if the meetings did not cease at once. The leader told me that
they had too much invested in the building so they had no choice but
to forbid this group to use the building.

Intimidation was once again successful.

Intimidation and Persecution

Intimidation uses the threat of violence to create fear of what will happen. With persecution, the threat is finalized.

Muslims like to picture themselves as being a persecuted religion. An overview of the history of the Muslim-Christian encounter, however, reveals the reality that it is much more likely that the Christian will be persecuted at the hands of the Muslim.

In his monumental work, *The World Christian Encyclopedia,* David Barrett cites the estimated number of Christian martyrs down through the ages. The numbers are staggering. Barrett reported that from A.D. 33 to A.D. 2000 approximately 69,420,000 men, women, and children have been killed because they were Christians. Of that total number, 9,101,000 Christians have been martyred by Muslims. Some of the worst situations of mass martyrdom in recent history were Idi Amin's Uganda massacres in 1971, the Sudan holocaust from 1963 to present, and the Rwanda genocide of 1994.[15] Today approximately 160,000 Christians are killed every year because of their beliefs.[16]

Today persecution of Christians by Muslims goes unabated. Those suffering the most are the citizens of the Muslim countries who want to live their lives peacefully as Christians in their native lands. The most intense persecution of Christians occurs in Egypt, Iran, Afghanistan, and Sudan. In these places persecution and intimidation seem to be intertwined in such a way that it is often difficult to distinguish between them. Some countries have no Christians left to persecute.

Persecution can be defined as having four levels:

- **Level One:** Persecution (or intimidation) that includes threats that lead to social disenfranchisement of the victim
- **Level Two:** Persecution that leads to material loss and limited possibilities for social advancement
- **Level Three:** Persecution that leads to isolation and separation from family, friends, and culture (prison, for example)
- **Level Four:** Persecution that leads to death and physical injury

There is no level three or four persecution in the West. This is true even among those from Muslim countries living in the West because there are laws against such actions. However, oftentimes the threats of death and injury have been so complete that the actual deed has not been necessary. For example, while a Muslim family will seldom kill a daughter who converts to Christianity, the fear of the possibility will often lead to the desired result of keeping her from following Christ.

Levels one and two are practiced on a regular basis both in Muslim countries and among Muslims in the West. These levels are not only much more prevalent but possibly more effective. In the Islamic culture, the extended family provides jobs, training, housing, food, insurance, etc., to its own. When a person disobeys and the family converts away from Islam, the isolation and threats begin immediately. A person who has grown up with the security of the family network begins to look to the church for such help but usually finds little. In Western society we look to the government to supply those needs. Thus, the new convert is left without a real support foundation. At a recent high-level conference on Middle East evangelism, one authority stated that approximately 80 percent of all converted Muslims return to Islam, not because of theological considerations but because of cultural needs.

The second level of persecution may be less visible, but it could be considered the most insidious. For those living in Muslim countries, becoming a Christian or blaspheming Islam generally means that the person is condemning himself to a life on the lowest social level. This makes it difficult or impossible to provide for their family. This may play out in the following ways:

1. A burned-out business
2. Children being denied entrance into the better schools
3. The unavailability of government sponsored housing
4. Inability to gain both an exit and a reentry visa
5. Transcripts not allowed to be sent outside of the country, and
6. Lack of promotion on the job.

In one Muslim country, I met with an anonymous national Christian who had just been released from prison. He had a well-respected position at the main airport. A coworker became jealous of him and reported him as a Christian. In this country they take pride in saying that there are no citizens of their country who are Christians, thus, to punish him would go against this belief. They questioned him and asked if he kept Ramadan the last time. Since he was a Christian, he answered truthfully that he did not. The police then sent him to jail for six months for failure to keep Ramadan. While he was in prison, his family began to suffer financially because they had no money coming in and socially because of the stigma of having a father in prison.

After four months he was very discouraged, but while walking in the prison yard one day, he saw a little section of a newspaper. It was printed in English, and he was one of the few prisoners who knew English. The newspaper came from England, and the small piece he found had a "Today's Devotion" section in it. As he read the Bible verse, he was assured that God had not forgotten him. The Scripture was Romans 8:38–39: "For I am convinced that neither death nor life, neither angels nor demons, neither the present nor the future, nor any powers, neither height nor depth, nor anything else in all creation, will be able to separate us from the love of God that is in Christ Jesus our Lord."

Several days later the man learned that some Christians had heard about his plight and had begun to help the family. After he was released, his director felt that he had been unfairly punished and gave him his pay for the six months and even promoted him.[17] While persecution is an important part of the Islamic strategy, by the grace of God many are able to stand up under the pressures that are brought to bear.

CONCLUSION

The struggle continues between the world's two largest religions. Even if it is an unpleasant thought, it is a fact that power encounters exist between the two in the twenty-first century. The religion promoting such encounters is Islam, but the church is strong and able to defend itself. The battle will continue and even intensify as a part of the present and coming clash of civilizations.

chapter **eight**

Muhammad, the Message, and the Mass Media

Distortions and Manipulation

After the hijacked passenger jets slammed into the World Trade Center and the Pentagon, the authorities tried to determine who was responsible. In a short time it became apparent that radical Islamists associated with Osama bin Laden were behind the planning and execution of these disastrous events. Many Muslims living in America were braced for the expected backlash. There were more than one thousand reported acts of violence against Muslims and mosques in the United States, but these were in most cases isolated events. The media broadly condemned such actions, and Americans were told not to judge a world religion on the basis of the actions of just a few radicals.

Most observers also expected that this would be a black mark against the Islamic faith, one that would be difficult to recover from in a short period of time. On the contrary, Islam did not suffer but rather made a giant leap forward. What was not known was that the Islamic strategists had been working for several years in the area of public relations.

Not only did Islam not suffer in America during this period, but it actually experienced growth in the six-month time frame after the events of September 11. Mosques all over the United States and Europe were ready with programs to take the bad news and use it to their advantage. In most mosques there were open houses where the public was invited to come and to learn about the "real Islam." *Imams* were invited to take part in ecumenical worship services—something that had been limited prior to 9/11.

Interest was greatly increased in the minds of the Americans and they asked, "Who are these Muslims?" Those in the mosques then said, "Come and visit us and we will show you the true Islam." Those who came were told that Islam was a religion of peace, love, and forgiveness and that there were few real terrorists in their faith. They did such a convincing job that some converted and others became vocal supporters of tolerance for Islam in their communities.

Already during the middle of the twentieth century, Muslim strategists realized that they needed to do a better job of public relations in the West. They began to put into place a strategy designed to change the image of Islam. In the beginning they did not have the experience or the resources to accomplish their goals, but they did lay the foundation for what was later to become an efficient program of lifting the image of their faith.

According to Daniel Pipes, author of the article "How Dare You Defame Islam," the change in Islamic fortunes actually began with the Salman Rushdie affair in January 1989. The Ayatollah Khomeini, the revolutionary ruler of Iran, called upon "all zealous Muslims to execute" not just Salman Rushdie as the author of *The Satanic Verses* but "all those involved in its publication and who were aware of its contents."[1] After Khomeini's pronouncement, the British press splashed the affair in the headlines of their papers. Television made it a major story and everyone was talking about the threat. The story was detrimental to Islam since it portrayed them as having values that are completely different from those in the West.

However, it was this event that seemed to mark the change in both tactics and efficiency of the public relations effort by the Muslims. Pipes goes on to state: "During the decade since 1989, many efforts have been undertaken by the forces of Islamism—otherwise known as Muslim fundamentalism—to silence critics. Ranging from outright violence to more subtle but no less effective techniques, they have produced impressive results."[2] Between 1989 and 2001 there was a change in reporting of events that involved the Islamic religion. Not only did the press begin to change and write more positive articles about Islam, but they also became quite negative to anyone who went against the political correctness of supporting Islam. One journalist from Salt Lake City, Gwynne Dyer, said in satirical words:

> Rule One: When covering terrorist attacks, do not discuss the political context of the attacks or the terrorists' motives and strategy. . . . Rule Two: All terrorists' actions are part of the same problem. . . . Rule Three: All terrorists are Islamic fanatics. Most of the Western media now knows (these rules) by heart.[3]

The point of Dyer's dripping sarcasm is that she felt the Western media did not treat terrorism or Islam fairly. Her editorial reads as if it was written by an indignant Muslim journalist expounding the prejudices of Western media against what is, after all, a religion of peace.

ISLAM AND THE MEDIA

Islam is no longer ready to sit back and allow the Western media elite to cover world events unchallenged. Instead, they are taking the initiative in bringing the news to a global audience. Of course, their coverage is biased, but they say that the Western media is also biased—so what's the difference? Al-Jazeera, the Arabic television and press agency well known worldwide for upstaging the illustrious CNN with its coverage of the American war in Afghanistan and for suspiciously exclusive access to Osama Bin Laden, has launched an English language TV channel in Europe and is increasing its Washington, DC, bureau from six to twenty-four staff members. The Western media scene is not just open; it is actively seeking Muslim input.

CNN, not to be outdone in the Muslim world, with its large audience has launched CNN-Arabic in an attempt to reach the vast Muslim television audience worldwide. Following the September 11 events, the British Foreign Office established an Islamic Media Unit to "focus on the Arab media to which it reaches out through personal interaction for an exchange of views."

The Islamic world is now focusing more firmly on spreading Islam through the use of mass media. Dr. Roushdy Shahata, a professor at Halawan University in Egypt, said, "The journalists must always have a good Islamic bias."[4] Being a religious journalist, he can write his subjects from the Islamic point of view. He asserts that the goal of the Islamic media is to broadcast to the entire world.

The main organization that is promoting a better use of the media is the World Islamic League. It has an alliance with several large media organizations. Recently they held a conference together in Jeddah, Saudi Arabia, concerning ecumenical media. Dr. Turaky, president of the World Islamic League, emphasized once again the importance of the mass media in the spread of Islam. They made a plan of cooperation between them in order to proclaim Islam and display it in a better light. Turaky also insisted that all the mass media cooperate with the *Da'wah* organizations.[5]

There appears to be several components in their unprecedented attempt to communicate their message to the West. These components are:

"We are not..."

This is an attempt to change the negative stereotypes of Muslims in the Western world by the emerging Muslim media leaders. For a century the Arab has been seen as a rather dim-witted fellow living in an inhospitable part of the world. When there was the need of comedy relief for a film, the directors could generally do well by inserting an Arab into the script. With the emergence of the "political correctness" fad, all minorities benefited from the new unwritten rules concerning stereotypes.

For the Arabs, the use of petrodollars, along with the efforts of some very capable men, gave a new impetus toward escalating this change. Several organizations were formed that had as a part of their purpose statement the influencing of the media. One such organization is the Council on American-Islamic Relations (CAIR), a Washington-based institution founded in 1994. Daniel Pipes has written: "CAIR presents itself to the world as a standard-issue civil-rights organization whose mission is to 'promote interest and understanding among the general public with regards to Islam and Muslims in North America and conduct educational services.'"[6]

CAIR has proven to be a very active organization that has taken part in defending Islam, especially in the media. In its short history it has been involved in various means to intimidate news organizations that portray Islam in an unacceptable light. Among their targets have been writers such as Steven Emerson, Daniel Pipes, Shaykl Palazzi, and a host of others who dare to take issue with Islam today. One example occurred when President George W. Bush nominated Islamic scholar Daniel Pipes to the board of directors of the United States Institute of Peace.

Charles Krauthammer of the *Washington Post* wrote, "This nomination has resulted in a nasty eruption of McCarthyism. Pipes's nomination has been greeted by charges of Islamophobia, bigotry, and extremism."[7] Among organizations that have heard from them or felt their criticism are the *National Post, New Republic, Los Angeles Times, Dallas Morning News, Weekly Reader's Current Events* (a children's magazine), and many others too numerous to name.[8] In some cases CAIR will picket the offices of the targeted organization or organize a letter writing campaign. In some undocumented instances, there have been threats addressed to the personnel in the organizations and the facilities where they are located. Whenever there is a terrorist attack or a Muslim is on trial, the news media will have a representative from CAIR or one of the other Muslim organizations defining their faith.

The English-language paper *Gulf News* recently reported on the Islamic Affairs Department of the government of Dubai—a member of the United Arab Emirates. The goal of this department, according to its manager, is to "project real Islamic teachings and correct faulty notions. Many non-Muslims and even Muslims maintain devious impressions about the religion. Thus, our task is to correct their faulty understandings."[9] An entire article in the *Washington Post* was devoted to Muslims' efforts to shake off negative stereotypes, chronicling the lives of three American Muslims who work for the United States government. All said their jobs help break down stereotypes about Muslims.[10]

The movies and television have proven to be a problem for Islam. In the past, several movie producers have suggested the making of a movie on the life of Muhammad. There was fierce opposition to this because Muslims believe that it is a sin to make an image of their leader. One producer decided to make the movie without an actor playing Muhammad but rather the space the actor would normally occupy would be left free. This also did not meet the approval of the Muslim community.

A few years ago another attempt was made to chronicle the life of Muhammad, "presenting the story of the seventh-century Islamic prophet to an American audience largely unfamiliar with the religion he founded."[11] They decided to go ahead and not show the face of the prophet. They had the film about two-thirds finished when the events of September 11, 2001, took place. They were about to end the project when it was suggested that they make it into a two-hour documentary titled *Muhammad: Legacy of a Prophet*. The documentary told the story of Muhammad together with interviews with scholars and modern-day United States Muslims.

The Public Broadcasting Service first presented it on December 18, 2002, right before the Christmas show. Rather than just being a film about the prophet, it became a tool for Muslim propaganda. It received raves from the secular press but was considered by many to be a film seeking to win converts to Islam. It is of interest to note that "the largest source of funding (for PBS) comes from the Corporation for Public Broadcasting, a private, non-profit corporation created by Congress that in fiscal 2002 received $350 million in taxpayers funds."[12] The same network aired another documentary in 1998 on the life of Jesus where the main emphasis was from critical scholars who questioned much of the historicity of Jesus. Islamic leaders have learned that they need not be afraid of films today but rather can use them to their advantage.

Muslim strategists did have a setback in the early 1990s when the film *Not Without My Daughter* was produced. It chronicled the life of an American woman whose daughter was taken back to Iran, the homeland of the girl's father. She was not allowed to leave the country; she basically became a slave in a Muslim context where women have little or no rights. She finally did escape over the mountains into Turkey. One author notes: "The 1991 film . . . set Muslims back about ten years in the effort to improve their public image."[13]

Islam has been very successful in the last ten years in redefining who they are and who they are not. But before the Muslim community can communicate positively to its skeptical Western audience, it must first convince them that Islam is not all bad, and that the Islamic faith is not the same as Palestinian suicide bombers and women abusers.

It is amazing to see how big a change there has been in a little over ten years on how Americans view Islam and Muslims. This was no accident but rather the results of a well-planned strategy that only now is really becoming effective. I doubt that there will be many articles, TV productions, movies, or magazine statements that stand out as negative toward Islam. This is definitely not the case in respect to Christians and the church.

"We are . . ."

The first element of the Muslim media message, dispelling negative views of Muslims, often works in partnership with the second element—projecting positive views of Muslims. As much as possible, the desire is to show that Muslims, particularly American Muslims, are decent, hardworking, loving, kind people. In short, American Muslims are just as American (or just as Western) as any other ethnic group in the great American "melting pot."

This, in fact, was the clear message of a series of public service announcements produced by the Islamic Media Foundation and aired to more than two million viewers across America in November 2002. The series, titled *Your American Muslim Neighbors,* showed American Muslim families in quintessential American activities: at Little League games, visiting Mount Rushmore, going to worship together (albeit to a mosque), etc. The images were altogether wholesome, positive, patriotic, and serene.

The Islamic Media Foundation has also run a series of public announcements that are in keeping with the group's objectives of "letting others know our contributions to the well-being of this society."[14] Adds the *Muslim News,* "Muslim communities across America are on a PR mission to explain what their religion is all about. . . . From political fundraisers and food drives to open houses at mosques."[15] Once again it is clear to see that their message is that Muslims, far from being bomb-bearing fanatics, are in fact paragons of charity to their American neighbors.

"We believe . . ."

The atmosphere of multiculturalism in American schools are an excellent place to bring in Islamic propaganda. At the same time that Christians are fighting the ACLU to obtain certain basic rights in the schools, Muslims seem to have an open door to come in and proselytize. As mentioned previously, one textbook used in California schools presented Islam in a very favorable light and suggested that the students might want to dress up like Muslims and experience such activities as the food they eat and how they pray. The students often were asked to take Muslim names and role-play being a follower of Muhammad. If this were done with a Christian context, lawsuits citing separation of church and state would surely follow.

Recently one of the principals of a California school gave me a letter that was addressed to all principals and district superintendents. It was from the Islamic Speakers Bureau. In the letter there were announcements suggesting that the teachers have the students turn on the above mentioned TV film *Muhammad: Legacy of a Prophet* as well as other TV programs showing in their area. They also offered "An Arts and Craft Kit for Presenting Ramadan and Eid During the Winter Holiday Season." In the letter were suggestions that all teachers and administrators attend a staff development training seminar titled "Staff Development Training for Educators and Administrators: Incorporating Islamic Cultural Studies in the Curriculum and Interacting with Muslim Students." They offered to send speakers to the schools to teach classroom courses for grades seven to twelve titled "Orientation on Islam and the Muslim World in the Context of World History and Social Science." Another course for the tenth to twelfth graders was called "Women in Islam." I have included a copy of the letters that made these free offers in Appendix B. I was informed that those sending the letters received many requests for speakers.

Five government-employed Muslims interviewed by the *Washington Post* said clearly that they each felt obliged to reach out to non-Muslims and educate people about Islam, especially at the start of Ramadan. Similar to the Christian observation of Christmas or Easter in terms of its universal practice and high importance to each faith's followers, Ramadan is a frequent starting point for Muslims educating non-Muslims about their faith.

WBAY TV, an ABC-affiliated station in the Green Bay, Wisconsin, area, included a brief explanation of Ramadan in a recent broadcast about the local Muslim community.

> Muslims from around the Fox Valley gathered to celebrate the beginning of Ramadan. Ramadan will last for one month. It requires Muslims to fast from sunrise to sunset for the next month and to refrain from several vices listed in the *Qur'an.* . . . Ramadan is time for prayer and fasting. It's also a chance to show the world what Islam is all about. . . . It's an ongoing effort to change the way Americans view the Islamic faith.[16]

The *Muslim News* adds: "Many of the nation's approximately 7 million Muslims will use the month of fasting and spiritual renewal . . . to continue their quest to make inroads into the mainstream."[17]

It's not just during Ramadan that the push for education takes place. The online version of the Saudi Arabian English daily, *Arab News*, has a hyperlink to a long feature on the life of the prophet Muhammad, for the benefit of its English readers who may wish to know more about the Muslim faith. It is likely that there are few, if any, Arab-language newspapers in the West that would include a link to a feature of any length of the Christian view on Jesus Christ.

Following September 11, numerous books by various "experts" appeared on the market purporting to educate their readers on Islam. The *Christian Science Monitor* reviewed one of these, *The Heart of Islam*. Jane Lampman wrote: "In 'The Heart of Islam', a renowned Muslim scholar offers to people 'interested in authentic Islam teachings, as well as its external expressions in law, history, art, and community."[18] Glowing reviews such as this further the educational thrust of the Muslim identity through use of media. In short, the message is clear: "Let us tell you what we really believe." They do, however, report only the side that the westerners want to hear.

"Come and see . . ."

As Muslims correct and improve their image and educate westerners about their faith, their next step is to begin to convert others to the faith. As Yusuf Mohammed, an attorney in the United States Labor Department, says, "There is a great opportunity forced on us by 9/11. A lot of people have become curious about Islam and want to know more."[19] Adds Anwar Hansan, founder and president of the Maryland-based Howard County Muslim Council, "We're trying to reach out to the community now, to remove the fear and ultimately make America a better place."[20]

While this kind of encouragement for outreach may take place Friday after Friday in mosques around the United States, it means little to the wider public until it is published in mainstream media. What is significant is the way local Muslim leaders are now being interviewed, quoted, and highlighted in print, radio, and television reports. Through Muslim use of media, readers, listeners, and viewers who were already curious about Islam are more exposed to this exotic faith and could become prime candidates for future conversion.

One article explained that Omar Muhammad Bashar Arafat of Baltimore "often preaches to fellow Muslims of their responsibility to reach out to other faiths."[21] Arafat tells the worshipers, "It is your duty as a Muslim living in the country, which celebrates democracy, which celebrates religious freedom, to show the beauty and true meaning of Islam. . . . I think it is the duty of every mosque in America to hold dinners, to hold banquets and invite people."[22]

"Let us tell you . . ."

Overarching each of these other components of the Muslim message is the desire to have an active voice in the mainstream media, that is to be heard loud and clear in every discussion of issues that relate to faith and in particular to the Islamic world. This is the strategy behind much of the work of the Islamic Media Foundation, which provides training and resources to help local Muslim leaders become resource people for the mainstream media. In one article leaders of this foundation wrote:

> Injecting Islam's solutions to matters of importance to the American public in national forums of debate. It is imperative to have a Muslim resource group that knows how to handle the media, so that mainstream media have easy access to Islamic scholars and specialists whenever they need an Islamic perspective or need commentary on situations involving Muslims.[23]

To that end, the foundation has organized the Islamic Media Access Network, a grassroots structure consisting of Muslims interested in media activism. This organization has plans to establish an Islamic

Broadcasting Network. It also produces *On Sight,* a weekly news magazine program that can be used by communities on their local television station. *On Sight* reports on events and issues from a Muslim perspective.

Muslim communities around the world are catching this wave. The *Muslim News* touts itself as

> . . . the only independent monthly Muslim newspaper in the U.K.—it is neither backed by any country nor by any organi- zation or party. It is financed by subscriptions, advertising and British Muslim businessmen. . . . "The Muslim News" reports on what the mainstream media refuses to report.[24]

Another news agency reported that in the United States there was a Muslim television network in the making. Two Arab-Americans, Mo Hassan and Omar Amonat, plan to develop the "first nationwide English-language Muslim television in the United States by the sum- mer of 2004."[25] The founders said that they "hope to help the Muslim community gain acceptance and increased understanding through the forum of media, as 'Telemundo' and 'Black Entertainment Televi- sion' have for Hispanics and blacks living in America."[26]

Many other newly created Muslim media groups are being orga- nized in order to propagate the faith. The most successful of the new attempts for Islamic entrance into the world of media was the Arab news network Al-Jezeera, which was launched in 1996 with funding from the government of Qatar. An estimated 150,000 viewers see the channel in the United States.[27]

During the 2003 Iraq war, daily updates about the war were car- ried around the world. Al-Jazeera was active in its coverage. While the Western media was covering the advance and success of the coalition forces, Al-Jazeera was covering problems and the killing of civiliza- tion caused by the troops. Anyone watching the reports from the two perspectives would swear that they were covering two different wars. Al-Jazeera, which was watched by the majority of the citizens of the Middle Eastern countries, was able to sway sympathies away from the

West. They proved their worth in one short war by replacing CNN as the main news agency watched by Muslims.

There is also the potential that Islamic interests will soon be influencing the mainstream media more. In an article in *Newsweek,* the writer Michael Isikoff interviewed Prince Al-Walid bin Talal, the multibillionaire investor who made headlines when he offered $10 million for the 9/11 victims and was turned down by Mayor Rudy Giuliani. During the interview, the prince complained about how the Zionists had "infiltrated" every part of the United States government. What infuriated him most was the "Jewish lobby's power over the media."

As Isikoff continued, he noticed on his desk the emblems of the many United States corporations, portions of which are owned by the prince: AOL Time Warner (his stake $1 billion), NewsCorp ($1 billion), and Disney Corp. ($50 million), not to mention his $10 billion stake in Citicorp the banking giant. Isikoff suggested, "But still . . . Surely, prince, given your holdings, you've got a little influence with the American media yourself." "Oh, yes, he told me; he talks to the top executives of these firms all the time. 'I try to tell them not to be biased,' he said."[28]

INFLUENCE THROUGH ECONOMICS

Today's global economic system is both centralized and yet greatly diffused at the same time. Gigantic multinational corporations control an ever-increasing share of wealth and influence but are susceptible to boycotts organized by dissatisfied consumers. In most cases boycotts, some of which are publicized, have little or no effect on the large corporations due in part to their size. If, however, a significant homogenous group does seek to bring pressure, it must be heard.

In the 1970s, 1980s, and even up through today, there have been attempts to have all Muslims boycott brands that are sold in Israel. Their purpose was to deny Israel the more commonly used products of the contemporary world. Varying degrees of success were achieved in that some companies' products (soft drinks being one) had to make a decision whether to sell to Israel or the surrounding Arab states. Those boycotts would ebb and flow depending on a number of issues and were not always related to politics. Businessmen seemed to always find a way around the boycotts so that their own interests were satisfied.

During and after the second Gulf War, businesses and even states were jockeying for use of the world situation for their own benefit. The American public was called upon to order "freedom fries" instead of French fries and to stop buying French perfume, French wine, and French automobiles as a way to show displeasure with France's lack of support for the American position. Citizens in France did much the same by boycotting American goods and even attacking a few American businesses such as McDonald's. One source of this economic battle has been the growing influence of Islam France.

The war caused a variety of commercial protests against America. Some of the reported protests include:

- Almost one out of four people in the Asian-Pacific region said they have avoided purchasing American brands.
- German bicycle maker Reice and Mueller has canceled all business deals with American suppliers.
- The Qibla Cola Company, a soft drink maker based in Great Britain that markets to the Muslim community, called for a boycott of United States global brands.
- Consumers in Europe and the Middle East have snapped up 4.5 million bottles of Mecca-Cola, an anti-American soft drink launched in October 2002. Mecca-Cola—with the motto that translates as, "Don't drink stupidly, drink responsibly"—has orders for fourteen million more bottles. The cola is also sold in Middle Eastern neighborhoods in the United States: in Detroit, and soon in New Jersey.[29]

Later in the same article the following was reported:

- Mecca-Cola founder Tawfik Mathlouthi also plans to open Halal Fried Chicken restaurants, to be called HFC, a jab at the

KFC chain. His aim: "People will stop eating and drinking American goods and using American goods," he says, "and that will increase the social problems in the United States and increase joblessness, and Americans will awake from their long sleep and maybe ask the United States government to respond."[30]

Muslims will continue to attempt to leverage their increasing purchasing power to both increase their own wealth and, in many cases, also to damage American culture.

INFLUENCE THROUGH POLITICS

All minorities in America now feel that even with their small percentage of the total population they can influence public opinion through politics. Recently the announcement was made that the largest minority group in America are the Hispanics, now approximately 13 percent of the population. If the statistics put out by the Muslims, who claim they now have seven million in the United States, are correct, then they would have about 2.8 percent of the population. It should be noted, however, that the real figures are approximately one-half of that estimated by the Muslims. Because of the parity between the Democrats and the Republicans, this small amount can make a large difference. The more they grow, the more political power they can have. Many Muslims have claimed that they put George W. Bush into the presidency because they overwhelmingly voted for him in Florida.

Fundamentals within Islam have learned very well how to use democracy to their own end. The minority Muslim population of Malawi, South Africa, was able to win the election mainly through the investment of tremendous amounts of funds into the electoral process. Both Algeria and Turkey are countries where the fundamentals came close to succeeding. In other countries Islamic candidates have been thwarted not because they did not have the votes but because of fear of what would happen if they did take over the government politically.

Islamic involvement in the political process is much more advanced in Europe than in the United States. In England there is now a shadow government that has been created by the Muslims to act on their own issues but also to be prepared if the opportunity ever comes to take over the government. In Belgium, an Islamic delegation arrived in the country to hold a meeting with the government, and in turn the whole of Europe since Brussels is fondly called the heart of Europe. Dr. Turaky of the World Islamic League said, "The European parliaments are a very good way to reach within the countries." He also noted that there are many Muslims in the parliament of Belgium, making good progress in the proclamation of Islam. Because of the good relationship between the Muslims in the Belgium government and the country, the World Islamic League was able to do the following on their trip:

1. They received permission to teach the Islamic religion in Belgium's schools
2. They received permission to have a prayer room in the Brocksel airport
3. They received permission to build a new Islamic cemetery
4. They got some laws changed so that the Muslims can practice their religious commitments.[31]

In Holland there are seven Islamic parliamentarians in the parliament, many of them members in Dutch political parties. Dr. Marzouk, the president of the Islamic University in Holland, said, "The Muslims in this country must be ready to govern Holland because of the increasing numbers of Muslims and the decreasing numbers of the original people of Holland."[32]

A successful part of their megaplan is to bring both educators and politicians to the Islamic faith. Here are some examples of their successes.

1. Alexander Cronemar is involved with American foreign affairs. He has a master's degree in comparative religions from Harvard University. He has also worked in the Middle East.

He married an American Muslim woman and became a Muslim himself. He was the producer of the recently released film on the life of Muhammad.[33]

2. Dr. Kasper Ibrahim Shahin became a Muslim on June 10, 2002. He is a scientist, economist, and the professor of technology at a state institution in the United States. He is also the president of this institution and is very well known by former presidents George Bush and Ronald Reagan. He became a Muslim as a result of the influence of his Islamic friends. It was stated that "he too wants to bring Islam to other scientists and prominent people in America by the use of mass media, but first he wants to bring his family into Islam."[34]

3. Dr. Hofman Murad, the former German ambassador to Algeria. It was reported that "he found Islam as the logical religion and one that was very close to the human mind. He found that Christianity is a faded religion. He is using all of his influence to spread Islam in Germany and around the Globe."[35]

4. The son of the president of the BBC became a Muslim and married a Muslim woman and changed his name to Yehia Beart. It was reported that his goal is to spread Islam in the United Kingdom and help his family embrace Islam.[36]

These are just a few of the names of prominent converts as reported in the *Middle East Newspaper*. Islam sees the need to concentrate on the main policy makers. One of the many rumors surrounding the death of Princess Diana was that she was killed by the secret service because she was considering marrying a Muslim. The rumor was probably false, but the concern about the possibility of Muslim royalty was real.

CONCLUSION

In the seventh century, Muhammad learned much from the Christians and Jesus concerning the belief in one God. So now Islam is learning much from them again, but this time in the realm of public relations. Radio, television, the Internet, and the printed media are now full of the battle for the minds and souls of the present generation. Encouraged by recent successes and well financed by oil dollars, Islam has come out of the dark ages.

To say Islam is close to surpassing the West in public relations would be a gross overstatement. But it is also foolish and incorrect to dismiss their efforts in this arena. Only time will determine if their efforts will be successful enough to make great gains in influencing the thinking of the average westerner.

chapter **nine**

What in the World Is Allah Doing?

An Overview of the Present-Day Expansion of Islam

One friend from Europe, who was a practicing Muslim, spoke with me after making the *hajj* into Mecca. He told me that there was a large sign on the road just outside of the Holy City that stated, "Islam now has over One Billion Adherents." Islam is without question the largest non-Christian religion in the world. The exact numbers are hard to come by, but one highly respected demographer, Patrick Johnstone, gave the following figures for Muslims and Christians at the turn of this last century:

Religion	Population Percentage	Adherents	Annual Growth
Christian	32.54%	1.973 billion	1.43%
Muslim	21.09%	1.279 billion	2.17%[1]

He goes on to add that only the religions that have a growth rate of over 1.39 percent are increasing faster than the world's population. Many will question these numbers, but they appear to be the most accurate ones available. Muslims often say that they are the fastest growing religion in the world, and Johnstone seems to support this claim; although if evangelical Christianity is separated out of the larger Christian church body, then their growth rate would be larger than that of Islam. Johnstone claims that the growth rate of evangelicals in the world is 4.7 percent and that of the Pentecostals is 4.5 percent.[2]

Today Islam is spreading by both peaceful and militant means. There needs to be a distinction made between conversion and forced submission, the first depending on *Da'wah* and the second being related more to *jihad*. Also, it should be noted that the greatest increase in Islam, particularly in the West, is coming not by conversion but rather by migration and large families. These arguments must be put aside because the focus of our discussion needs to be on the Islamic strategy for the future. It will not be feasible to take an in-depth look at all the countries of the world to see what Islam is doing, but rather we shall look at the major areas of the world and, in some cases, concentrate on some of the key countries where Islam is either growing or using innovative means for expansion.

THE MIDDLE EAST

To be sure Islam dominates the Middle East, but this is not satisfactory for those who seek a more radical Islam. There are undercurrents of dissatisfaction that runs deep in countries that have not put *Shariah* in place or who have failed to declare that they are Islamic republics. Countries that fall into this more moderate category are Egypt, Jordan, Lebanon, Kuwait, and Iraq.

Prior to the second Gulf War, Iraq was ruled by the Baath party and thus did not have an extreme Islamic government. In chapter 1, it was stated that the second step of Ayatollah Khomeini's plan for world dominance was encouraging the creation of Islamic republics in the surrounding Muslim countries whether by revolution, war, or negotiation. The Iran-Iraq war of the 1980s ended in a deadlock, thus Ayatollah's plans were blocked. However, the success of the coalition forces in defeating Saddam Hussein gave the Shiites new hope.

Soon after the end of the war it was reported, "Beating their chests and chanting praises to Allah, tens of thousands of Shiites flooded the southern city of Basra on Saturday to welcome home their exiled leader [Ayatollah Mohammed Baqir al-Hakim] whose brand of hard-line Islam could play a decisive role in shaping the religious and social face of the new Iraq."[3]

Later in the article, al-Hakim was quoted as saying, "*Shariah* has to lead this country."[4] The battle for Iraq continues between those who support a Western form of democracy in a Middle Eastern country and those who desire an Islamic republic.

The sad history of contemporary Lebanon writes another chapter in the attempt of Islam to have complete dominance over all of the Middle East. The war left the country and its beautiful capital city, Beirut, in ruins. Pierre Francis, a Christian leader in Lebanon, wrote his Th. D. dissertation on the causes and effects of the war. He wrote, "Lebanon has been an area of continued struggle between the power of Islam and that of Christianity. According to results, and not necessarily motives, the Civil War in Lebanon of 1975 to 1992 constituted a contemporary link in the chain of the Muslim conquest from the perspective of Islam."[5] In his dissertation, Francis's main theme is that the cause of war was Islam's attempt to replace the Christian led country with an Islamic republic, thus removing the only Christian state in the area. They almost succeeded.

The number of Christians in the Middle East continues to decrease due mostly to immigration. They feel that they have a brighter future in the West.

AFRICA

Possibly no part of the world shows more clearly the violent side of Islam than Africa. The continent has experienced bitter warfare in

Algeria, terrorist attacks in Kenya, genocide in the Sudan, massacres of Christians and the burning of their churches in northern Nigeria, just to name a few. Johnstone's statistics for this continent are as follows:

Religion	Population Percentage	Adherents	Annual Growth
Christianity	48.37%	379.4 million	2.83%
Islam	41.32%	324.1 million	2.53%[6]

Both of the two major religions continue to make rapid advancements at the expense of native tribal religions, but neither of them is outdistancing the other at this time.

One international activity that is unfolding before our eyes has to do with Muammar Qaddafi, the president of Libya and a known Muslim fundamentalist. In recent years the Organization of African Unity (OAU) had been declining and, for all practical purposes, was dead. Recently President Qaddafi called for the creation of a new pan-African organization. He has taken the lead in the formation of an alternate to the OAU. Up to now no final structure has been formed, but the name most often mentioned as the head of the new organization is Qaddafi. The Muslim North is very active in trying to place their people in influential positions of leadership for future expansion. For the sake of clarity the continent should be seen as having two parts: the first being what is often called North Africa, which is predominately Muslim, and the other is all of Africa south of the Sahara, which is more Christian.

North Africa

Islam retains a strong hold in this area, but it continues to try to convert the remnant of Christians living in the countries that extend from Morocco to the Sudan.

The first country we will look at is Egypt, which is approximately 13 percent Christian, most of whom belong to the Coptic Orthodox church that traces it beginnings back to the conversion of the Ethiopian eunuch in Acts 8. There are also pockets of Roman Catholics, Presbyterians, and Baptists to name a few.

This very populous country was the birthplace of the Muslim Brotherhood, one of the first of the modern fundamentalist movements. This extreme form of Islam has had a history of exploiting economic problems to mount a series of attacks against Christians, tourists, and any others who blocked them from achieving their aims. Christians, particularly in the southern part of the country, have suffered much from economic and physical persecution.

Once when I was in a large town in the south, an older Christian Egyptian woman came to me in tears and wanted me to help her find her granddaughter. I was told that the thirteen-year-old had been kidnapped by the Muslims and would be held hostage until she converted to Islam. Later I was informed that this was a common practice in that part of the country. Another Christian told me that his pharmacy had just been burned down for the second time, and he had been warned either to convert to Islam or leave.

Among other activities practiced by Egyptian fundamentalists are:

1. Demanding that all non-Muslims be considered *dhimmi* thus losing most political rights
2. Imposing dress and behavior codes on all
3. The incitement of various forms of discrimination against Christians
4. Takeover of professional organizations: examples are the bar and medical associations
5. Destabilizing the country so as to take over the country and declare an Islamic republic
6. Persecute and even assassinate secular critics
7. Construct new mosques but forbid new churches from being started or church buildings being repaired or built

Further to the west in Algeria, economic failures and an attempt at democracy after the War of Liberation in 1962 led to a situation where it appeared that the Islamic Political Party would take control of the government, but the results were annulled by the government unleashing a civil war, which has caused over one hundred thousand deaths. Many of the Christians, who constitute less than 1 percent, were also killed. Once again political instability was used as an excuse to persecute the Christian minority.

Ravages of war has had an unusual result in that today there is more growth of the Christian church there than any other country of North Africa. All of the countries of North Africa have seen some limited growth, but the efficiency of the Muslim persecution and the Islamic-leaning governments have slowed down this growth.

Sudan is possibly one of the saddest examples of the abuse of Islam in their road toward world domination. In 1983 it was declared to be an Islamic republic. This decision included the institution of a form of *Shariah* in the country that applied to both Muslims and non-Muslims alike. Since about one-fourth of the country was Christian, this caused hardships on this minority.

The constitution offers some religious liberty, but reality has shown that there has been, and still is, a brutal attempt to convert the Christians to Islam. There have been countless examples: the bull-dozing of churches, persecutions of individuals, denial of human rights, death by starvation, and the destruction of Christian institutions such as hospitals and schools.

Over one million have been killed in the predominately Christian southern provinces. Sudan remains the most gruesome example in the world today of *jihad* being practiced in order to further Islam.

Sub-Saharan Africa

Sub-Saharan Africa is an entity of its own and is separated from the predominately Muslim North Africa by a large desert region. According to Patrick Johnstone, the number of Muslims in this area by mid-2001 was 7.14 million.[7] In this part of the world the countries with the largest Muslim population are Mozambique, Malawi, Madagascar, and South Africa.

The growth of Islam in this area came from two historical movements. The first was the expansion by trade down the East African coast on to Mozambique from 750 to A.D. 1500. The second was the migration from 1500 to the present into the coastal areas of Western Africa, Central Africa, Sudan, Ethiopia, and Uganda. This includes South Africa in the eighteenth and nineteenth centuries.

Several years ago during a dialogue meeting with some Muslim leaders in Europe, one of them told me what their strategy was for this area. It was quite simple and has proven to be successful. He said the plan called on Islam to make a march to the south. It would start in the northern part of the continent and move south trying to win black African countries one at a time. If they came across a country or an area that was difficult and would require more time, then they would just jump that area and continue to the south.

He stated to me that Kenya was one that had proven to be harder than expected. Nigeria is an excellent example of this strategy at work in that the north is Islamic while the south is strongly Christian. They continue to move to the south burning churches and causing problems with those who resist. As already stated, they are building a new mosque every mile close to the main highway that leads to the south as a visual expression of their march southward.[8]

Every type of strategy spoken about previously in this book has been and is being utilized in Africa. They see education as being an important step toward their goal. One Christian missionary who was speaking about Rwanda stated that one in four of the college professors at the National University are Muslims. This is compared to 90 percent of the students being non-Muslim. About a dozen Egyptian and Pakistani professors are working at the university at no cost to the country. The government of Saudi Arabia is paying their salary.[9]

Oil dollars are readily available for the Islamic work in southern Africa. A good example of how the use of strong finances has been successful is the example of Malawi, the country of David Livingston. Christianity has a long and illustrious history here. Today a little over three-fourths of the 9,670,000 citizens are Christian. Islam only has approximately 15 percent. In one of the recent democratic elections, one of the candidates for president was a Muslim. Large amounts of money came in from foreign sources and Bakili Muluzi, a Muslim, won the election.

In a 1998 report titled "Religious Freedom in the Majority Islamic Countries," it was stated, "Numerous signs point to a growing Islamic influence in the country. Many Muslim students have obtained scholarships to study in Saudi Arabia and other Islamic countries, the number of mosques has grown enormously, following a precise expansion strategy."[10]

Some say that there will be little growth of Islam despite the political pressures, but others see that Islam has been revitalized by the president's election.

The key to conquering southern Africa is the Republic of South Africa. It is the jewel of the region because of its strong economy and governmental structure. Prior to the radical changes brought on in South Africa because of the collapse of apartheid, it was generally viewed as a Western nation and thus considered in the Christian camp. Now it is considered a neutral state, and some of the countries of the Middle East feel that it could be tilted toward their culture, religion, and way of life.

By the mid-1990s over 81 percent of the population considered themselves Christian. This compared to the eight hundred thousand or 2.4 percent who claimed to be Muslims. Most of the latter came from Southeast Asia and were centered on the coast. Once again the strategists in Mecca could read the political changes in the country, and they began to make plans to exert a misappropriate amount of pressure for their mission cause. As the newly, predominately black government began to take place, few noticed that there were inroads made by the Islamists.

In an interview with a theologian from South Africa, Martinus Pretorius, now the professor of systematic theology at the Evangelical Theological Faculty in Leuven, Belgium, stated, "Even though in South Africa they have only about 2 percent of the population they constitute

20 percent of the cabinet. Two portfolios they occupy are the Ministry of Justice and the Ministry of Radio and Television. During the Apartheid period they were very busy laying a foundation for *Da'wah* among the blacks. Now they are reaping a degree of success."[11]

In concluding with Africa south of the Sahara, it is apparent that the battle for the hearts and minds of its population will be active in the future. Those who follow Jesus Christ would be well advised that they cannot put this part of the world on the back burner but rather should become involved in the activities of this volatile region.

ASIA

Asia is extremely large both in land mass and in population. It has a surface area of 23.5 percent of the world's land, when you include Russia east of the Ural Mountains. Approximately 61 percent of the world's population lives in this area.[12]

Asia is the only continent where Christianity is not the largest religion. Islam points to Asia proudly and claims that it is on this continent that they have had their most successful *Da'wah* experience. The number of Muslims is over 900 million and still growing. The Muslim country with the largest population is Indonesia with over 171 million. Justin Long, in an evaluation of the growth of Islam, stated:

> Islam's Growth . . . shows no sign of tapering off. Though it, like Christianity, got off to a slow start, it has now claimed more than 25% of Asia, and could well approach 30% by 2050. The contest between Islam and Christianity now faced in Africa will shortly be seen in Asia as well, as Islam grows as a majority in many Asian nations, and a substantial minority in others (including China).[13]

In many parts of Asia, Islam crept in quietly at the beginning but now has decided to take a more aggressive approach. They are faced with some huge problems, one being the diversification of Islam due to the many deep, preexisting religious beliefs and practices, resulting in different expressions of faith than those practiced and expressed in the Middle East. John L. Esposito wrote in his book *Islam in Asia:*

> The expansion of Islam in Asia produced a variety and diversity of Islamically informed societies. All Muslims shared a common faith, a confession of their belief in the one God and in his Book and the teachings of his prophet. However, Islam encountered peoples of vastly different historical backgrounds, languages, ethnic/tribal identities, loyalties, customs, and cultures. In a very real sense an Arab Islam was transformed into Persian, South Asian, and Southeast Asian Islam through the process of assimilation and synthesis. Despite the common core of belief and practice epitomized by the Five Pillars of Islam, Muslim societies differed in the extent and manner to which religion manifested itself in public life—politics, law, and society.[14]

As a result, the growth of Islam in Asia has and continues to be manifested in a variety of ways. All methods seem to be used in this strategic part of the world including *jihad* and *Da'wah.* Because Asia is where most of the world's Muslims live, it is an especially appropriate place to examine the growth of Islam.

The size of the area is such that we shall divide it into four subareas. They are South Asia, Southeast Asia, East Asia, and the Pacific. Even with this breakdown, the complexity of the area has many overlapping movements and ideologies within Islam.

South Asia

Another term for South Asia could be "The Indian Subcontinent"; this area would include the countries of Pakistan, India, Afghanistan, and Bangladesh. In this part of the world, Islam has an important impact on political stability. These four countries have a total of approximately 282 million followers of Islam. The percentages of the population range from 99 percent in Afghanistan to 12 percent in India.

Pakistan with over ninety-one million has been described as the "only state explicitly established in the name of Islam."[15] It was established because of political and religious strife in India in order to provide a state where Islam could be expressed both politically and socially. Despite this, however, the role of Islam in the country remains unclear until now.

Up until recently Pakistan's Muslims, like other Muslims in the region, tend to follow a school of Islam that is less conservative, and hence the support for strongly and overtly religious parties has been minimal. Santu Limaye argues that because Islam was spread primarily through the preaching of Muslim *Sufi* saints and since the *Sufi* teachings contrast with the more conservative teachings in the Middle East, the former Hindu converts are less conservative.[16]

Today there is an ever-increasing influential fundamentalist movement. Acts of terrorism such as the murder of the journalist Daniel Pearl and the bombing of Christian schools and churches demonstrates that radicalism is alive today. There is a battle within Islam itself in the region. Both the moderates and the fundamentalists are seeking to control the future of the Islamic movement.

Because the subcontinent is heavily Muslim, much of the growth of Islam in this part of the world is due mainly to large families. Intense dislike and conflict between Hindus and Muslims have threatened war in the area but has not led to mass conversion to Islam. At one time, some of the leaders of the "Outcasts," or the lower casts of India, were suggesting that it was foolish for them to remain Hindus since they were so ill-treated. Suggestions were made that this caste would in total convert to another religion such as Christianity, Buddhism, or Islam. One of their key leaders, Ram Raj, has said that he and other leaders "have been investigating the Muslim and Buddhist religions, as well as Christianity. Muslim and Buddhist leaders have assured them that they would do whatever was needed to bring the 300 million outcast Hindus into their camp."[17]

When they met with Christian leaders, they were told that the Christians could not help them because they would not be able to handle the repercussions from the Indian government.[18] Ram Raj said that he was "keenly disappointed to hear this as Christianity had been his first choice."[19] Because of the lasting conflicts and also because of the bitter history, the leaders of the outcasts excluded Islam as a possibility. No final move to either of the other two religions has taken place.

The situation in India is rather different since they comprise only 12 percent of the total, but their impact on the stability of the country is significant. This minority status puts Muslims in another situation. Shahabuddin and Wright, in writing on India, stated:

> The role of Islam, and therefore of Muslims, in public life both potentially and actually differs fundamentally in countries with only a minority of Muslims in their populations from those with Muslim majorities. Extremists on both sides, Muslims and non-Muslims, may think that the minority situation can be changed into a majority one by religious conversion, higher birthrates, or immigration, but the chances of this reversal happening in India are highly unlikely.[20]

Hindu-Muslim violence continues today with little change. As tensions rise at the regional level between India and Pakistan especially over Kashmir, Islam seems to have lost its focus. At the international level, this area continues to gain attention. The war against the Taliban in Afghanistan, the nuclear arms of India and Pakistan, and political unrest all add to the newsworthiness of Southern Asia. The Muslims have increased their connections with the Middle East and with international Islamic movements, thus showing that there are strong undercurrents that continue to support the expansion of Islam in South Asia. Their strong presence throughout the region cannot be ignored.

Even though Islam was probably brought to South Asia through peaceful means centuries ago, it seems as if Islam continues to grow today in the region through conflict and conquest as well as large families.

Southeast Asia

Most historians date the entry of Islam into Southeast Asia around the thirteenth century. Islam was introduced to the region primarily through Gujarati traders from the Indian subcontinent and the preaching of *Sufi* sages. The region is composed of a string of islands along a route connecting India and China. It includes as its major countries Indonesia and Malaysia.

Many of the Muslim communities of South and Southeast Asia remain discrete and separate, both in the ideal norms they profess and in the day-to-day practices they pursue.

An example is Indonesia where approximately 87 percent of the population is Muslim. Johnstone and Mandryk have made three distinctions within that 87 percent. They write that approximately 30 percent are "high identity, high practice"; approximately 35 percent are "high identity, low practice"; and approximately 35 percent are "low identity, low practice."[21]

Although Indonesia has resisted becoming an Islamic republic, it still remains a strongly Islamic country. According to Lemaye,

> Islam has never played a central role in the country's politics. Nevertheless, there has been persistent tension between those advocates of a more prominent and formal role for Islam in the country, and those who resist making Islam an organized political actor. . . . A central point about the Islam in Indonesia is that it is not monolithic.[22]

It is Indonesia that only recently became the hotbed for radical Islam. When al Qaeda was forced out of Afghanistan, this country with its strong fundamentalist movement was considered the heir apparent especially for the Pacific region. They have had a history of attacking Christians and other non-Muslims in rather brutal fashion.

Reports continue to flow that tell of forced conversions and atrocities against those who refuse to come to Islam. I have had the opportunity of working for some time in Indonesia, and I am kept well informed of what is happening in that country. Because the country is composed of thousands of islands, the central government cannot and truly does not want to exert control over the Islamic extremists. The war against Christians goes on unabated.

Because of my contacts I receive constant updates of events. The number and depth of the atrocities are such that it would take another book just to describe. Here are just a few statements written to me from the area.

> In the early hours of Sunday morning (August 4, 2002), as the seaside village of Matako, 32 km east of Poso slept peacefully, *jihad* terrorists struck terror into this Christian community. The attack began at 3:30 A.M. with cries of— Allahu Akbar! Allahu Akbar! . . . six homes of the church's members were burned down. . . . The Presbyterian Church was also attacked and damaged. . . . Five members of the church were shot.[23]

> On Monday, July 22, 2002, at 11 A.M., in the Mayoa rice-fields, near the city of Pendolo, 36 km south of Tentena, three Christians from the village of Mayoa were working in their rice-field and clove plantation when they were attacked by a group of armed *jihad* warriors when they were shot near the Koropanghk group irrigation unit.[24]

There are literally thousands of examples where radical Muslims have attacked Christians, burned down their churches, and intimidated the believers. This continues today.

Today in Malaysia, approximately 55 percent of the population is Muslim. In several of the states the leaders have declared themselves an Islamic republic and said that their form of law would be *Shariah*. There has not been support from the central government nor the police for such action thus the proclamations have not been enforced. The number of attacks against non-Muslims has not nearly reached the intensity of Indonesia.

Concerning Malaysia, Caesar Farah writes, "Islam is so solidly identified with the Malay culture that *masuk melayu* (lit. 'To become Malay') is the designation for becoming a Muslim . . . Islam is still a significant and integral factor in Malay culture as reflected in their world view, in their literature, and oral traditions."[25] The Islamic resurgence is leading to political uncertainly in the country and the radicals seem to be growing.

In conclusion, Islam is deeply imbedded in Southeast Asia. The battle now is between the fundamentalists and the moderates as to who will control the fate of the governments. In only the last few years, those advocating *Shariah* and Islamic republics have been winning converts to their side. The Christians and the non-Muslims have been on the sidelines with the radicals attacking them and attempting to force them out by means of *jihad*. There seems to be little interest in the more quiet and subtle tactics used in *Da'wah* in the West.

East Asia

The dominant country is this area is China where, according to Farah:

> (Islam entered China) in 651, second year of Yonghui of the T'ang Dynasty. . . . Shortly thereafter, Arab and Persian Muslim merchants began to arrive by sea and by land. . . . The extent of contacts can be judged by the fact that Chinese annals record thirty-seven formal missions from Muslim rulers to China by the launch of the ninth century.[26]

During these early penetrations, the people known as the Hui emerged, and they were the most responsive to the message of Islam. They have been the primary propagators of Islam throughout China. They represent an interesting mix of Chinese, Middle Eastern, and Central Asian cultural, religious, and historical traditions. Today, it is the Hui that are the most dominant of the ten Muslim minority groups recognized by the communist government.

The Hui Muslims have a significant presence throughout China, while the other Muslim minorities are primarily concentrated in the northwestern part of China. At the present time the major Islamic influence is coming in through the Islamic countries of Central Asia. Three of the central problems faced by the Muslims of China are (1) cultural assimilation into the country, (2) continued pressure from the Communist state, and (3) factionalism among their believers.

Islam must face the problem of having more freedom than prior to 1990 but still functioning under definite restrains. Lemaye reports that "there are now more mosques open in China than there were prior to 1949, and Muslims travel freely on the *hajj* to Mecca, as well as engaging in cross-border trade with co-religionists in Central, the Middle East, and increasingly, Southeast Asia."[27]

The division among the different factions has much to do with their interaction with the various branches of Islam now present in the world. The new freedom does afford them the opportunity to practice *Da'wah* among the citizens of their own country. *Jihad* is not an option.

PACIFIC REGION

Many historians date the entry of Islam into the Philippines around the fourteenth century, two centuries prior to the arrival of the Spanish colonizers. Farah notes that "in the sixteenth century the islands of the Philippines were in advanced stage of Islamization when King Phillip of Spain . . . gave the orders to his admirals 'to conquer the lands and convert the people [to Catholicism].'"[28] However, Muslims in the southern islands were able to resist the attacks. With the arrival of the Spanish, the northern islands of Luzon and the Visayas were converted to Christianity while the southern islands of Mindanao and Sulu were Muslim converts.[29]

Known as the Moros, Filipino Muslims comprise approximately 5 percent of the entire population of the Philippines and are centered in the southern islands close to Indonesia. In 1983, an Islamic *Da'wah* Council of the Philippines was organized for the purpose of bringing all Muslim organizations under one umbrella. Some very high-profile terrorist attacks as well as kidnapping of westerners has given an international face to the Muslim rebellion. The political and social instability in the region has not been a source of any significant growth in the area. *Jihad* is practiced thus putting the lives and property of Christians in danger in the south.

EUROPE

Of all the continents of the world, Europe is probably the number one target by the Muslim strategists who are seeking world dominance—Eastern Europe, because of the fall of Communism and the vacuum left in the spirits of people; Western Europe, because they perceive it as being decadent, they feel that it will collapse from the inside, leaving its population desperately seeking for an answer to life's questions to which they feel that they have the answers.

The two areas, East and West, were separated for about eighty years by the Iron curtain and only now are seeking new means to come together. Because of this historical separation at least for most of this generation, I shall also separate Europe into two parts to help in our understanding of how Islam hopes to take over this continent.

Eastern Europe

Demographers generally separate the former Soviet Union into two parts; the area east of the Ural Mountains are placed in Asia and generally referred to as Central Asia, while the area west of the Urals is in Europe. For our purposes of looking at the advance of Islam, we will include the Asian part of the U.S.S.R. in with Eastern Europe.

The dominant religion of most of this area is Christian but with a strong Islamic presence. In broad terms it can be said that the indigenous peoples of countries such as Kazakhstan, Kyrgyzstan, and Uzbekistan are Muslims, while the Russians and their related people groups are Christians. Both the ethnic and the religious separation have caused problems in the past, and a strong sense of nationalism

in some of the states since the fall of the wall has intensified this conflict. Nationalism and a sense of anti-Russian feelings have given rise
to those calling for a nationalism that is defiled by both race and the
Islamic religion.

After the collapse of Communism, many of the Muslim countries
to the south of the Soviet Union saw their opportunity to do *Da'wah*
in the north. Turkey, Iran, and Saudi Arabia targeted these areas and
began to flood the area with both *da'ais* (missionaries) and funds.
Because of the strong religious persecution under Communism, all
religions had only a nominal presence. Islam suffered and many were
willing to obey the laws of the land and to cease to be active Muslims.
However, with the fall of the atheistic government, the breakup of the
U.S.S.R. and the hefty influence from the south, there was a revival of
Islam in Central Asia.

It is not only Islam that is being propagated but a militant Islam
with many different organizations vying for the hearts and heads of
the people. Such groups have exacerbated the problem that the governments have in Central Asia as the extreme form of Islam, propagated by Osama Bin Laden and others, continues to have a growing
influence. When Russia invaded Afghanistan, the resistance used the
concept of *jihad* to fight against their enemies from the north. After
the defeat of the Soviets in Afghanistan, the Muslims continued to
use the same tactics in attempting to drive the Russians (and thus
Christians) out of the former U.S.S.R. states.

In his book *Jihad, The Rise of Militant Islam in Central Asia*,
Ahmed Rashid describes a number of radical movements now growing in Central Asia. One of the most popular, widespread under-
ground movements in Uzbekistan, Kyrgyzstan, and Tajikistan is the
Hizb ut-Tahrir. Rashid states: "The HT has a vision of uniting Central
Asia, Xinjaing Province in China, and eventually the entire *ummah*
(Islamic world community) under a Khilafat (Caliphate). . . ."[30] He
goes on to say: "HT leaders believe that Central Asia has reached what
they call 'a boiling point' and is ripe for takeover."[31] The point at hand
is that they see world conditions as such that Central Asia can become the center of the reestablishment of the unified Islam.

In countries such as the Balkans and others to the west, Islam has had a long history of conflict. Bulgaria and Bosnia have strong communities of Muslims. They hope to use these communities as beachheads that can lead to the conversion of that area. In the Bosnian war, much physical support in the way of arms and financing came in from the Islamic countries. The same is true in Chechnya. The main effort for advancement in these areas could be called a combination of *jihad* and *Da'wah* depending on the circumstances. It should be noted that there have not been many converts to Islam in this area recently.

Western Europe

Western Europe has been flooded with Muslims who have come from almost all the Muslim countries. Who are they and where did they come from? Here is an overview. They are:

- **Guest workers.** These are generally to be found in Germany, Austria, and Switzerland. At first they were blue-collar workers that came to fill the menial and poorly paid positions in these countries. There was a great need for such workers since there was radical economic growth in these countries. It was the intentions of both the host and the guest that they would return home. Many came to earn funds that could then be used to buy land or a house in the home country. With time, the men brought their families with them, and they began to set down roots.
- **Immigrants.** These differ from the guest workers in that their original intent was to live in the new country. The majority of Muslims in England and France fall into this category. They had certain rights, since they lived in areas that were colonized by the host country. Often these immigrants find it hard to accept that they are anything but a citizen of the European country where they find themselves. In most cases the immigrants came to the west as a family unit.
- **Refugees.** As wars and famines hit areas in Asia, Africa, and

the Middle East, many refugees are created and a small number of them find their way to Europe. They can be single persons or complete family groups. Their stay is often considered as temporary, but with time they become more established.

- **Students.** Numerous young people come to Europe for a period of up to seven years in order to study at one of the European universities. They often are very bright people who plan to return to their homes and often become leaders in their countries.
- **Businesspeople.** With the economic strength of the Middle East countries, many businesspeople have bought second homes in Europe and spend a great amount of time there.
- **Tourists.** Again, due to favorable economic strength of the Middle East countries, many Muslims have made Europe their vacation and shopping choice. They will often spend extended periods of time in Europe.
- **European Muslims.** There is a small but growing group of indigenous Europeans who have converted to the Muslim faith and are active in the practice of their faith.

Beginning in the 1970s and 1980s, the Islamic communities of Europe began to find their own identity and even realized that they had an obligation to their religion to try to encourage other Muslims to live their faith in the foreign land. This then led them to see that it was possible for them to perform *Da'wah* with the Europeans, thus Islam became much more dynamic and some would say more radical. All the methods of *Da'wah* described in the previous chapters are now being used in Western Europe with some success.

I estimate that the number of European Christians who convert to Islam is roughly the same as the number of Muslims living in Europe who convert to Christianity. The Muslim growth is mostly through an increase of immigration and the fact that they have a tendency to have large families. Some of their success is in the area of public relations. It is here that they spend many resources.

THE AMERICAS

South America and the Caribbean

The Arab immigrants that have moved into this area over the last two hundred years practice Islam in Latin America. They come from three different sources: the Indo-Pakistani immigrants, the descendants of East Indian indentured laborers, and African-American converts to Islam in the West Indies. Latin America seems to be one of the target areas for conversion. They are building magnificent mosques in all the countries that are financed mostly by the oil-rich Muslim countries.

While making a trip to Carracas, Venezuela, I was shown a beautiful large mosque across from the Hilton Hotel. I was told that it was one of the largest in South America and also housed a training center. Another example is the new megamosque in Buenos Aires, Argentina. It has a fifty-meter high ceramic white dome. The project began in 1995 and had a construction cost of $15 million, paid by King Falid of Saudi Arabia. The land was donated by the Argentinean government.[32] They have translated and published a large number of their books into both Spanish and Portuguese. One of the organizations that are active in the region is the fundamentalist Jamat-e-Islami. They are having some success in converting the native Latinos to their faith as well as the black South Americans.

The total number of Muslims in the area is quite small when compared to Christians. Johnstone states that 91.65 percent of the population is Christian while only 0.34 percent are Muslims. They number roughly 1.4 million.[33] There are some indications that Islam is targeting Hispanics in the United States with the hopes that it will affect the southern part of the continent in the future.

North America

Much of what has been written has looked at the plans now being used in North America. The total numbers range from Johnstone's

4.6 million to the Muslim's estimate of over seven million. At this point a word of caution should be given. Muslims do not always have accurate statistics and they often will greatly exaggerate their numbers. This does not take away from them or their growth, but it does warn us not to take all the figures about size too seriously.

In America it is mostly African-Americans who are converting to orthodox Islam, and not just to the Nation of Islam. There are some Anglos and some Hispanics but these numbers are few. In studying the strategy, one would have to say that the area where they are committing most of their resources in the West include Western Europe and North America. Once again their main emphasis is to do the work by an expanded use of *Da'wah*.

Areas of success, apart from their work with the minorities, could be said to be the building of mosques, student work, work with prisoners, and the effective public relations endeavors that has changed how people in Canada and the United States perceive Islam.

CONCLUSION

Islam continues its march forward as does Christianity. However, it is a sad commentary that in countries where Islam rules, Christians struggle to stay alive. Conversion to Christianity in lands ruled by Islam can mean more than prison . . . it can be a death sentence. In the West, Muslims are free to proselytize and grow and they are taking advantage of Western religious tolerance in order to expand their base for world dominance.

After the attacks on the World Trade Center on September 11, many were quoted as saying, "The world will never again be the same." There was no catastrophic change in the world's demography, but rather the change was more of perception. Suddenly, news concerning conflicts involving Muslims now landed on the front pages of newspapers instead of being buried on the back pages.

The changes between Islam and the West are hard to understand or map out for the future. However, as one begins to study this encounter, it becomes apparent that Huntington's "Clash of Civilizations" and Woosley's "Fourth World War" are now realities. Islam is now on the march in many parts of the world. They have their strategy and battle plans in place, but they still have many weaknesses that they seem unwilling to acknowledge. It seems that the non-Islamic world is not ready to lie down and surrender.

What in the world is Islam doing? Although they are doing much, their real successes come into question.

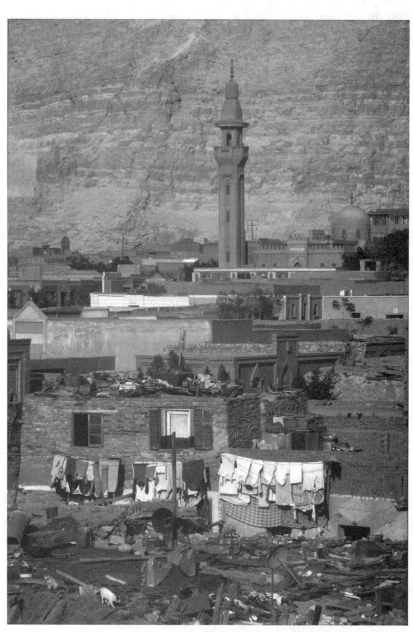

Poverty of the people in the shadow of a mosque in a Middle Eastern city.

chapter **ten**

Measuring Success
One Country at a Time

Will Islam Really Take Over the World?

H ow *Islam Plans to Change the World*—the title of this book
seems to make the assumption that Islam will be successful, but
this is very much in question. Of course, the ultimate aim of Islam is
complete world dominance, and many Muslims feel that it is inevitable.

As noted earlier, Islam is the world's fastest growing major religion,
and they are having some success in most regions of the globe. They have
tremendous financial resources and momentum on their side. But is it
realistic to say that they can and will conquer the world in the future?

Let's look at the facts and try to determine if they can accomplish this
monumental task. I have identified twelve successes and twelve failures.

TWELVE SUCCESSES

No religion can carry the title of the world's fastest growing major
religion without doing some things right. In trying to evaluate what
Islam is doing right, it will help to bring together all the activities and
strategies that have led them to where they are today—a growing
faith. Following is a list of their successes:

1. They have been successful in having a global strategy. Islam is the only major world religion with a megastrategy. The only other one that I am aware of is the Mormon church, but rather than being a major world religion, they fall more into the category of a sect. Even the evangelical and Pentecostal branches, both of which have a higher growth rate than Islam, do not have a solid megastrategy in place. A megastrategy means that all the resources of an organization are in place and working together for a common goal. Because Islam does not compartmentalize life into different and often conflicting areas, it has an opportunity of utilizing its followers to promote their faith. An example concerns their diplomats who are active in various countries in the building of mosques and in the proclamation of Islam. In the Christian world, the Christians among the diplomats might go to church but do little to really promote missions. In Islam's strategy they have tried to combine all the different facets of life into one for the purpose of a global witness.

2. They have been successful in using international trade as a tool for growth. In the history of the expansion of Islam, trade played an important part in the extension of the faith of Muhammad. On the other hand, history shows that the large trading companies, formed by the colonizing powers, were more often against the missions rather than helpful. Today international businesses with bases in the Christian West are of very little help in the promotion of the Christian faith. However, Muslim businessmen are actively promoting their faith and are helping to build mosques all over the world. The average Muslim businessman sees a responsibility to promote the growth of Islam.

3. They have been successful in using their students to do *Da'wah*. Generally the students going to study overseas and especially in the West are focused upon the task of influencing others to their faith. Not all students are actively engaged in the promotion of their faith, but student work and work in

schools remains a high priority, receiving both finances and encouragement.

4. They have been successful in reaching the blacks of the world, both in Africa and in the West, especially in North America. They have played the race card very effectively and have made many to believe that Christianity is really racist while Islam is for all races. The success of their African strategy is to make people believe that Islam is the only religion that accepts a person for who they really are. They use such things as the slave trade of the past to discredit Christians, without making mention that history has shown that blacks were the leaders in this trade.

5. They have been successful in portraying their theology to westerners in terms that can be accepted by them. They use terms such as love, grace, forgiveness, fellowship, and compassion in effective ways to try to communicate Islam. These terms are not dominant in Arabic; the concepts have been made to refer to Islam when in reality this is not the case. Most people in America and Europe see Islam as comparable to Christianity in content because of Muslims' carefully planned strategy of communicating their faith in the West.

6. They have been successful in the use of the large amounts of the petrodollars that have been made available to them by the Gulf States including Saudi Arabia. This is probably the single most important success that they have. The readiness to use these resources has made the task much easier in many of the other areas.

7. They have been successful in the prisons in the West. As already mentioned, they win mostly young minorities to their faith when they are in prison. They give converts a new name and identity as well as taking care of their families until they are released. They also help in getting the person started again in society. Also to be noted is that these converted persons are often good recruits for the more radical forms of Islam, which advocate terrorism and intimidation.

8. They have been successful in the use of intimidation. Through terrorism and other means, they have been able to bring fear into the lives of many in the world. It remains to be seen if this fear leads to growth, but in some cases the intimidation has led some weaker Christians to accept Islam instead of fighting. This is true in such countries where Islam has a large majority and the Christians and others are weak. Several examples of this are Egypt and Indonesia.

9. They have been successful in the use of force. *Jihad* in some parts of the world has been helpful in adding to the growth. Possibly the best example is that of Sudan. As Islam becomes the dominant religion in some areas of the world more *jihad* activities can be expected to bring growth to the area conquered.

10. They have been successful in changing the image of Islam. This is true especially in North America and Western Europe. The picture of the slow-minded Arab on a camel is no longer shown, but it has now been replaced with the image of a dedicated Muslim who takes his or her religion very seriously. They have upgraded their literature and are using the mass media in a very effective way. Their greatest failure in this area has been with the Israel-Palestinian conflict where they have come up as losers because of the more effective Jewish control of the issues in the media.

11. They have been successful in the construction of numerous mosques in the world, many of them large and beautiful. There is no question that their physical presence in so many different countries has given Muslims much to boast about. It is not only the size and beauty of the buildings that is impressive but also the numbers and locations in so many countries of the world.

12. They have been successful in the portrayal of both the simplicity and the piety of their religion. The five pillars are known all over the world and form an easily understandable basis for their religion. Most see them as being genuinely reli-

gious, which is a large plus factor for them. This simplicity of faith has been a great asset for their growth in the urban areas around the globe.

TWELVE FAILURES

1. Muslims are not growing as fast as they claim. They have failed to prove that they are a rapidly growing community. Most observers will certify that they do have growth, but they have not been able to show truly how rapid of a growth they really have experienced. It is generally believed that Muslims have a tendency to exaggerate their growth, and since they do not keep the same type of records as is kept in the West, it becomes very difficult to verify the growth rate. The number of persons who change to Islam because of a real conversion is small. It is believed that most of the growth comes from either a forced conversion or from having large families.

2. They have failed to contextualize Islam into the more dominant world cultures. To become a Muslim means that the women must take on a semblance of the same type of dress as in the Middle East. Simply said, to become a Muslim often means a rejection of one's cultural norms, values, and background and the taking on of a foreign way of life. This will continue to be a hindrance for seeing large numbers convert to Islam in other cultures.

3. They have failed to convince the world that they are a peaceful religion. The continued use of *jihad* and terrorism has helped growth in some areas but also worked against them and their rather effective public relations strategy. Every new attack and atrocity is a constant reminder that there is an inseparable tie between Islam and conflict. Many have been turned off from this religion because of the facts that are now available to all in the global environment. It seems that they have conflicts with most of the major religions of the world thus making their chances of success in some parts of the world less probable.

4. They have failed to convince practicing Christians that Islam is better than Christianity. Because Islam is a post-Christian faith, many of their leaders proclaim that it is superior and even use texts from both the Bible and the *Qur'an* to show that Jesus was expecting the coming of Muhammad to make his revelation to the world perfect. This teaching simply has not been accepted, thus putting into doubt that there will ever be a mass turning from the faith of Jesus Christ to that of Muhammad.

5. They have failed to stop Christian missions. They see Christian missions as their number one enemy. At this time the Christian church continues to grow in Islam's backyard. I doubt that the numbers worldwide that convert from Islam to Christianity are more or less the same as those who convert from Christianity to Islam. The exit through their back door is much bigger than they want or will admit.

6. They have failed to fill the many mosques that they have built. In many parts of the world the mosques stand empty. They expect and hope that soon they will be filled with people from the areas around the mosques, but only time will tell if this will happen. Just the building of a mosque does not always mean a change of faith by those who live close to it.

7. They have failed to make people believe their threats. Over the last twenty years many voices have come out of Islam declaring *jihad* against a country or a people, or they have spoken of their destruction for not obeying Allah. Many of these threats go unrealized to the point that they are not taken as seriously as before. It is very similar to the boy who always cried "wolf." This has had a tendency to discredit their religion.

8. They have failed to form a Muslim country with a democracy that could appeal to the modern-day person. They continue to lag in this area, and thus those who might convert must think twice about what a Western Islamic country would really look like. The creation of an Islamic republic in Iran has had the effect that many from that country have become disillusioned with Islam and are looking to leave.

9. They have failed to provide an education system that will prepare their young people for life in the modern world. So much of their education is rote memory of the *Qur'an;* thus they fail to encourage the creative process in children. This leads to a lack of advancement as well as to a lack of improvement of the average Muslim's standard of living.

10. They have failed to relieve the fear that is so deeply ingrained in their faith. New believers begin to experience this and they soon become disappointed in their new belief, but fear stops them from expressing their doubt. Essentially, their fears feed upon their fears.

11. They have failed to give assurances to their followers for the future. They have not developed a strong theology for the future outside of a worldwide *ummah* and they certainly have not provided a personal assurance of a victorious life with God after death.

12. They have not been able to completely dispel the stereotype of the Muslims being people who live in the desert in the Middle East. Because of their monoculturalism, this image continues despite strong attempt to change how they are perceived.

In observing the facts, I believe that Islam will have constant growth in the future but mostly among those people groups that already adhere to Islam. This growth will be "biological," or better said, because of large families. If Christian missions were not present in the world today and were not as dynamic as they are today, then the growth of Islam would be much greater.

Christianity remains the number one buffer against Islam, a fact readily recognized by those who seek a worldwide *ummah.* Christianity and Islam will remain the two largest religions, both seeing converts from the other and both seeking to win the world to their belief. Both will have approximately the same growth that is a little better than the world's growth rate.

The main hindrance to both of the religions will be secularism with its many different facets. A few other world faiths will show some growth—but none are in a position to challenge the two leading ones at this time.

LOOKING INTO THE FUTURE

Some historians say that history is cylindrical, that it continues to repeat itself, while others say that it is liner, or that repetition is not necessary and thus more difficult to predict. What does the future hold for the two great religions? Will there be a clash of these two cultures that will result in a war?

Huntington writes: "A global war involving the core states of the world's major civilizations is highly improbable but not impossible. Such a war . . . could come about from the escalation of a fault line war between groups from different civilizations, most likely involving Muslims on one side and non-Muslims on the other."[1] There are other possibilities.

Three key questions must be asked:

1. Is a decline of the West and Christianity, as has happened in all other advanced societies, inevitable?
2. Is Islam destined to realize its dreams of a worldwide *ummah*?
3. Is it possible for Islam and Christianity to live together with a real appreciation of the other's religion and culture?

The inclination of most westerners, quite naturally, is to answer the first two questions with a strong "no" and the last one with a weak "maybe." Those from the Middle East would answer differently. They would say a strong "yes" to the first two and a reluctant "maybe" to the third. The answers would come from an allegiance to their own history and values recognizing a hope and not particularly the facts.

Both Islam and Christianity have a strong eschatology (view of the end times) that comes from their worldview. Both turn to their holy books to substantiate their view.

VIEWS OF THE END TIMES

Islam

Once while visiting the "Great Mosque" in Damascus, my guide pointed to one of the tall, graceful minarets, "the minaret of Jesus." Muslim tradition says that on the summit of this minaret, Jesus will descend, not in judgment but to kill the Antichrist and the people of Gog and Magog, as well as to proclaim Islam as the true religion. The world's improvement will be during the reign of Jesus, who will live for about forty years on earth. He will die while waiting for the Day of Judgment.

Islam does believe in a great judgment day, a time when all will be judged for the kind of life they have led. But prior to this, the world will continue to improve until the day comes when the whole earth will live under the banner of Islam and all its peoples will live under *Shariah* law. After this has occurred, the judgment day will come. Even during the dark ages of Islam, this hope of conquering the world was kept alive in the hearts of the *Imams*. They have a tendency to look at all world events as leading up to their takeover of the world. Their somewhat illogical actions must be understood in light of this theology. Many could not see why a man like Saddam Hussein would continue to stand up against the West even when all logic pointed to a defeat of Iraq. He kept feeling that Allah was going to intervene and give him victory. When the tragic accident of the Columbia spaceship occurred, Saddam, who was facing an attack from the United States, published a statement declaring that Columbia's destruction was the "beginning of Allah's punishment upon the United States and its Mid-east Zionist ally." The statement noted that the Israeli astronaut killed in the shuttle breakup, Ilan Ramon, had participated in the 1981 Israeli Air Force destruction of Iraq's nuclear reactor near the town of Osirak.[2]

Islam feels that the West will ultimately fail from within. They point to a number of reasons for this belief. Huntington gave five reasons why he sees the West in danger. Islam would point to the same deficiencies. They are:

1. Increases in antisocial behavior, such as crime, drug use, and violence
2. Family decay, including increased rates of divorce, illegitimacy, teen-age pregnancy, and single-parent families
3. At least in the United States, a decline in "social capital," that is, membership in voluntary associations and the interpersonal trust associated with such membership
4. General weakening of the "work ethic" and rise of a cult of personal indulgence
5. Decreasing commitment to learning and intellectual activity, manifested in the United States in lower levels of scholastic achievement.[3]

Huntington goes on to say that "The future health of the West and its influence on other societies depends in considerable measure on its success in coping with these trends, which, of course, gives rise to the assertion of moral superiority by Muslims and Asians."[4]

Most Muslims with whom I have spoken feel that the last great power that must be overcome before the world rule of Islam can begin is the United States; thus, the term that is used all over the Islamic world to describe the United States is "The Great Satan." For them the Devil will use this bastion as his last holdout before Islam will be successful. With a philosophy like this, there seems little hope that Islam will ever come to a place of compromise with the West.

Christianity

The Christian view of the last days is both simple and complicated. Simple, in that most Christians feel that the world will continue until Jesus Christ returns and that there will then be a day of judgment. At that time those who have disobeyed God will be separated from him and cast into hell, while those who have accepted Jesus Christ will reign with him for eternity. It is, however, far more complicated in that there are large varieties as to what will take place before the Day of Judgment comes.

A basic concept is that there will be a thousand-year reign of Jesus Christ before the final judgment. This is based on Revelation 20. There are three differing ideas to when and how this thousand-year period will take place. Some say it will be before Christ returns (postmillennialism); some say after his coming (premillennialism); and some say there will be no literal thousand-year reign (amillennialism).

The postmillennialists would be more comparable to the Muslims, in that this view says that the world will get better and better (and more Christian) until man has developed a near-perfect world and Jesus can simply come and set up his kingdom. This would mean that the church would conquer all evils (including Islam) until the end. This was a very popular concept in the 1920s and the 1930s. Many said that man had conquered alcohol (with Prohibition), war (with the League of Nations), and other evils. Hitler even used this belief as a theological basis of his formulation of his thousand-year *Reich* (Kingdom). After the rise of fascism in Germany and Italy and the Second World War, postmillennialism became very unpopular and few in the church today would see this as a real possibility.

Both the amillennialists and the premillennialists would see a somewhat darker side of the future. They take literally the words of Jesus in Matthew 24 when he said that before he returned:

> You will hear of wars and rumors of wars. . . . Nation will rise against nation, and kingdom against kingdom. There will be famines and earthquakes in various places. . . . [Y]ou will be handed over to be persecuted and put to death, and you will be hated by all nations because of me. . . . [A]nd many false prophets will appear and deceive many people. (Matthew 24:6–11)

Those holding to this view are not surprised by the persecutions and problems coming from the revival of Islam. They state that this has been predicted and the words of Jesus are now coming true. They see Muhammad as one of the false prophets who were mentioned by Jesus.

The premillennialists have a tendency to look at every world event and see a biblical fulfillment of prophecy. The war with Iraq (Babylon), the creation of the State of Israel, and its Muslim opposition all point to the return of Jesus Christ. They have a tendency to point to different systems, religions, and persons as the Antichrist.

One interesting theory that is gaining some allegiance by the more radical premillennialists is that there will be a joining together of the Roman Catholic Church (whom they pointed to as the Antichrist before the rise of Islam) and Islam. For them the rallying point will be Mary; they believe it is no coincidence that Mary is revered as the Lady of Fatima (where she appeared to some peasant children), which is the name of Ali's (the fourth Caliph) wife. Proponents believe that both Islam and Roman Catholicism will accept Mary, join together, and thus become the Antichrist who will attempt to take the world away from God. It would be safe to say that very few accept this theory as being credible.

Most Christians do not attempt to predict what will happen between Islam and Christianity. They are concerned that Islam is growing but are still satisfied with the prominent position that they enjoy as the world's only superpower. Some see an immediate and dangerous challenge to their way of life by Islam and are concerned for the future.

SCENARIOS FOR THE FUTURE

In the emerging world of multiculturalism, mass immigration, and changing worldviews, we must attempt to predict what will be the logical consequences of the events of today.

History has shown us that life on earth is, if nothing else, unpredictable; thus, one who tries to make a prediction is often playing the fool. What is now being predicted is done in light of the conflict of the two great religions. It does not take into account the other civilizations such as China, who will play an ever-increasingly important role in world affairs. Theology and eschatology will be brought to bear. Also, missiology will help in looking at growth and decline of religions in the world this century. Here are five possible scenarios for the future.

1. There will be a rise of influence of the moderate branches of both Islam and Christianity. As this happens, there will be better conclusive dialogue between the leaders of the two faiths. Both sides will see that they must find a way to coexist and will create a framework whereby this will be possible. Intense competition that leads to physical conflict will decrease to an extent that both will find strength from each other. The fact that both share a common heritage and a common belief in the one God will be the base from which this cooperation can begin. They would realize that they must share the stage with other ideologies such as secularism, Buddhism, Hinduism, etc. Both would continue to do their missions and *Da'wah,* but within agreed upon limits and bounds. Civilization would benefit immensely from such a solution. This would be the best possible alternative to the present conflict. My problem with this possibility is that at the present time the moderates are not only ceasing to grow in influence in their perspective faiths, but rather they are losing adherents.

2. The Islamists will be correct. Islam would continue to gain adherents through both *Da'wah* and *jihad.* There will be minor wars of liberation together with persecutions of non-Muslims in such a way that the "Path of Muhammad" would increase in both size and power. One by one countries would become Islamic republics. The first big step toward this end would be the capitulation of Israel. This would then be followed by either the conversion or ousting of all non-Muslims from the Middle East and other areas controlled by Islam. Of the Western powers, Europe would convert to Islam first with the United States being the last great stumbling block before Islam. America would fall because of the excellent propaganda from Muslims combined together with the moral decay of a failed Christian society.

3. The apparent status quo between the two religions will continue. Islam will continue on its course for world dominance, reverting to ways that have led to their resurgence. There will be a continuance of persecution and attempts at *jihad*. The rest of the world would not continue to tolerate such action and there will be an ever-increasing division of the world into two or more major camps. Two of these civilizations would constantly wage war against each other. These wars would be wars of words combined with economic war, propaganda war, and actual physical conflict. The phrase "The Clash of Civilizations" would become reality and relations between the two would deteriorate. The results of such conflicts would depend upon a number of factors, which includes not only the inner strength of each society but also their military might. In the near future the Western civilization would have the upper hand.

4. As Islam and Christianity continue to have conflict with each other, one of the other world-class civilizations such as China would gain such strength that it would become the dominant force in bringing in a "Brave New World" society. Because of the drained strength of the two great religions, they will have little or no stamina to defend themselves.

5. Islam will continue to grow and will become more brutal in its attempts to conquer the world. There will be a rise of terrorism in all parts of the non-Muslim world since they have discovered how effective this can be. The nations of the world will be subject to suicide bombings. A number of wars such as those against Iraq and Afghanistan will take place but will be ineffective since Islam has learned to fight not from a position of military strength but from the shadowy back alleys of the urban societies. Christians especially will be marked for death and persecution. Islam will never completely take over the world but will have successes and there will be some growth. In this scenario, the world would face a long period of instability.

What are my feelings? After spending much time trying to under-stand the two civilizations that are the theme of this book, and in studying the eschatology of both religions as well as looking at the political realities of the complex world in which we live, I have devel-oped some ideas as to what will happen.

I see somewhat of a status quo developing with neither making much gain at the expense of the other. Islam will have the upper hand in some parts of the world such as Black Africa and Central Europe. There will also be a growing Islam in Western Europe, not by convert-ing the ethnic Europeans but by an increase in immigration and large families. Blacks in America will continue to come to Islam for a short period of time, but there will be a revival among the Christian blacks that will slow the growth of Islam.

I tend to accept the last of my five scenarios. There will be continued conflict between the two civilizations. It will lead to many losing their lives by both conflict and persecution. Ultimately there will be one large conflict before Jesus Christ does return, not to proclaim the mer-its of Muhammad but rather to establish his kingdom. The ultimate victor in this process will not be the Christians but rather Jesus Christ.

In trying to predict the future, I am reminded of the time when I was watching the movie *Apollo 13* on video. Some children were present and during the movie it looked as if the spacecraft would be lost and all in it killed. One of the children was greatly concerned and began to cry. I said, "Don't worry; everything will be all right."

The somewhat emotional child said, "How do you know?"

My reply was simple: "I already know how the movie is going to end."

Christians who are concerned about the present situation as well as the future only need to go to the Bible to see that God has already told us what the real ending will be. We shall be victorious in Jesus Christ, the only true King of Kings and Lord of Lords (Revelation 19:16).

As I mentioned in the preface, the real antidote for the problems be-fore us is clear. Let's become much more active in living out our Chris-tian faith and proclaiming the truth as found in Jesus Christ.

Together, let's dedicate ourselves anew to these all-important tasks.

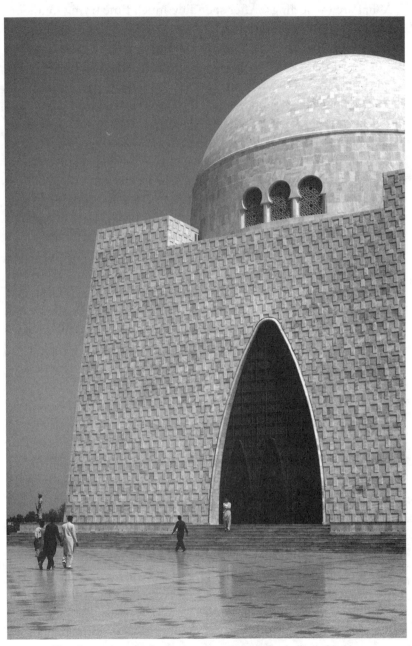

Massive and expensive new mosques are being built worldwide.

appendix **a**

Quotes from
Middle Eastern Sources

In an attempt to better understand the current thinking on *Da'wah* and the strategy on the part of both Muslim scholars and the Islamic media, I asked one of my doctoral students to do research in sources written in Arabic and readily available in the Middle East. This student now lives in Germany but was born and grew up in one of the core countries of the Middle East. He spent several months studying numerous sources, the main one being the *Middle East Newspaper*. He did the translations from Arabic into English since he is fluent in both languages.

The endnotes are somewhat different than those generally used in the West, but one can still determine both the validity and the source of the statements. The purpose of this addition to the book is to help the reader see that much of what has been written thus far is not fictitious. There is definitely a prevailing attitude in the Middle East that both sets Islam against the West and seeks to further the growth of Islam in the world.

The following are the seven parts of appendix A:

1. Connecting Islamic Religious *(Da'wah)* Institutions with Aid Organizations and Other Institutions
2. The Use of Dialogue in *Da'wah*
3. The Ecumenicalization of *Da'wah*
4. Political Ambitions and How They Help *Da'wah*
5. The Constitution of the Islamic Infrastructure
6. The Institutionalization of *Da'wah* in the Western Context (Para-Mosque)
7. Statistics Around the World

FIRST: CONNECTING ISLAMIC RELIGIOUS *(Da'wah)* INSTITUTIONS WITH AID ORGANIZATIONS AND OTHER INSTITUTIONS

The cooperation between the Islamic organization *(Da'wah)* and other Islamic institutions is very important to fulfill one goal: the proclamation of Islam as soon as possible. Through this cooperation, the organizations are saving time and efforts in the establishment of an Islamic nation and law *(Shariah)*.

Connecting Works with Aid Work Organizations

Shaik Aqil Alaqil, the chairman of the Mecca relief institutions Al Haramain and Al Shariefain, confirmed that all *Da'wah* works and relief work in the West have overcome all of the problems incurred since September 11. According to Shaik Aqil, the work of these organizations, besides the relief work, also includes *Da'wah* to Islam. In this newspaper article, it also stresses that the first goal of this organization is *Da'wah* non-Muslim to Islam. This organization has thirty-one branches inside Saudi Arabia and twenty-two other branches all over the rest of the world, including the United States. One of the goals of the organization is to help prisoners by providing them different ways to experience Islam. Sometimes the organization will pay the small amount required to purchase the release of these prisoners.

They have also established *Qur'an* teaching circles, and they build prayer rooms. The organization has also built approximately one hundred mosques around the world and has held conferences in which Islamic beliefs were taught. This organization paid 1.3 million Reial ($400,000 United States) in their support of *Qur'an* teaching circles. They have paid approximately one million Reial ($250,000 United States) in their support of helping prisoners.[1]

Concerning the Relief World Islamic Organization (located in Kuwait), the chairman stresses that they are involved with six thousand charity projects around the globe. One of the main thrusts of these charity projects centers on the proclamation of Islam. Other projects include building mosques, schools, universities, hospitals, clinics, orphanages, and other educational institutions. They have spent the equivalent of millions of United States dollars during the last six months in the carrying out of these projects. Some of the members of this organization are leaders in the *Da'wah* field. The president stresses that all Islamic organizations should coordinate with each other. These organizations deal with Islamic Institution for Education, Science, and Culture.[2]

Along with the relief projects, the Ad Al Azir Bin Baz relief institution is helping the Islamic *Da'wah* organizations in the proclamation of Islam to the Muslim minority in the West as well as the non-Muslim majority. Recently this organization produced a film called *True Islam,* which introduces the religion to the world. It was produced in English and French and will be broadcast by the biggest broadcasting companies in the Western world (United States, Europe, and Australia). One of the goals is to have this film translated into all of the vital languages around the globe.

The primary subjects of the film are:

- The Islamic role in building the world culture through history
- Focusing on the normality and mediation of Islam
- The importance of dialogue between Islamic nations with other nations and religions
- The roll of Islam in giving mankind freedom through Allah

- Focusing on Islamic roles within scientific research
- The Islamic role in establishing Western culture

The primary goals of the film are:

- The proclamation of Islam to the world
- Displaying Islamic teachings and principles
- Explaining Islamic beliefs
- Encouraging non-Muslims to embrace the religion[3]

Recently, the ministry of Islamic affairs held a conference in Jadah, Saudi Arabia, concerning the Islamic organizations under the religious administration and their spheres of influence. All Islamic organizations present confirmed that the most important relief work they can give to the non-Muslim world is presenting Islam . . . the acceptable religion before Allah (*Qur'an* 3:19).[4]

Da'wah Through the Mass Media, Governmental Institutions, and Organizations

The Islamic world is now focusing more firmly on spreading Islam through the use of mass media and governmental organizations. One of the primary ways this occurs is through the Islamic relief organizations. Dr. Roushdy Shahata, a professor at Halawan University in Egypt, said, "The journalists must always have a good Islamic bias. Also, being a religious journalist, he can write his subjects from the Islamic point of view." He assures that the goal of the Islamic media is to broadcast to the entire world.[5]

There are many cases of cooperation between Islamic institutions and media organizations. Recently, the Islamic Institution for Education, Science, and Culture met with an Islamic online organization. The purpose was to set up conferences, educational meetings, and Islamic studies for access on the Internet. This will give a better view for Islam in the West via the Internet. They also dealt with the translation and publishing of Islamic science and cultural books.[6]

Dr. Fahad Al Tajash, the chairman of a Saudi company for research and publishing, confirmed that the cooperation between his institution and the World Islamic League was regarded as a major step in helping the Islamic nation and in spreading Islam. He also emphasized the importance of such cooperation between all Islamic organizations around the globe. This would help the spread of Islam and also help it to be seen in a better way.[7]

The relationship between the World Islamic League and a newspaper in the Middle East is considered the most significant of the reported organizational alliances. Six months ago they held a conference together in Jadda, Saudi Arabia, concerning ecumenical media. Dr. Turaky emphasized once again the importance of the mass media in the spread of Islam. They made a plan of cooperation between them in order to proclaim Islam and display it in a better light. Turaky also said that all of the mass media must cooperate with the *Da'wah* organizations.[8]

SECOND: THE USE OF DIALOGUE IN *Da'wah*

Dialogue is one of the main strategies in the proclamation of Islam to the Western world. After the discovery that the religion could not be spread in the West through the use of war, they started employing another strategy . . . living in the Western countries and gradually spreading Islam and establishing the Islamic nation. Therefore, the Islamic organizations are now having some type of dialogue with the entire world.

Thoughts About Dialogue from an Islamic Perspective

When dialogueing about Islam in the West, members of an Islamic organization will refrain from making references to the Islam of Medina. This includes all of the scriptures that deal with killing all of the non-Muslims and treating them badly. The scriptures also say that the only acceptable religion is Islam and that the whole earth must become an Islamic nation. Instead, the dialogue revolves around the Islam of Mecca. This is when Muhammad was a weak man and didn't have many followers. He would show love and mercy, saying that his new religion is a peaceful one that respects all other nations and religions. The Islam of Medina is known as the bloody side of Islam, and the Islam of Mecca is known as the good side of Islam. Furthermore, Allah has promised to all Muslims that he will establish them on earth if they believe and do righteous deeds (*Qur'an*, an-Noor 24;5S).[9]

Dr. Jussif Quaradawy, one of the more famous Islamic scholars, confirmed that Allah has allowed the Islamic religion to spread into the whole world through the use of wars. But because they are no longer able to do this, they must use another way to proclaim Islam. We can see from this statement that Allah had legislated the war against anyone who is not Muslim and anyone who stands against Islam. But they do not say this during any dialogues with Western officials.[10]

Along the same lines as Dr. Quaradawy, Dr. Turaky, the president of the World Islamic League, said, "We must learn many things from the battle of Bader (a war that was led by Muhammad during the 2nd year of establishing Islam in Ramadan against the non-Muslim in Mecca during their way to the north of Mecca to do business)." In this battle, many men were killed from both sides. Yet we see Dr. Turaky referencing it as something that we must learn many things from.[11] In addition to these, we also have one of the most famous Islamic priests (Shack Ibin Athemin) confirming that there is only one party before Allah, which is Hezeb Allah (God's Party), which basically means that the only religion acceptable to God is Islam.[12] Ibin Baz is also quoted as saying that the only people who are close to the heart of God are Muslims.[13]

The Islamic nation would still condone the spread of Islam through the use of warfare. They are not able to do this because of the Western abilities in warfare and sometimes must even avoid the subject in their history.

Islamic Dialogue (with the Western Government)

The Islamic organizations in the West always display the Islam of Mecca during their dialogues so that the Western world may only see the peaceful side of the religion. The side that loves Allah and other nations and respects their decisions to choose the religion that they want. The side that proclaims that Islam is against any kind of terrorism, especially the kind that is to proclaim Islam. During the last meetings of the World Islamic League, Dr. Turaky confirmed that Islam is against any kind of terrorist activity and that Islam is a tolerant religion.[14]

Generally, all of the Islamic organizations and their leaders emphasize that Islam is against terrorism and does not distinguish itself among other religions that are not Muslim. Dr. Abed Al aziz Bin Authman Al Tuaigy (the president of the Islamic Institution for Education, Science, and Culture) said that Islam is a tolerant religion that loves all mankind.[15]

Dialogue with the Professors and the Educational Institutions

Having dialogues with professors and educational institutions is very important because it is through them that access will be gained into the government, thus beginning the change of Western legislation. This will allow the Islamic minority to practice their beliefs and proclaim Islam. During a meeting for the Islamic intellectuals in the Muslim world, they emphasized the importance of all professors having training and exposure to the true Islamic beliefs, so they can display those beliefs during global conferences.[16]

Another approach in reaching the Western intellectuals is through the scientific study of the *Qur'an*. The Muslim scientists purposefully seek out Western scientists for this very reason. Dr. Turaky said, "It is very important to reach the academics in the west, to visit the colleges which have orientation studies, and to dialogue with their professors in order to display the good side of Islam." He said this before his visit to a college in Scotland.[17]

Dr. Turaky and a large Islamic delegation visited Germany on June 17, 2002. The aim of the visit was to have a meeting with the scholars and politicians in Germany and then in the whole of Europe, and finally in the United States. During the visits, the delegation explained the Islamic teachings about war and terrorism.[18] After finishing the visit to Germany, the delegation went on to the U.K. for the same purpose.[19]

As we can see, the most important Islamic organization in the Islamic world is the World Islamic League, which is supported by Saudi Arabia. This league contains sixty Islamic organizations gathered from the entire Islamic world and plays a very vital role in the displaying of Islam to the Western world, especially within the governments and educational institutions.[20]

Dialogue Through Conferences, Global Meetings, and Exhibitions

During a humanity conference, the participants emphasized the importance of dialogue with the West and Christians, and the necessity of presenting the good principles of Islam to the Western masses and their governments.[21]

It wasn't long ago that an Islamic delegation participated in the earth summit in Johannesburg. Dr. Turaky and many Islamic leaders accompanied them. This conference was considered the largest one in the world. The aims of the Islamic delegation were:

1. To show the importance of Islamic toleration with (and within) other nations.
2. Helping other nations get rid of their problems by the application of Islamic solutions to earth-related problems. These solutions were offered by Allah through the *Qur'an*.
3. Dr. Turaky said that the main goal in this conference is to proclaim Islam to the whole world.[22]

During an exhibition, Yussif Islam—a British Da'l (who embraced Islam years ago and wants to proclaim it through his exhibition in London)—confirmed that the main goal is doing and proclaiming Islam to non-Muslims. One of the participants was the Islamic British photographer Abed.[23]

Sometimes the Islamic minority has held their exhibitions in Christian churches. One such event happened in Amsterdam, Holland.

One of the visitors was the queen of Holland, and she said that it is time to learn many things from the Islamic culture and people should get used to seeing a Muslim woman in parliament.[24]

THIRD: THE ECUMENICALIZATION OF ISLAM

The ecumenicalization of Islam, or the Islamic law, is also one of the Islamic World League's strategies to proclaim Islam to the world. The organizations are using this approach because of the danger of the worldly ecumenical focus to the stability of the Islamic nation in the West and also in the Islamic countries. This is why the whole of the Islamic organizations are holding meetings and conferences to deal with this new wave of ecumenical focus.

Recently, most of the Islamic organizations met in Mecca to submit their suggestions about how to deal with this. The mass media perspective simply confirmed that the journalists must have religious training and know basic Islamic teachings. Dr. Turaky said that it is very important for journalists to know the major principles of Islam so that they can give the Islamic solutions to the world problems. He also called for cooperation between all Islamic organizations with the mass media in the Arab world and in the West. He also said that the Islamic organizations are preparing to have an Islamic mass media institution.[25]

Dr. Gaffer Edrissi, the president of the Islamic American University, said, "I'm not against the ecumenical movement. . . . I see it will insure that Islam is a global religion and its prophet Muhammad is a prophet for the entire world. Through the ecumenical movement, the world will be like a small village and this village doesn't need more than one prophet, which is Muhammad. Furthermore, the Islamic legislations are very flexible and we can apply them in any time and in any place."[26]

King Fahad, the king of Saudi Arabia, said, "We must get benefit from the ecumenical movement because it is still in the beginning and we must Islamize it as soon as possible to help the Islamic nation."[27]

FOURTH: POLITICAL AMBITIONS AND HOW THEY HELP DA'WAH

Political and Administrative Activities

An ambition of Islamic organizations is to have a representative in the American Congress, in the European Parliament, and in a scientific society or institution that has good relationships with prominent people. Dr. Turaky stresses, "We must reach the scholars and the politicians in the West because their governments depend on their decisions within research."[28]

The executive chief of the Islamic American Council, Nihad Awad, said, "The Muslim minorities are working hard to be a powerful instrument during the next presidential election in the United States." He added that there are one hundred thousand Muslim votes from seven big states. Furthermore, the Muslims have finished establishing an educational and religious infrastructure in North America, so now it is time to establish an Islamic political infrastructure.

The American Islamic Council is working hard to train Muslim leaders to be politicians. Only in this role can the Muslims ensure a strong future in North America and Canada. After what happened on September 11, 2001, this strategy became more than a hobby it became a must for Muslims.[29]

Paul Findley, a member of the Middle East committee in Congress, confirmed that Muslims are now in very sensitive and important positions in America. They are making their presence known within public political decisions as well. They helped George Bush get elected by contributing sixty-thousand votes to the critical state of Florida. With this on their side, they are pushing Islamic organizations to cooperate with any future presidential candidates.[30]

An article on an Islamic Web site (www.islamway.net) pointed out that there are many Islamic students who want to get involved with politics. Islamic institutions and organizations are training them to be powerful elements in the support of Islam in the future politics of the West. This article also pointed out that Muslim men getting married to non-Muslim women will increase the number of votes for an

Islamic political candidate because of their tendency to vote along with their husbands.[31]

In Belgium, an Islamic delegation arrived in the country to hold a meeting with the government and, in turn, the whole of Europe. Dr. Turaky said, "The European parliaments are a very good way to reach within the countries." He also said that there are many Muslims in the parliament of Belgium and that this is good because it is making good progress in the proclamation of Islam. Because of the good relationship between the Muslims in the Belgium government and the country, the World Islamic League was able to do the following on their trip:

1. Obtain permission to teach Islam in Belgium's schools
2. Have a prayer room in the Brocksel airport
3. Build a new Islamic cemetery
4. Encourage some legal changes so that the Muslims can practice their religious commitments[32]

In Holland there are seven Islamic parliamentarians in the parliament. Many Muslims are members in Dutch political parties. Dr. Marzouk Awlad, the president of the Islamic University in Holland, said, "The Muslims in this country must be ready to govern Holland because of the increasing numbers of Muslims and the decreasing numbers of the original people of Holland."[33]

Islamize the Politicians: The Shortcut to Reaching the Western Governments

Sometimes the strategies of dialogue, the Internet, and sending delegations are not enough. So some have been implementing another method for the past fifty years. It is to simply Islamize the governor, prominent people, and politicians of the West. Through these individuals, Islam can be shown in a good light to the general populace.

Alexander Cronemar is involved with American foreign affairs. He has a master's degree from Harvard University. He has worked in the Middle East. He married an American Muslim woman and became a Muslim himself. Now he is producing a film on the life of Muhammad. This film will be a big step in the proclamation of Islam to non-Muslim people in the United States. It is scheduled to be broadcast on PBS.[34]

On June 10, 2002, Dr. Asper Ibrahim Shahin became a Muslim. He is a scientist, economist, and speaker from the upper class, and a professor of technology at a state institution in the United States. He is also the president of this institution and well known by former presidents George Bush and Ronald Reagan. He became a Muslim as a result of the influence of his Islamic friends. He too wants to bring Islam to other scientists and prominent people in America by the use of mass media. But he first wants to bring his family into Islam.[35]

More Examples

Dr. Hofman Murad, the German ambassador in Algeria, found Islam is the logical religion and very close to the human mind. He found that Christianity is a faded religion. He is using all of his influence to spread Islam in Germany and around the globe.

The son of the president of the BBC became a Muslim and married a Muslim woman. He changed his name to Yehia Beart and his goal is to spread Islam in the United Kingdom and help his family embrace Islam.[36]

FIFTH: THE CONSTITUTION OF THE ISLAMIC INFRASTRUCTURE

In order to guarantee a good future of the Islamic nation in the West, it is important to have an Islamic infrastructure that will have the ability to take care of the Islamic people in every aspect of life. They are going to need the proper religious training in order to keep the Islamic nation strong all over the globe. It is useless if they have mosques that teach only a few individual people without having an educational infrastructure that can reach the whole Islamic generation. The educational institutions can implant the Islamic beliefs in a better way than can the mosques.

The Constitution of Islamic Educational Infrastructure and Religious Infrastructure

Many Islamic organizations in the West have helped their people by building them schools and Islamic institutions, thus giving them a higher profile in the society. The students of Al Azhar University are presently studying how to plant new Islamic colleges in the United States and Europe that will teach Islamic law and how to make *Da'wah* among non-Muslims, while also learning the Arabic language.[37]

According to Dr. Turaky, the Saudi Arabian government has established thousands of mosques and Islamic educational institutions and schools around the globe in order to proclaim the Islamic religion to the non-Muslim West.[38]

It is easy to see the role of Saudi Arabia in the spreading of Islam. In the United Kingdom, London and Edinburgh are the centers for Islamic activity. Islamic books (approx. 92,000) concerning the Islamic *Da'wah* have been given to these locations for distribution. Almost 500 copies of the *Qur'an* and about 34,100 "bunches" of other books have also been distributed. This type of activity is apparently normal according to the Islamic leaders of these areas.[39] The establishment of a European Islamic university is a primary goal of the World Islamic League. It will teach religion, law, medicine, engineering, etc.[40]

Right now it is difficult to establish an Islamic infrastructure of education in America. But there are enough mosques. However, there is a school in New Jersey that is Islamic and has seven hundred students. There are plans to build two similar schools in the near future.[41]

Dr. Ali Qara Daghi, President of the Belief Section of the Islamic University in Qatar and a member of the European Council for Islamic research says "The educational infrastructure should continue to be a focus even after the religious infrastructure is in place."[42]

In the August 10–16, 2002 edition of the *Economist,* a special report on Muslim activity in Western Europe was featured. It focused on whether there were some things about Islam that make it impossible for it to integrate into Western liberal societies. The conclusion was that there is nothing in Islam that makes integration impossible but that there are several obstacles that must be overcome. One obstacle concerns the prayer leaders of the mosques and their involvement with the community. They apparently are ignorant about the countries in which they are placed. Forward thinking *Imams* said that if Europe is to be served appropriately, then *Imams* must be trained in Europe rather than in the Middle East, Pakistan, or North Africa. This leads to the suggestion of European states establishing and funding these schools in order to counter this problem.[43]

Establishing a Global Islamic Infrastructure for the Islamic Mass Media

The need for an Islamic mass media is increasing day by day, especially after what happened in New York and Washington, D.C., on September 11, 2001. Obviously, it isn't enough to only have local Islamic mass media in Islamic countries when their felt need is to show the good side of Islam across the world. In order to make this happen, they must establish a global infrastructure of mass media that will have the ability and the capacity to display the Islamic point of view to the Western world within a short period of time.

Recently, a Saudi businessman revealed that an Islamic satellite for the West will soon be built. All of the Islamic *Da'wah* materials will be in English and French, and soon they will produce programming in all vital languages of the world. The aim of this channel will be to proclaim true Islam to the West and to help the Islamic world financially by encouraging the Western investors to do business with Islamic countries.[44] Egypt has also developed a satellite channel, which proclaims Islam to the Muslim world as well as to the Western world. It provides a defense for the Islamic religion.[45]

Saaid Tantawee, Al Axhar high priest, said, "The Islamic nation must have this kind of mass media to help our people live in the western countries and (for the) spreading of Islam without any kind of problems from the western nations."[46] The Islamic Institution for Education, Science, and Culture said that it "will adopt this project to help the Islamic nations . . . to be a powerful instrument in the future."[47]

The Islamic channels currently broadcasting their programs to the West are the:

1. Islamic Channel, sponsored by Saudi businessman Shaui Saleh Kamel
2. Andaloos Channel from Spain
3. Al Manar Islamic Channel from Lebanon, sponsored by *Hazeb Allah* (God's Party)
4. *Al Rahman* Channel (the Mercy One Channel) from Indonesia
5. Islamic City Channel in the United States, which reaches 2.5 million Muslim viewers
6. MTV Channel from the United Kingdom (selected programming)[48]

There is a possibility that Muslims will soon rent a Western channel to broadcast Islamic programs every Sunday morning. There are Islamic channels in Arabic nations.[49] And there is an Egyptian sponsored channel in Germany that also has programs in the Middle East and North Africa.[50]

SIXTH: THE INSTITUTIONALIZATION OF *Da'wah* IN THE WESTERN CONTEXT (PARA-MOSQUE)

A para-mosque is any spiritual ministry whose organization is not under the authority of a local Muslim congregation or body.[51] Or a para-mosque is an organization, which was formed as an alternative to those established in previous centuries.[52] This federation goes out of its way for the advancement of the religious, cultural, and social aspects of all Muslims on the American continent. It is working toward Muslims becoming strong through their Islamic heritage, the interpretation of its teachings, and the setting forth of its lofty principles, which it shares together with other religions whose adherents live among the non-Muslims of America. This federation will be a powerful agent in the spreading of the Islamic culture to the widest possible boundaries among America.[53]

The objectives of this agency are as follows:

1. To present the Islamic way of life as defined by the *Qur'an* and *Aunna*
2. To strengthen bonds of brotherhood among Muslim communities and individual Muslims
3. To promote mutual appreciation and friendly relations between Muslims and non-Muslims
4. To stimulate Islamic thinking and action in the North American setting
5. To coordinate activities of member communities and communicate with the entire Muslim world[54]

The Islamic Information Center of America

Musa Qutab is from Jerusalem and was educated in the Quaker community. He established the Islamic Information Center of America in 1983 with John Merenkov, an American doctor. The center has three objectives:

1. To deliver the message of Islam
2. To inform non-Muslims about Islam
3. To aid United States Muslims in delivering the message to others[55]

These goals are fulfilled by contacting people, giving lectures, conducting seminars, publishing writings, handing out literature, and utilizing the mass media.

The Muslim Student Association and Islamic Society of North America

The Muslim Student Association and Islamic Society of North America started in 1963 with seventy-five students at the Urbana campus in Illinois. It sought to improve students' knowledge of Islam, to perpetuate the Islamic spirit, explain Islam to Americans, and promote the restoration of Islam in student's home countries. They have a magazine called *Al Ittihad* (which is the Muslim's answer to *Christianity Today*). One of their brochures states that the "important task is *Da'wah* among non-Muslims, because the campus is where the most curious, the most inquisitive, and the most open-minded audience for Islam (is)."[56]

Rabitat al-Alam al Islami (The Muslim World League)

The Muslim World League was founded by the Saudi government in 1962. It is a low-church organization dedicated to *Da'wah* in those countries where Islam is a minority religion. It assists Islamic centers, youth camps, and summer schools. It provides teachers and *Imam*s, and develops prison ministry, fellowships, and grants. It produces television and radio programs as well as a Muslim newspaper. Mohammed Ali al Harakan felt that the World League was to "perform the obligation to *jihad*, to propagate Allah's religion, and move firmly into the activist camp."[57]

There are many more Muslim organizations in the United States.[58] Some of them are:

- The Association of Muslim Scientists and Engineers
- The Islamic Medical Association
- Islamic Societies of Georgia and Virginia
- Islamic Circle of North America (located in Canada)
- The Ahmadiyya (nonorthodox organization)

SEVENTH: STATISTICS AROUND THE WORLD

Islamic Population in the Western World

- Australia 100,000
- Belgium 250,000
- Denmark 60,000
- France 3,000,000
- Germany 2,500,000–3,000,000 (half million have German nationality)
- Greece 150,000
- Ireland 5,000
- Italy 500,000
- Luxembourg 1,000
- Netherlands 408,000
- Norway 22,000
- Portugal 15,000
- Spain 450,000
- Sweden 100,000
- Switzerland 100,000
- United Kingdom 2,000,000
- United States 5,000,000–7,000,000
- Canada 250,000
- Latin America 2,500,000[59]

Islamic Mosques

- There are 325 mosques in Germany[60]
- There are 250 mosques in Holland[61]

Islamic Schools

- There are 360 Islamic schools in the United States[62]
- There are 800 Islamic schools in Belgium[63]

appendix b

Islamic Speakers Bureau

In December 2002, many principals and other education supervisors in California received an offer from the Islamic Speakers Bureau to provide speakers and courses for public schools. Their argument was that many Muslim students were experiencing or might experience "discrimination or harassment," thus they wanted access to the classrooms as steps to reduce the level of intimidation.

A random checking of schools shows that some administrators have accepted these offers under the topic of "multicultural understanding."

The following are copies of one set of letters that was received by a school administrator in the San Francisco area.

Islamic Speakers Bureau

(408) 296-7312 or (888) 296-7312

December 2002

Dear Curriculum & Multicultural Supervisors and In-service Training Managers, Greetings of Peace!

Islamic Speakers Bureau (ISB) is a program of Islamic Networks Group (ING), a nonprofit organization that supplements existing education about Islam and Muslims in the context of World History and Social Studies in middle and high school classrooms. As we enter our eleventh year of operation, the ISB delivers over 1200 presentations a year.

Muslim students of various racial and ethnic backgrounds make up an increasing percentage of the school population. There are approximately 250,000 Muslims in the Bay Area, with over 20,000 Muslim students in public schools.

In the aftermath of the tragic events of September 11th and the threat of war with Iraq and possibly other Muslim populated nations, Muslim students, more than ever are the targets of prejudice, harassment, and even hate incidents. Even if Muslim students do not experience such obvious discrimination or harassment, it is excruciating to hear the constant negative discussions of Muslims and even Islam in the news, the classroom, and among students. Muslim students may often be experiencing real trauma that they are unable to discuss with their peers or teachers, for fear of humiliation. Parents are often unaware or helpless to alleviate the situation.

An understanding teacher, counselor, or administrator can make an enormous difference in a student's life and school experience. We suggest the following training seminars and presentations in the classroom as steps to reduce the level of discrimination or harassment:

STAFF DEVELOPMENT TRAINING:

Title: "Staff Development Training for Educators and Administrators: Incorporating Islamic Cultural Studies in the Curriculum and Interacting with Muslim Students"

Intended audience: All Educators and Administrators

Subject matter:
- Common Stereotypes
- Sources of Stereotypes
- Overview of Islamic Culture
- Incorporating Islamic Culture Studies in the Curriculum, Grades K–12th: Tools and Resources
- Understanding Muslim Religious Practices
- Tips for Interacting with Muslim Students

Training Period:
1.5–2.0 hours

Training format:
Interactive, where questions can be asked throughout.

Handouts:
- Booklet titled, "An Educator's Guide to Islamic Religious Practices," published by CAIR
- Booklet titled, "Discover Islam, The Reader," published by Transcom International
- "Catalogue for Teachers & Librarians, Grades K–12th," published by Islamic Speakers Bureau

Fees:
Negotiable, based on available district funding. Willing to provide it at no cost if funding is not available.

Equipment needed:
Overhead projector & screen, or laptop, LCD projector and screen

PRESENTATION IN THE CLASSROOM FOR GRADES 7TH–12TH:

Title: "Orientation on Islam and the Muslim World in the Context of World History and Social Science"

Intended audience: Students, Grades 7th–12th who are studying a subject relating to Islam or the Muslim World. (Note: California's Social Studies Content Standards include a unit on Islam in seventh grade, and units on other parts of the world including the Muslim world in ninth, tenth, and twelfth grades).

Subject matter:
- Terminology
- Islamic History
- World Population of Muslims
- Islam versus Culture
- Islam in America
- Beliefs and Practices of Muslims
- Islamic Holidays

Presentation period:
40–90 minutes, depending on teacher's request

Presentation format:
Interactive, allowing questions to be asked in the course of the presentation.
    Presentation also includes visual aids and display of cultural symbols and ethnic clothing.

PRESENTATION IN THE CLASSROOM FOR GRADES 10TH–12TH:

Title: "Women in Islam"

Intended audience: Students, Grades 10th–12th who are study-

ing a subject relating to Islam or the Muslim World, with particular emphasis on women's studies.

Subject matter:
- Stereotypes
- Sources of stereotypes
- Women's conditions in pre-Islam Arabia
- Identity based on *Qur'an* & Sunnah
- Women's spiritual nature
- Relationship with men in the public sphere
- Relationship with men in the domestic sphere
- Muslim female role modes
- Important women in early Islam
- Muslim women today
- Muslim women tomorrow

Presentation period:
20–90 minutes, depending on teachers request

Presentation format:
Interactive, allowing questions to be asked in the course of the
presentation.
   Presentation also includes visual aids and a display of cultural symbols and ethnic clothing.

About our Speakers:

• ISB speakers adhere to the First Amendment Centers "A
Teachers Guide to Religion in the Public Schools," which we
also apply to all public facilities. For more information on the
guidelines, visit hftp://www.freedomforum.org/.
• ISB speakers are also certified after a rigorous process of
training, testing, and observation in a live setting by veteran
trainers, whom have a combined training experience of 50 years
or more.

- ISB is also a founder and active member of NNASB (National Network of Affiliated Speakers Bureaus), whose charter can be found at hftp://www.ing,org/about/page.asp?num=11

TEACHER'S KIT FOR PRESENTING RAMADAN AND EID, GRADES K–6TH:

Especially important in the winter holiday season, this kit was designed for public schools teachers and Muslim parents to provide tools for incorporating Ramadan and Eid holidays in schools arts and crafts programs.

Kit includes two books as follows:

Book 1:
Islamic Speakers Bureau School Series
Presenting Ramadan and Eid in Elementary School Grades K–6
Kit for Parents and Teachers, 4th Edition
Islamic Networks, Inc. 2001, 127 pgs.

Table of Contents:
Part One: Introduction
Part Two: Presenting Ramadan and Eid in Grades K–6 (actual presentation scripts)
Part Three: Teaching Materials for Grades 4–6
Part Four: Coloring Activities
Part Five: Art Projects
Part Six: Lunar Activities
Part Seven: Supplemental Activities

Book 2:
Ramadan Activities
Teacher Created Materials, Inc. 2000, 16 pgs.

Table of Contents:
Islam: A Brief Overview
Ramadan—The Month of Fasting
Comprehension Questions
Ramadan Word Search
Ramadan Activity Calendar
Make Your Own Tasbih (Muslim prayer beads)
"An Ordinary Day" Instructions
"An Ordinary Day" Game board
Write Your Name in Arabic
An "A-Mazing" Trip to the Mosque
Muslim World Matching
Extension Activities and Resources
Answer Key

Kit's order form is enclosed with this letter.

Also attached is a Calendar of Important Islamic Holy Days

For further information, please do not hesitate to call our office
at 408-296-7312. You may also schedule a speaker through our
website at hftp://www.ing.org

Sincerely,

Maha ElGenaidi & Ameena Jandali
Hosai Mojaddidi
ISB Co-Founders
ISB Scheduler

Islamic Speakers Bureau
(408) 296-7312 or (888) 296-7312

Announcements
Visit our website at

http://www.ing.org/speakers/subpage.asp?num=1
&pagenum=1

For Islamic Resources for Research Topics Relating to Islam &
the Muslim World.

Tune in to KQED, Television Channel 9 for the following
programs:

• **Wednesday, December 18th at 9:00 p.m.** for the national
broadcast premiere of **Muhammad: Legacy of a Prophet.** This
special tells the story of the 7th-century prophet who changed
world history in 23 years and continues to shape the lives of
more than 1.2 billion people. This lively, thorough and honest
portrait of the man and the prophet takes viewers to ancient
Arabian sites where Muhammad's story unfolded and into the
homes, mosques and workplaces of some of America's approximately seven million Muslims to discover the many ways in
which they follow Muhammad's example. With some of the
world's leading scholars on Islam providing historical context
and critical perspective, viewers learn not only who
Muhammad was, but also what most American Muslims believe Islam teaches and how their beliefs are increasingly shaping society. Actor Andre Braugher narrates.

• **Wednesday, December 18th at 11:00 p.m. for Muslims in
Appalachia.** A documentary exploring the hidden life of Mus-
lims living in the heart of the Bible Belt. Interviews with local
Muslims along with comments by Yvonne Haddad of
Georgetown University and others combine with scenic footage

of the Appalachian Mountains in all seasons to provide the viewer with a portrait of Islam's presence, contributions, and tensions with modern Appalachian life. The program explores the ways in which minority status affects individual faith and community life. By filmmaker Steve M. Martin.

• **Thursday, December 19th at 9:00 p.m.** for a special re-broadcast of **FRONTLINE: Muslims**, produced by Independent Production Fund. The events of September 11 left many Americans questioning how such atrocities could be perpetrated in the name of religion: specifically, the religion of Islam. Yet even as United States opinion polls reflect a collective sense of mistrust toward a religion few Americans know much about, Islam continues to be the fastest growing religion in the United States today. What is Islam? What do Muslims believe in? And how does their faith shape their lives, their identities, and their political ideologies? Frontline explores these and other questions in this special report that examines the fundamental tenets of Islam and the causes behind its current worldwide resurgence. Through interviews with dozens of ordinary Muslims from such diverse countries as Iran, Malaysia, Turkey, and the United States, Frontline illuminates the perspectives, conflicts and tensions that are shaping today's Muslim world.

New mosque in a rural area in Southeast Asia.

Outline of a large mosque by night.

appendix c

Distribution of Muslim Populations by Nation-State

The *Muslim Almanac* lists the "Distribution of Muslim Populations by Nation-State," which includes area of the country, population, percentage of population that is Muslim, and the capital city.[1] That list is included below.

Afghanistan

Area: 250,000 sq. mi. (647,500 sq. km.)
Population: 16.4 million (1991 estimate)
Percent Muslim: 100. More than 75 percent are Sunnis; the remainder are Shia
Official Language: Pashtu and Dari
Capital: Kabul

Albania

Area: 11,100 sq. mi. (28,750 sq. km.)
Population: 2.5 million (1994 estimate)
Percent Muslim: 65
Official Language: Albanian
Capital: Tirana

Algeria

Area:	919,595 sq. mi. (2,381,740 sq. km.)
Population:	27.9 million (1994 estimate)
Percent Muslim:	over 99
Official Language:	Arabic
Capital:	Algiers

Azerbaijan

Area:	33,436 sq. mi. (86,600 sq. km.)
Population:	7.4 million (1992 estimate)
Percent Muslim:	87; 70 percent are Shia and the remainder are Sunnis
Official Language:	Azerbaijani
Capital:	Baku

Bahrain

Area:	239 sq. mi. (620 sq. km.)
Population:	508,000 (1991 estimate)
Percent Muslim:	All indigenous Bahrainis are Muslims. Over 70 percent are Shia and approximately 30 percent are Sunnis
Official Language:	Arabic
Capital:	Manama

Bangladesh

Area:	55,599 sq. mi. (144,000 sq. km.)
Population:	112.8 million (1992 estimate)
Percent Muslim:	87 percent of Bengalis are Muslims, making Bangladesh the third largest Muslim country after Indonesia and Pakistan
Official Language:	Bengali
Capital:	Dhaka (formerly Dacca)

Benin

Area:	43,483 sq. mi. (112,620 sq. km.)
Population:	5.3 million (1994 estimate)
Percent Muslim:	13–15
Official Language:	French
Capital:	Porto-Novo

Bosnia-Herzegovina
Area:	19,781 sq. mi. (51,233 sq. km.)
Population:	4.6 million (1993 estimate)
Percent Muslim:	40
Official Language:	Serbo-Croatian
Capital:	Sarajevo

Brunei Darussalam
Area:	2,228 sq. mi. (5,770 sq. km.)
Population:	260,482 (1991 estimate)
Percent Muslim:	63
Official Language:	Malay and English
Capital:	Bandar Seri Begawan

Bulgaria
Area:	42,823 sq. mi. (110,901 sq. km.)
Population:	8.9 million (1994 estimate)
Percent Muslim:	9–13
Official Language:	Bulgarian
Capital:	Sofia

Burkina Faso
Area:	105,869 sq. mi. (274,200 sq. km.)
Population:	10.2 million (1994 estimate)
Percent Muslim:	25
Official Language:	French (indigenous language Moré spoken by 55 percent of the population)
Capital:	Ougadougou

Cameroon
Area:	183,568 sq. mi. (475,440 sq. km.)
Population:	12.3 million (1994 estimate)
Percent Muslim:	25
Official Language:	French and English
Capital:	Yaoundé

Canada
Area:	3,851,808 sq. mi. (9,976,140 sq. km.)
Population:	28.5 million (1993 estimate)
Percent Muslim:	less than 3

Official Language: French and English
Capital: Ottawa

Central African Republic
Area: 240,535 sq. mi. (622,980 sq. km.)
Population: 3.1 million (1994 estimate)
Percent Muslim: 5, primarily in the north
Official Language: French is the official language (the national language, Sango, is spoken by the majority)
Capital: Bangui

Chad
Area: 495,755 sq. mi. (1,284,000 sq. km.)
Population: 6.2 million (1993 estimate)
Percent Muslim: 44
Official Language: French and Arabic
Capital: N'Djamena (formerly Fort-Lamy)

China
Area: 3,646,448 sq. mi. (9,44,292 sq. km.)
Population: 1.1 billion
Percent Muslim: 5 (1990 estimate)
Official Language: Mandarin Chinese
Capital: Beijing

Comoros
Area: 838 sq. mi. (2,170 sq. km.)
Population: 530,000
Percent Muslim: Almost 100
Official Language: French and Arabic
Capital: Moroni

Cote d'Ivoire
Area: 124,502 sq. mi. (322,460 sq. km.)
Population: 14.5 million (1994 estimate)
Percent Muslim: 24
Official Language: French
Capital: Yamoussoukro

Cyprus
Area: 3,571 sq. mi. (9,250 sq. km.)

Population: 725,000 (1992 estimate)
Percent Muslim: 18.7
Official Language: Greek and Turkish
Capital: Nicosia

Djibouti
Area: 8,494 sq. mi. (22,000 sq. km.)
Population: 542,000 (1991 estimate)
Percent Muslim: 94, primarily Sunni with a small Shia minority
Official Language: French and English. Somali and Afar are widely spoken
Capital: Djibouti

Egypt
Area: 386,662 sq. mi. (1,001,450 sq. km.)
Population: 58.2 million (1994 estimate)
Percent Muslim: 90
Official Language: Arabic
Capital: Cairo

Eritrea
Area: 46,842 sq. mi. (121,930 sq. km.)
Population: 2.6 million (1992 estimate)
Percent Muslim: 50
Official Language: No official language has been designated. Arabic and Tigrinya are the working languages of the Eritrean government
Capital: Asmara

Ethiopia
Area: 435,186 sq. mi. (1,127,127 sq. km.)
Population: 55 million (1994 estimate)
Percent Muslim: 45
Official Language: Amharic
Capital: Addis Ababa

France
Area: 211,209 sq. mi. (547,030 sq. km.)
Population: 56.6 million (1990 census)
Percent Muslim: 1.2

Official Language: French
Capital: Paris

The Gambia
Area: 4,363 sq. mi. (11,300 sq. km.)
Population: 1 million (1993 census)
Percent Muslim: 85
Official Language: English; principal vernaculars are Wolof and Mandinka
Capital: Banjul (formerly Bathurst)

Georgia
Area: 26,911 sq. mi. (69,700 sq. km.)
Population: 5.4 million (1989 census)
Percent Muslim: 11
Official Language: Georgian
Capital: T'bilisi

Germany
Area: 137,804 sq. mi. (356,910 sq. km.)
Population: 80.2 million (1991 estimate)
Percent Muslim: 3
Official Language: German
Capital: Berlin

Ghana
Area: 92,100 sq. mi. (238,540 sq. km.)
Population: 17.1 million (1994 estimate)
Percent Muslim: 12
Official Language: English
Capital: Accra

Guinea
Area: 94,927 sq. mi. (245,860 sq. km.)
Population: 7.7 million (1995 estimate)
Percent Muslim: 90
Official Language: French
Capital: Conakry

Guinea-Bissau
Area: 13,946 sq. mi. (36,120 sq. km.)

Population:	1.1 million (1994 estimate)
Percent Muslim:	38
Official Language:	Portuguese is the official language. A Guinean "Crioulo" or Africanized version of Portuguese is the lingua franca
Capital:	Bissau

Guyana

Area:	83,000 sq. mi. (214,970 sq. km.)
Population:	808,000 (1992 estimate)
Percent Muslim:	9
Official Language:	English
Capital:	Georgetown

India

Area:	1,269,345 sq. mi. (3,287,590 sq. km.)
Population:	919.1 million (1994 estimate)
Percent Muslim:	11
Official Language:	Hindi and English
Capital:	New Delhi

Indonesia

Area:	741,000 sq. mi. (1,919,440 sq. km.)
Population:	184.3 million (1992 estimate)
Percent Muslim:	87
Official Language:	Bahasa Indonesia
Capital:	Jakarta

Iran

Area:	636,296 sq. mi. (1, 648,000 sq. km.)
Population:	59.8 million (1992 estimate)
Percent Muslim:	93.8; Sunnis constitute about 6 percent
Official Language:	Farsi
Capital:	Tehran

Iraq

Area:	168,754 sq. mi. (437,072 sq. km.)
Population:	19.2 million (1992 estimate)
Percent Muslim:	95; 60 percent Shia; 35 percent Sunni
Official Language:	Arabic
Capital:	Baghdad

Jordan

Area:	32,175 sq. mi. (83,335 sq. km.)
Population:	3.9 million (1992 estimate)
Percent Muslim:	92
Official Language:	Arabic
Capital:	Amman

Kazakhstan

Area:	1,049,155 sq. mi. (2,717,300 sq. km.)
Population:	17 million (1992 estimate)
Percent Muslim:	40
Official Language:	Kazakh is the national language with Russian spoken widely by all ethnic groups
Capital:	Almaty

Kenya

Area:	224,962 sq. mi. (582,650 sq. km.)
Population:	27.8 million (1995 estimate)
Percent Muslim:	16
Official Language:	Swahili and English
Capital:	Nairobi

Kuwait

Area:	6,880 sq. mi. (17,820 sq. km.)
Population:	1.4 million (1994 estimate)
Percent Muslim:	90; 63 percent Sunni and about 27 percent Shia
Official Language:	Arabic
Capital:	Kuwait City

Kyrgystan

Area:	76,641 sq. mi. (198,500 sq. km.)
Population:	4.7 million (1995 estimate)
Percent Muslim:	52
Official Language:	Kyrgyz
Capital:	Bishkek

Lebanon

Area:	4,015 sq. mi. (10,400 sq. km.)
Population:	2.8 million (1992 estimate)
Percent Muslim:	57 (including Druze)

Official Language:	Arabic; with French as a second language
Capital:	Beirut

Libya
Area:	679, 362 sq. mi. (1,759,540 sq. km.)
Population:	4.7 million
Percent Muslim:	97
Official Language:	Arabic
Capital:	Tripoli

Madagasgar
Area:	226,657 sq. mi. (587,040 sq. km.)
Population:	13.4 million (1994 estimate)
Percent Muslim:	1.7
Official Language:	No official language is given. Principal languages are French and Malagasy
Capital:	Antananarivo

Maldives
Area:	116 sq. mi. (300 sq. km.)
Population:	214,000 (1990 estimate)
Percent Muslim:	100
Official Language:	Divehi
Capital:	Malé

Mali
Area:	478,767 sq. mi. (1,240,000 sq. km.)
Population:	8.9 million (1994 estimate)
Percent Muslim:	80
Official Language:	French
Capital:	Bamako

Malyasis
Area:	127,581 sq. mi. (329,750 sq. km.)
Population:	17.5 million (1991 estimate)
Percent Muslim:	53
Official Language:	Bahasa Malaysia or Malay
Capital:	Kuala Lumpur

Mauritania
Area:	397,955 sq. mi. (1,030,700 sq. km.)

Population:	2.1 million (1994 estimate)
Percent Muslim:	99
Official Language:	Arabic, Wolof, Peular, Soninke are spoken in southern Mauritania and recognized as national languages
Capital:	Nouakchott

Mauritius

Area:	718 sq. mi. (1,860 sq. km.)
Population:	1.1 million (1994 census)
Percent Muslim:	17
Official Language:	English
Capital:	Port Louis

Mongolia

Area:	604,250 sq. mi. (1,565,000 sq. km.)
Population:	2.2 million (1992 estimate)
Percent Muslim:	4
Official Language:	Khalka Mongolian
Capital:	Ulaanbaatar

Morocco (including Western Sahara)

Area:	172,414 sq. mi. (446,550 sq. km.)
Population:	27.8 million (1994 estimate)
Percent Muslim:	99
Official Language:	Arabic
Capital:	Rabat

Mozambique

Area:	309,496 sq. mi. (801,590 sq. km.)
Population:	16.3 million (1995 estimate)
Percent Muslim:	25
Official Language:	Portuguese
Capital:	Maputo (formerly Lauenco Marques)

Myanmar (formerly Burma)

Area:	261,970 sq. mi. (678,500 sq. km.)
Population:	43.6 million (1992 estimate)
Percent Muslim:	4; mostly Pakistani extraction
Official Language:	Burmese
Capital:	Yangoon (formerly Rangoon)

Netherlands

Area: 14,413 sq. mi. (37,330 sq. km.)
Population: 15 million (1991 estimate)
Percent Muslim: 2
Official Language: Dutch
Capital: Amsterdam

Niger

Area: 489,191 sq. mi. (1,267,000 sq. km.)
Population: 9 million (1994 estimate)
Percent Muslim: 88
Official Language: French; Hausa is also spoken all over the country as the language of trade
Capital: Niamey

Nigeria

Area: 365,670 sq. mi. (923,770 sq. km.)
Population: 126 million (1995 census)
Percent Muslim: 48–50
Official Language: English, Hausa is spoken widely in the north and Yoruba in the south
Capital: Abuja

Oman

Area: 82,031 sq. mi. (212,460 sq. km.)
Population: 2 million (1990 estimate)
Percent Muslim: 100, mostly Ibadi
Official Language: Arabic
Capital: Muscat

Pakistan

Area: 310,403 sq. mi. (803,940 sq. km.)
Population: 125.2 million (1993 estimate)
Percent Muslim: 95
Official Language: Urdu
Capital: Islamabad

Philippines

Area: 115,831 sq. mi. (300,000 sq. km.)
Population: 60.5 million (1990 estimate)
Percent Muslim: 5, primarily Sunni

Official Language: Philippino; English
Capital: Manila

Qatar
Area: 4,247 sq. mi. (11,000 sq. km.)
Population: 486,000 (1990 estimate)
Percent Muslim: 99.9
Official Language: Arabic is the national language, but English is widely spoken and Farsi is used by smaller groups in Doha
Capital: Doha

Russian Federation
Area: 6,592,771 sq. mi. (17,075,200 sq. km.)
Population: 148.6 million (1993 estimate)
Percent Muslim: 12
Official Language: Russian
Capital: Moscow

Saudi Arabia
Area: 756,985 sq. mi. (1,960,582 sq. km.)
Population: 16.9 million (1992 estimate)
Percent Muslim: 100
Official Language: Arabic
Capital: Riyadh

Senegal
Area: 75,749 sq. mi. (1,196,190 sq. km.)
Population: 8.3 million (1995 estimate)
Percent Muslim: 93
Official Language: French; Wolof is widely spoken
Capital: Dakar

Sierra Leone
Area: 27,699 sq. mi. (71,740 sq. km.)
Population: 4.6 million (1994 estimate)
Percent Muslim: 40
Official Language: English; Krio, a Creole language derived largely from English and African languages is the lingua franca
Capital: Freetown

Singapore

Area:	244.2 sq. mi. (632.6 sq. km.)
Population:	2.8 million (1993 estimate)
Percent Muslim:	16
Official Language:	Chinese (Mandarin dialect), Malay, English, and Tamil
Capital:	Singapore

Somalia

Area:	246,202 sq. mi. (637,660 sq. km.)
Population:	7.4 million (1994 estimate)
Percent Muslim:	99
Official Language:	Somali, Arabic, and English
Capital:	Mogadishu

Spain

Area:	194,885 sq. mi. (504,750 sq. km.)
Population:	39.4 million (1991 census)
Percent Muslim:	Less than 1
Official Language:	Spanish is the national language; Catalan, Basque, Galician, Bable, and Valencian are also official in respective autonomous communities
Capital:	Madrid

Sudan

Area:	967,490 sq. mi. (2,505,810 sq. km.)
Population:	29.7 million (1994 estimate)
Percent Muslim:	70
Official Language:	Arabic
Capital:	Khartoum

Surinam

Area:	63,039 sq. mi. (163,270 sq. km.)
Population:	416,000 (1994 estimate)
Percent Muslim:	20–25
Official Language:	Dutch; English is widely spoken
Capital:	Paramaribo

Syria

Area:	71,498 sq. mi. (185,180 sq. km.)
Population:	12.9 (1992 estimate)

Percent Muslim: 90
Official Language: Arabic
Capital: Damascus (Dimashq)

Tajikistan
Area: 55,251 sq. mi. (143,100 sq. km.)
Population: 6.1 million (1995 estimate)
Percent Muslim: 62
Official Language: Tajik (Persian)
Capital: Dushanbe

Tanzania (including Zanzabar)
Area: 364,901 sq. mi. (945,090 sq. km.)
Population: 29.7 million (1994 estimate)
Percent Muslim: 35
Official Language: Swahili (or Kiswahili) is the lingua franca. English and Swahili are the official languages
Capital: Dar es Salaam

Thailand
Area: 198,456 sq. mi. (514,000 sq. km.)
Population: 56.3 million (1990 census)
Percent Muslim: 4
Official Language: Thai
Capital: Bangkok

Togo
Area: 21,927 sq. mi. (56,790 sq. km.)
Population: 4.2 million (1994 estimate)
Percent Muslim: 15
Official Language: French
Capital: Lome

Trinidad and Tobago
Area: 1,981 sq. mi. (5,130 sq. km.)
Population: 1.2 million (1990 census)
Percent Muslim: 6
Official Language: English
Capital: Port of Spain

Tunisia

Area:	63,170 sq. mi. (163,610 sq. km.)
Population:	8.7 million (1994 census)
Percent Muslim:	99
Official Language:	Arabic
Capital:	Tunis

Turkey

Area:	301,384 sq. mi. (780,580 sq. km.)
Population:	56.4 million (1990 census)
Percent Muslim:	99; mostly Sunni, but substantial Shia minority exists
Official Language:	Turkish
Capital:	Ankara

Turkmenistan

Area:	188,456 sq. mi. (488,100 sq. km.)
Population:	4 million (1995 census)
Percent Muslim:	72
Official Language:	Turkmen is mandatory in schools. Russian continues in use in government and business
Capital:	Ashgabat

Uganda

Area:	91,136 sq. mi. (236,040 sq. km.)
Population:	20.8 million (1995 estimate)
Percent Muslim:	6
Official Language:	English
Capital:	Kampala

United Arab Emirates

Area:	29,182 sq. mi. (75,581 sq. km.)
Population:	1.9 million (1991 estimate)
Percent Muslim:	100
Official Language:	Arabic; English is widely used in business
Capital:	Abu Dhabi

United Kingdom

Area:	94,526 sq. mi. (244,820 sq. km.)
Population:	97.9 million (1994 census)
Percent Muslim:	2

Official Language:	English
Capital:	London

United States

Area:	3,618,773 sq. mi. (9,372,607 sq. km.)
Population:	248.7 million (1990 estimate)
Percent Muslim:	3
Official Language:	English
Capital:	Washington, D.C.

Uzbekistan

Area:	172,742 sq. mi. (447,400 sq. km.)
Population:	23 million (1995 estimate)
Percent Muslim:	75
Official Language:	Uzbek
Capital:	Tashkent

Yemen

Area:	203,850 sq. mi. (527,970 sq. km.)
Population:	11.4 million (1995 estimate)
Percent Muslim:	100, Zaydi Shia majority
Official Language:	Arabic
Capital:	Sana

Notes

CHAPTER 1: DON'T PANIC

1. John Esposito, *Unholy War: Terror in the Name of Islam* (New York: Oxford University Press, 2002), 117.
2. Patrick J. Buchanan, *The Death of the West* (New York: Thomas Dunne, 2002), 118.
3. Ihsan Bagby, Paul M. Perl, and Bryan T. Froehle, "The Mosque in America: A National Portrait", (April 26, 2001). This report is available online at http://www.cair-net.org/mosquereport/.
4. This statistic was taken from the work published by the Population Division of the United Nations in *World Population Prospects: The 2000 Revision, Highlights,* released February 28, 2001. The report also shows that by 2050 Germany's 82 million people will have fallen to 59 million and that Europe's population of 728 million today will crash to 600 million.
5. Muslim *Imam*, interview by author, Germany, September 14, 1993. For security reasons, the name of the *Imam* cannot be published.
6. Steven Emerson, *American Jihad* (New York: Free Press, 2002), 194.
7. Cited in the editor's review of Ronald de Valderano, *Terror: The War Against the West,* http://www.libertyhaven.com/Politicsandcurrentevents/crimeandterrorism/terorwar.shtml (accessed online 13 August 2002).
8. Ibid.

9. Dr. James Slack, interview by author, Mill Valley, Calif., August 14, 2002.

10. Jerilyn Watson, "This in America—Muslims in America," aired on Voice of America, December 17, 2001, posted online at http://www.manythings.org/voa/01/01121tia_htm (accessed 15 January 2003).

11. Fatema Mernissi, *Islam and Democracy* (Cambridge, Mass.: Perseus, 2002), 44.

12. Buchanan, *Death of the West,* 16.

13. Ralph D. Winters, *The Twenty-five Unbelievable Years 1945–1969* (South Pasadena, Calif.: William Carey Library, 1970). Winters has written an excellent study on the radical changes that took place during these years. It concentrates mostly on the effects of this period on religion and, particularly, on Christian missions.

14. Ibid., 12.

15. Mernissi, *Islam and Democracy,* 190.

16. Larry A. Poston, *The Changing Face of Islam in America* (Camp Hill, Pa.: Horizon, 2000), 14.

17. Jane I. Smith, *Islam in America* (New York: Columbia University Press, 1999), 179.

18. Ibid.

19. Mernissi, *Islam and Democracy,* 130.

20. Elisabeth Siddiqui, quoted in *A Brief History of Islam in the United States,* http://www.islamamerica.org/history.cfm.

21. Fareed Zakaria, "The Politics of Rage: Why Do They Hate Us?" *Newsweek,* October 15, 2001.

22. Buchanan, *Death of the West,* 9.

23. Nelson Black, quoted by Buchanan, *Death of the West,* 187.

24. James Kurth, "The American Way of Victory," *National Interest* (summer 2000): 5.

25. Samuel P. Huntington quoted by Buchanan, *Death of the West,* 126.

26. A. J. Bacevich, *Books in Review: The Clash of Civilizations and the Remaking of World Order,* http://www.firstthings.com/ftissues/ft9705/reviews/bacevich.html. This review was on Huntington's major work, which was a follow-up to his widely read article on the same subject published in *Foreign Affairs* in the summer of 1993.

27. Emerson, *American Jihad*, 162.

28. Dale Hurd, "Hijacking Tolerance: Radical Islam's War with Christianity," CBN News, May 12, 2003, posted online at http://cbn.com/CBNNews/News/030512a.asp.

29. Ibid.

30. The World Muslim League was created in 1962 with one of its purposes as the promotion of Islam worldwide. It has a permanent staff and its headquarters are in Mecca.

31. Emerson, *American Jihad*, 160.

32. Peter Finn, "Saudis Say Iran Cooperating in War on Terror," *Washington Post*, August 11, 2002.

CHAPTER 2: THE QUIET REVOLUTION

1. Jane I. Smith, *Islam in America* (New York: Columbia University Press, 1999), 160.

2. Dr. Ghassan Khalif, interview by author, Spain, July 3, 2002.

3. Ibid.

4. Jamal Badawi, *Islamic Da'wah in the West*, video lecture (London: Islamic Foundation, 1988).

5. Lisa Beyer, "Saudi Arabia: Inside the Kingdom," *Time*, September 15, 2003, 50.

6. Badawi, *Islamic Da'wah in the West*.

7. Stuart E. Brown, *Meeting in Faith* (Geneva: WCC Publications, 1989).

8. Fatema Mernassi, *Islam and Democracy* (Cambridge, Mass.: Perseus, 2002), 34.

9. Ibid.

10. Marsha S. Haney, *Islam and Protestant African-American Churches* (San Francisco: International Scholars Publications, 1999), 122.

11. Wayne Perry, "Hip-hopping on Faith," *San Francisco Chronicle*, January 3, 2003, D10.

12. George Braswell, *What You Need to Know About Islam and Muslims* (Nashville: Broadman and Holman, 2000), 3. It should be noted that various authors state different numbers for the number of mosques in the United States. In this book, we have quotes giving between 1,200

and 3,600 mosques in the United States. The wide variation is due to two reasons: (1) different ways of defining what constitutes a mosque, and (2) the lack of adequate statistics coming out of the Islamic community in the United States.

13. Brian Connor, *Islam Taught in California Schools,* http://www.cbn.com/CBNNews/CWN/020802IslamTaught.asp. The article gives a list of statements from the book as well as opinions of California parents concerning the class.

14. Ibid., 2.

15. Ibid., 3.

16. William J. Bennetta, *A Review of Islam: A Simulation of Islamic History and Culture, 610–1100,* http://www.textbookleague.org/filth.htm (accessed online 7 May 2003).

17. Ibid.

18. Perry, "Hip-hopping on Faith," D10.

19. Mernissi, *Islam and Democracy,* 49.

20. Smith, *Islam in America,* 165.

21. This was taken from an interview with an area director of the Prison Fellowship Ministry on April 14, 2002. The name of the person cannot be given because of security reasons.

22. Quoted by Haney, *Islam and Protestant African-American Churches,* 111.

23. John Ogletree, lecture at North American Mission Board meeting in Atlanta, Georgia, July 29, 2002.

24. *The Minaret,* July–August 1993, 38.

25. Dale Neal, "Attacks Continue to Sway Opinions on Islam," *Ashville Citizens Times,* September 11, 2002, 1.

26. Badawi, *Islamic Da'wah in the West.*

27. Ibid.

28. Smith, *Islam in America,* 67.

29. Ibid.

30. Ibid., 68.

31. Khurram Murad, *Da'wah Among Non-Muslims in the West* (London: Islamic Foundation, 1986), 9.

32. Ibid., 10.

33. Khurrram Murad, *Da'wah Among Non-Muslims in the West,* http://
www.masmn.org/books/Khurram_Murad/Dawah_among_
Non_Muslims_in _the_West/ (accessed online 6 August 2002).

CHAPTER 3: *Jihad*

1. Azlim A. Nanji, ed., *The Muslim Almanac* (Detroit: Gale Research,
1996), 499.
2. Sachiko Murata and William Chittick, *The Vision of Islam* (New York:
Paragon, 1994), 21.
3. Donna Abu-Nasr, "Bin Ladin's World Revisited," posted online at http://
www.lats.com/rights/register.htm (accessed online September 28, 2002).
This quote came from an undated press release. The dateline was Damascus. The author quoted from the book *Bin Ladin, Al-Jezeera, and I,* by
Jamal Abdul Latif Ismail. The book, which at the time is only in Arabic,
includes a fifty-four-page transcript of the complete 1998 interview that
was broadcast in abbreviated form on Al-Jezeera, a popular Islamic television program. The book was sold out in the Middle East.
4. Roland Armour, *Islam, Christianity, and the West* (Maryknoll, N.Y.:
Orbis, 2002), 31.
5. Hammudah 'Abd al 'Ati, *Islam in Focus* (Beltsville, Md.: Amana, 1998),
146.
6. George W. Braswell, *Islam: Its Prophet, Peoples, Politics, and Power*
(Nashville: Broadman and Holman, 1996), 74.
7. Christine Schirrmacher, "Islam and Christianity," *Journal of the Institute
of Islamic Studies of the Lausanne Movement Germany,* no. 1 (2000): 2.
8. El Fadl Khaled, "The Rules of Killing at War," *Muslim World* 89, no. 2
(1999) 160:8.
9. Section titled "Newswatch," *Press Democrat,* October 10, 2002, 2.
10. *Imad Shehadeh Self-Published Newsletter* in the hands of the author,
October 4, 2001, 2. It should be noted that various authors state
different numbers for the number of mosques in the United States. In
this book, we have quotes giving between 1,200 and 3,600 mosques in
the United States. The wide variation is due to two reasons: (1)
different ways of defining what constitutes a mosque, and (2) the lack

of adequate statistics coming out of the Islamic community in the United States.

11. Ibid., 3.
12. Malise Ruthven, *Islam in the World* (London: Penguin, 2000), 219.
13. Armour, *Islam, Christianity, and the West,* 177.
14. Ahmed Rashid, *Jihad: The Rise of Militant Islam in Central Asia* (New Haven: Yale University Press, 2002), 1.
15. Ibid.
16. Hussein K. al-Hussein, "Islamic Jihad: Some Misconceptions," *Muslim World League Journal* 16, no. 3 and 4 (1998): 36.
17. Armour, *Islam, Christianity, and the West,* 29.

CHAPTER 4: IF YOU BUILD IT, THEY WILL COME

1. Bryant L. Meyers, *The New Context of World Missions* (Monrovia, Calif.: MARC, 1996), 8.
2. Azim A. Nanji, ed., *The Muslim Almanac* (New York: Gale Research, 1996), 465.
3. Ibid.
4. Ibid., 471.
5. Jane I. Smith, *Islam in America* (New York: Columbia University Press, 1999), 129.
6. Martin Frishman et al., *The Mosque: History, Architectural Development, and Regional Diversity* (New York: Thames and Hudson, 1994), 30.
7. Ibid., 77.
8. Ibid., 41.
9. Ibid., 72.
10. Frank Charles Thompson, *The Thompson Chain-Reference Bible* (Indianapolis: B. B. Kirkbride, 1978), 1648.
11. J. Christy Wilson, *Afghanistan: The Forbidden Harvest* (Elgin, Ill.: Cook, 1981), 59.
12. Nigerian Background Information, *Cultural Mosaics of Nigeria,* http://www.uni.edu/gai/nigeria/background/standard10.html (accessed 10 May 2003).
13. Marsha S. Haney, *Islam and Protestant African-American Churches* (San Francisco: International Scholars Publications, 1999), 109.

14. Paul Johnson, "What Follows Saddam in Iraq," *Forbes*, August 19, 2002, 41.

15. Lisa Beyer, "Saudi Arabia: Inside the Kingdom," *Time*, September 15, 2003, 50.

16. Ibid.

17. CAIR (Council on American-Islamic Relations), *Number by 25 Percent of American Mosques Grows*, http://www.cairnet.org/mosquereport/Increase_in_Number_of_Mosque_Participants.htlm (accessed 6 August 2002).

18. Ibid.

19. Ibid.

20. Nabeel Abraham, "Arab Detroit's 'American Mosque,'" in *Arab Detroit: From Margin to Mainstream* (Detroit: Wayne State University Press, 2000), 280.

21. Nanji, *Muslim Almanac*, 478.

22. Islam Online, *Muslims Harassed for Praying in Cordoba Mosque*, http://www.islamonline.net/English/News/2002-03/04/article18.shtml.

23. *The World Seen from Rome*, http://www.zenit.org/english/archive9905/ZE990514.html (accessed online 14 May 1999).

24. This material was taken from the Daq-al-Islam Web site, which also describes the different ministries of the mosque in vague terms, posted online at http://www.digitalabique.com/pages/tours/caralislam_t.html (accessed 10 January 2002).

CHAPTER 5: IT'S THE LAW

1. Ghulam Sarwar, *Islam, Beliefs, and Teachings* (Chicago: Kazi, 1993), 161.

2. Stephen Schwartz, *The Two Faces of Islam* (New York: Doubleday, 2002), 42.

3. Ibid., 41.

4. *The Concept of Dhimma in Islam and Its Ramifications*, http://www.angelfire.com/az/rescon/DHILMMI.html (accessed 17 February 2003), 1.

5. Quoted by Anthony Flew, "Islam's War Against the West: Can It Abide a Secular State?" *Free Inquiry* 22 (spring 2002): 43.

6. Ahmed Rashid, *Jihad: The Rise of Militant Islam in Central Asia* (New Haven: Yale University Press, 2002), 9.

7. Ian Johnson and David Crawford, "In 'Law' Seminars: A Saudi Group Spreads Extremism," *Wall Street Journal*, April 15, 2003, A1.
8. Ibid., A10.
9. Ibid.
10. Lisa Beyer, "Saudi Arabia: Inside the Kingdom," *Time*, September 15, 2003, 47.
11. Bernard Lewis, *The Crisis of Islam: Holy War and Unholy Terror* (New York: Random, 2003), 113.
12. Ibid., 114.
13. Ibid., 114–15.
14. Ibid., 115.
15. Ibid., 116.
16. Ibid., 8.
17. Johnson and Crawford, "In 'Law' Seminars: A Saudi Group Spreads Extremism," A10.
18. David Wallechinsky, "The 10 Worst Living Dictators," *Parade Magazine*, February 16, 2003, 4.
19. Ibid.
20. John L. Esposito and John O. Voll, *Islam and Democracy* (New York: Oxford University Press, 1966), 65.
21. Ibid., 67–68.
22. Christiane Bird, *Neither East nor West* (New York: Washington Square Press, 2001), 51–52.

CHAPTER 6: THE WHOLE TRUTH AND NOTHING BUT THE TRUTH

1. *Is "Truth" Relative or Absolute?* (Staley Bride, U.K.: July 3, 2000), posted online at http://www.understandingislam.com/related/text.asp?type=questions&qid=31 (accessed 25 October 2002).
2. *Truth and Relativity*, last updated July 24, 2000, posted online at http://www.thewaytotruth.org/thinkingstraight/truthandrelativity.html (accessed 26 October 2002).
3. Ibid.
4. Ibid.
5. Posted online at http://www.lamblion.com.

6. Posted online at http://www.andromeda.Rutgers.edu/~rtavakol/engi/
   neer/ethics (accessed October 2002).

7. Ibid.

8. *Truth and Relativity* (accessed 26 October 2002).

9. Ibid.

10. Ibid.

11. Caesar E. Farah, *Islam* (Hauppauge, N.Y.: Barron's, 2000), 80.

12. Posted online at http://www.sharif.org (accessed 8 February 2003).

13. *Comparative Index to Islam: Lying,* http://answering-islam.org/ IndexL/
    lying.html (accessed 4 August 2002), 1.

14. Ibid.

15. Ibid.

16. Fatema Mernissi, *Islam and Democracy* (Cambridge, Mass.: Perseus,
    2002). The outline for the book can be found at the beginning of the
    book. A thorough study of the book will explain what the author
    meant by the different types of fear.

17. "Munkar and Nakeer are two of Allah's angels who appear to a person
    after Death. They are blue and black in color. After death they come and
    ask the person what he or she said or proclaimed in his life before, if he
    then states that he followed Allah and recites the confession of what he
    believed the angels will say that they knew he or she was going to say that
    which he did. His grave was then enlarged by seventy cubits by seventy
    cubits. The grave was also illuminated, where after the person was told to
    sleep like a bridegroom who will only be wakened by his beloved. He or
    she will remain that way until Allah raises him up. If the angels appear to
    a person who was a hypocrite and they ask him or her the same question,
    it is stated that he or she will answer that he or she only recited that which
    he or she heard the other peoples saying. Upon hearing these words the
    angels will tell him or her that they knew he was going to say that and
    commands the earth to crush him or her until his or her rib interlocked
    in which position he or she will remain until Allah raises him or her up."
    Posted online at http://www.allaahuakbar.net/barelwiyat/angels.htm (ac-
    cessed 6 November 2002).

18. *Imam* Ghazali, *Imam* Ibn Qayyim, and Ibn Rajah Hanbali, *The Signs of
    Fear of Allah: Its Reasons, Its Fruits and Some Poems: 1995* (London: Al-

Firdous Ltd., 1995), posted online at http://www.islam.com/Article.aspx?id=324 (accessed 6 November 2002).

19. Imam Ali Ibn Abi al'Izzal Hanafi, *Salvation Lies Between Fear and Hope.* Sharh Al'Aqidah at Tahawiyyah, *The Islamic Creed* (abridged), Al Attique Publishers, 2000. Posted at http://www.islam.com/Article.aspx?id=5318 (accessed 5 November 2002).

20. Iman Madaarijus-Saalikeen, *Remembering the Destination of Mankind in the Hereafter-A Cure for Weak*, http://www.islam.com/Article.asx?id (accessed 10 October 2002).

21. *Belief in the Hereafter: Pillars of Faith*, http://www.islaam.com/Article.aspx?id=50 (accessed 15 November 2002).

22. K. M. Islam, "The Infidel Hell," in *Extreme Islam: Anti-American Propaganda of Muslim Fundamentalism*, ed. Adam Parfrey (Los Angeles: Feral House, 2001), 310.

23. Ibid.

24. Paragraph on *Salvation: Islam a Religion of Hopelessness and Fear*, by N.S.R.K. Ravi, North American Mission Board, http://ontruth.com/islambyravi.html.

25. *Light of Life*, http://www.light-of-life.com/eng/ilaw/15721et.html (accessed 10 February 2003), 11.

26. Mernissi, *Islam and Democracy*, 13.

27. Ibid., 26.

CHAPTER 7: POWER SHORTAGE

1. Charles H. Kraft, *Anthropology for Christian Witness* (Maryknoll, N.Y.: Orbis, 1998), 453. Kraft is one of America's outstanding authorities on power encounter on a global scale.

2. From a speech given by the Hon. James R. Woolsey, former director of the Central Intelligence Agency, on November 16, 2002, titled *World War IV* (text in the hands of the author), 1.

3. Ibid., 1–2.

4. Debates and Speeches of Ahmed Deedat, posted at http://216.239.33.100/search?hl=en&q=cache:..../video-debates—speeches-of-ahmed-deedat.hdtml+Mosque%20DaWA (accessed 6 August 2002).

5. Steve Hawthorne and Graham Kendrick, *Prayer Walking: Praying on Site with Insight* (Lake Mary, Fla.: Charisma House, 1993), 85–87. The story has been condensed for the sake of brevity, but the complete story of the power encounter can be found in the above mentioned book.

6. *Egypt's Al-Azhar Clerics: We Declare War on America,* posted at http://www.memru.de/uebersetzungen_analysen/themen/islamistische_ideologie_egypt_02_11_01.html (accessed 17 December 2002), 2.

7. Ibid.

8. Ibid., 2–3.

9. *Webster's New English Dictionary* (New York: Simon and Schuster, 1994), s.v. "intimidation."

10. Daniel Pipes, *How Dare You Defame Islam,* http://danielpipes.com/Article/321 (accessed 27 January 2003), 1.

11. "Iraq's Tiny Christian Communities Brace for Heightened Persecution," *Baptist New Mexican,* March 29, 2003, 3.

12. Ibid.

13. *Muslims Urged to Kill Christian Fashion Writer,* http://www.bpnews.net/bpnews.asp?ID=14752, 1/218/2003 (accessed 6 February 2003), 1–2.

14. "Bomb Kills Christian Convert," News from Lebanon, http://www.into@barnabasfund.org (accessed 8 May 2003).

15. David Barrett, George T. Kurian, and Todd M. Johnston, *World Christian Encyclopedia* (New York: Oxford University Press, 2003), 1:11.

16. Ibid.

17. Private interview by author, 1990. Because of security concerns, I cannot name the person or the country.

CHAPTER 8: MUHAMMAD, THE MESSAGE, AND THE MASS MEDIA

1. Daniel Pipes, *How Dare You Defame Islam,* http://danielpipes.com/article/321, 4.

2. Ibid.

3. Gwynne Dyer, "Simplistic New Media Rules for Covering Terrorism," *Salt Lake Tribune,* November 4, 2002.

4. Islamic Net Article 200.08.2002-09-06 6. This was opened in the

Middle East and was in Arabic. This was the only information available in identifying the source.

5. "Islamic Cooperation," *Middle East Newspaper,* Religion, March 3, 2003.

6. Pipes, *How Dare You Defame Islam,* 3.

7. Charles Krauthammer, "Islamic Scholar Target of Political Onslaught," *Press Democrat,* August 15, 2003.

8. Pipes, *How Dare You Deface Islam,* 3–4.

9. Bassam Za'ar, "Insight: Projecting True Picture of Islam," *Gulf News,* online ed., November 2002.

10. Caryle Murphy, "Muslim U.S. Workers Hope to Break Image," *Washington Post,* November 6, 2002.

11. *US Filmmakers Tread Carefully in Mohammed Biography,* http://tv.yahoo.com/news/va/20021212/103972897200.html, 2.

12. Daniel Pipes, "PBS Caught Recruiting for Islam," *Baptist New Mexican,* January 25, 2003.

13. Osma Gull Hasan, *American Muslims: The New Generation* (New York: Continuum, 2000), 100.

14. Posted online at http://www.islamicmedia.net/mission1.htm (accessed August 2003).

15. Ursula Owre Masterson, "American Muslims Launch PR-style Campaigns to Defend Islam," *Muslim News* (Harrow, Middlesex, U.K.), November 6, 2002.

16. "Muslim Ramadan Begins, So Does Acceptance," WBAY TV (Green Bay, Wis.), November 8, 2002.

17. Donna Gehrke-White, "Moving Beyond the Mosque: Muslims Seek to Enter Mainstream," *Muslim News,* posted at http://www.muslimnews.co.uk/ramadan (accessed 15 January 2003).

18. Jane Lampman, "A Muslim Scholar Builds Bridges to the West," *Christian Science Monitor,* November 7, 2002.

19. Caryle Murphy, "Muslim U.S. Workers Hope to Break Image."

20. Masterson, "American Muslims Launch PR-style Campaigns to Defend Islam," 2.

21. John Rivera, *As Ramadan Begins, Cleric Urges Tolerance,* http://www.sunspoon.net/news/local/bal-md (accessed 6 November 2002).

22. Posted online at www.islamicmedia.net.

23. Posted online at www.muslimnews.co.uk.

24. Michael Isikoff, "It's All a Matter of Bias," *Newsweek,* December 30, 2002–January 6, 2003, 14.

25. Kari Dean, "Muslim TV Network in the Making," *Wired News,* posted at http://www.wired.com/news/print/0,1294,58773,00.html.

26. Ibid.

27. Ibid.

28. Noelle Knox and Theresa Howard, "Anti-war Protests Take Aim at American Brands," *United States Today,* April 4, 2003, 2B.

29. Ibid.

30. "Dr. Turaky Meeting with the European Parliament," *Middle East Newspaper,* Religion, May 24, 2002.

31. *Muslim Holland,* http://www.islamway.net.

32. "Meeting in America About Islam," *Middle East Newspaper,* Religion, May 8, 2002.

33. *Middle East Newspaper,* Religion, June 23, 2002 .

34. Ibid.

35. Ibid.

36. Ibid.

CHAPTER 9: WHAT IN THE WORLD IS ALLAH DOING?

1. Patrick Johnstone and Jason Mandryk, *Operation World: Twenty-first Century* (London: Bethany, 2001), 2.

2. Ibid., 3.

3. Danielle Haas, "Iraqi Crowds Welcome Ayatollah Home," *San Francisco Chronicle,* May 11, 2003.

4. Ibid.

5. Pierre Francis, *The Civil War in Lebanon (1975–1992) and the Christian Evangelical Message: Toward Survival, Extinction or Expansion* (Th.D. dissertation, Evangelical Theological Faculty, Louvin, Belgium, September 1993), 3. The dissertation looks at the causes of the war and its effects on the traditional Christian community. Francis sees the war as a continued attempt by Islamic forces to drive all remnants of Christianity out of the

Middle East. Beirut had been the center for evangelical Christian missions to the Middle East, but the war drove them out. Many mission agencies then placed their headquarters in either Cyprus or Western Europe.

6. Johnstone and Mandryk, *Operation World*, 21.

7. Quoted in the preliminary draft of a paper titled *Spreading the Word of God Among Muslims in South Africa*, 3. This draft was produced by the United Bible Societies. The date of the draft was September 26, 2002. The paper is in the hands of the author.

8. Christian missionary to Nigeria, interview by author, February 3, 2001. For the sake of security, the name of the missionary cannot be revealed.

9. Christian missionary to Rwanda, lecture given in Introduction to Missions at Golden Gate Baptist Theological Seminary, November 3, 2002. For the sake of security, the name of the missionary cannot be revealed.

10. *Religious Freedom in the Majority Countries, 1998 Report*, http://www.agonet.it/cristianita/acs/acs_english/report_98/malawi.htm.

11. Dr. Martinus Pretoria, interview by author, Leuven, Belgium, September 14, 2002.

12. Johnstone and Mandryk, *Operation World*, 41.

13. Justin D. Long, *Asia 1900–2025: The Rise and Fall of World Religions*, http://www.gem-were.org/mmrc/mmrc9723.htm (accessed 28 November 2002).

14. John L. Esposito, ed., *Islam in Asia* (New York: Oxford, 1987), 15.

15. Satu Limaye, *Islam in Asia: Asia-Pacific Center for Security Studies*, http://www.apcss.org/Publications?Report_Islam_in_asia_99.html, 3 (accessed 28 November 2002).

16. Ibid.

17. Indian Christian Fellowship, *Conversion of Millions in India*, http://www.webedelil.com/church/delhi411.htm (accessed 3 May 2003).

18. Ibid.

19. Ibid.

20. Syed Shahabuddin and Theodore P. Wright, "India: Muslim Minority Politics and Society," in *Islam in Asia*, ed. John Esposito, 152.

21. Johnstone and Mandyrk, *Operation World*, 339.

22. Limaye, *Islam in Asia: Asia-Pacific Center for Security Studies*, 11.

23. These were statements taken from prayer letters sent to me between

January 1, 2002, and March 30, 2003. The names of the missionaries cannot be given due to security reasons.

24. Ibid.
25. Caesar E. Farah, *Islam* (New York: Barrons, 2000), 262–63.
26. Ibid., 284.
27. Limaye, *Islam in Asia: Asia-Pacific Center for Security Studies*, 15.
28. Farah, *Islam*, 277.
29. Ibid.
30. Ahmed Rashid, *Jihad: The Rise of Militant Islam in Central Asia* (New Haven: Yale University Press, 2002), 115.
31. Ibid., 116.
32. Chris Moss, *Islam in Latin America: Latin America's First Mega-Mosque Open Eyes to Islam*, http://www.latinmuslims.com/history/megamosque.html.
33. Johnstone and Mandryk, *Operation World*, 33.

CHAPTER 10: MEASURING SUCCESS ONE COUNTRY AT A TIME

1. Samuel P. Huntington, *The Clash of Civilizations and the Remaking of World Order* (New York: Simon and Schuster, 1996), 312.
2. David Dolan Newsletter, *(Israel Update) Pieces on the Ground*, February 3, 2003.
3. Huntington, *Clash of Civilizations*, 304.
4. Ibid.

APPENDIX A: QUOTES FROM MIDDLE EASTERN SOURCES

1. *Middle East Newspaper*, Religion, May 3, 2002, interview with Shack Aquila al Aquila.
2. *Middle East Newspaper*, Religion, May 3, 2002, interview with Jussif Haji.
3. *Middle East Newspaper*, Religion, January 31, 2002, Abd a aziz bin baz institution.
4. *Middle East Newspaper*, Religion, March 11, 2002, meetings in Jadda.
5. Islamic Net Article, 8E20.02—09–06 6.
6. *Middle East Newspaper*, Religion, May 25, 2002, Islamic cooperation.

7. *Middle East Newspaper*, Religion, April 5, 2002, interview with Dr. Fahad al Taiash.

8. *Middle East Newspaper*, Religion, March 3, 2002, Islamic cooperation.

9. 'Abdallah 'Abd al-Fadin, *Is the Koran Infallible?* (Light of Life, first edition, n.d.), 143–46.

10. *Middle East Newspaper*, Opinions. February 26, 2002, what we can learn from the war in Afghanistan.

11. *Middle East Newspaper*, Religion, n.d., interview with Dr. Turaky.

12. *Middle East Newspaper*, Opinions, January 23, 2002, Sheik Ibin Taimeja.

13. *Middle East Newspaper*, Religion, May 3, 2002, Islamic delegation to Europe.

14. *Middle East Newspaper*, Religion, May 18, 2002, meetings concerning the dialogues with the West.

15. *Middle East Newspaper*, High Education Research, March 29, 2001, the American Company (amidst).

16. *Middle East Newspaper*, front page, May 10, 2002, new studies to understand *Qur'an*.

17. *Middle East Newspaper*, front page, March 11, 2002, Islamic delegation visiting the U.K.

18. *Middle East Newspaper*, Religion, June 17, 2002, Islamic delegation in Germany.

19. *Middle East Newspaper*, front page, March 11, 2002, Islamic delegation visiting the U.K.

20. *Middle East Newspaper*, Religion, February 19, 2002, interview with Dr. Turaky.

21. *Middle East Newspaper*, Religion, May 25, 2002, humanity studies from an Islamic point of view.

22. *Middle East Newspaper*, Religion, August 16, 2002, Islamic organizations in the earth summit.

23. *Middle East Newspaper*, Religion, March 29, 2002, the Da'l ussif Islam new exhibition.

24. www.ALJazeera.net, n.d., interview with Dr. Yussif Qaradawe.

25. *Middle East Newspaper*, Religion, March 20, 2002, meetings between Islamic organizations in Saudi Arabi.

26. *Middle East Newspaper,* Religion, April 13, 2002, interview with the president of the Islamic American University.

27. *Middle East Newspaper,* Religion, April 8, 2002, King Fahad interview.

28. *Middle East Newspaper,* Religion, June 21, 2002, meeting with Dr. Turaky about the relationship between Islam and the West.

29. *Middle East Newspaper,* Religion, February 2, 2002, meeting with executive chief of the Islamic American Council, Nihad Awad.

30. Al Jazeerah, August 2, 2002, Paul rejected the Islamic wrong ideas about Islam.

31. www.islamwav.net (accessed August 2, 2002).

32. *Middle East Newspaper,* Religion, May 24, 2002, Dr. Turaky meeting with the European Parliament.

33. www.islamwav.net (accessed August 20, 2002), Muslims in Holland.

34. *Middle East Newspaper,* Religion, May 8, 2002, meeting in America about Islam.

35. *Middle East Newspaper,* Religion, June 23, 2002.

36. *Middle East Newspaper,* Special Subjects, n.d.

37. *Middle East Newspaper,* Religion, May 16, 2002, new branches for Al Azhar University.

38. *Middle East Newspaper,* Religion, November 9, 2001, interview with Dr. Taricha.

39. *Middle East Newspaper,* Religion, February 2, 2002, the mosque of King Fahd.

40. *Middle East Newspaper,* Religion, February 8, 2002, conference for the World Islamic Universities.

41. Al Jazeerah channel, program (a Sharee'ah wal Haiat), December 7, 2000.

42. *Middle East Newspaper,* Religion, August 10, 2001, interview with Dr. Ali Quara Daghy.

43. ISIC *The Economist* August 10–16, 2002.

44. Islamic Net, July 3, 2002, interview with a businessman.

45. Islamic Net, July 13, 2002, Islamic media under the ecumenical.

46. *Middle East Newspaper,* Religion, May 3, 2002, interview with Shaik Tantawee.

47. *Middle East Newspaper,* Religion, September 20, 2002, conference for the leaders of an Islamic organization in South America.

48. Islamic Net, July 16, 2002, Islamic satellite.

49. Islamic Net, August 12, 2002, Islamic satellite.

50. *Middle East Newspaper,* TV, Radio, August 7, 2002, Arabic channel in Germany.

51. The Institutionalization of *Da'wah* in the West, Islamic *Da'wah* in North America, Allan Larry Poston, Northwestern University. Dissertation for Ph.D., 1988.

52. Da'wah *in the West,* Allan Larry Poston, published by Oxford University Press, 94.

53. Ibid., 97–98.

54. Ibid., 98.

55. The Institutionalization of *Da'wah* in the West, Islamic *Da'wah* in North America, Larry Allan Poston, Northwestern University. Dissertation for Ph.D., 1988.

56. Ibid.

57. Ibid.

58. Ibid.

59. Dr. Yvonne Y. Haddad, professor of Christian-Muslim Relations, Center for Muslim-Christian Understanding, Georgetown University, toward the craving of Islamic space in the West.

60. www.islam.de.

61. Islamic.net, Article, August 18, 2002, Muslims in Holland.

62. *Middle East Newspaper,* Religion, February 12, 2002, Muslims can change the political situations in the United States.

63. *Middle East Newspaper,* Religion, June 15, 2002, Muslims in Belgium.

APPENDIX C: DISTRIBUTION OF MUSLIM POPULATIONS BY NATION-STATE

1. Azim A. Nanji., ed., *The Muslim Almanac* (New York: Gale Research, 1996), xxix–xxxv.

Glossary

al-houdh. The pool of water in hell.

al-jisr. The bridge over hell.

Allah. The name for God in Islam.

Allahu akbar. "God is Greater"; phrase used by Muslims in the form of a battle cry, in the call to prayer, and often used in general conversation.

Ayatollah. "Sign of God"; title used since the twentieth century by a high-ranking Shiite leader.

Caliph. Successor to Muhammad's temporal, but not spiritual, authority over the Muslim community.

daa'i. A missionary in Islam.

dar-al-bughd. Term referring to the community of non-Muslims who are hated by Muslims.

dar-al-harb. "The house of war"; Islamic doctrine and language divides the world into two parts, the other being *dar-al-Islam*. This one is for the non-Muslim world and means the "unpeaced" abode.

dar-al-Islam. "The house of Islam"; the Islamic world.

dar-al-kuffer. Term referring to the community of non-Muslims or unbelievers.

da'wah. "Call or invitation" summoning others to heed the call of God to Islam; propagation of the faith.

dhimmi. A conquered Jew or Christian who lives under Islamic rule.

fatwa. An official pronouncement from a leader in Islam; also a nonbinding legal opinion.

fiqh. The legal system of Islam as practiced in the courts.

gharaba. "Strangeness"; it is a derivative of the Arabic that means "The West" (*ghareeb* meaning "strange").

gharb. The word in Arabic that means "The West"; also means "darkness" by implication.

Hadith. The Islamic writings describing the life and sayings of Muhammad.

Imam. In general usage it means the spiritual leader in a Muslim community.

Injil. The Gospels describing Jesus that are accepted by Islam.

irsalyaat. Negative word in Arabic that is used to describe Christian missions.

jihad. The word for struggle. It need not be physical but could be. Also used to mean holy war.

jizya. Poll tax for *dhimmis* living under Islamic rule. Payment of this tax exempted them from military duty.

Kaa'ba. The most sacred shrine in Islam and is located in the courtyard of the Grand Mosque in Mecca. Believed to have been erected by Abraham.

mahdi. The awaited one, the *Imam* who will return and unite all Muslims into one *ummah,* according to Shiite Muslims.

minaret. The tower of the mosque, from which the call to prayer is issued five times daily.

mosque. From the Arabic *masjid;* a place of Muslim worship.

Muslim. Literally, "one who submits himself to the will of God"; a follower of the religion of Islam.

Qur'an. The Holy Book of Islam, a transcript of God's word as revealed to Muhammad.

Ramadan. Ninth month of the Muslim lunar year and the month of fasting during daylight hours.

shahada. The profession of faith, a statement of fundamental belief in Islam. It states, "There is no god but Allah and Muhammad is the messenger of Allah."

Shariah. The code of laws and rules governing the life and behavior of Muslims; comprises not a single book but various compilations of precedents.

Shiite. A follower of Islam in the *Shia* branch of Islam. Shiites differs from the main branch of the Sunnis in that they accept the spiritual authority of Ali, the cousin and son-in-law of Muhammad and the fourth Caliph.

Sufism. Islamic mysticism; brotherhoods of Sufis, or mystics, exist throughout the Muslim world.

Sunnite. A Muslim of the majority *Sunni* grouping that follow the *Sunna* or practices of Muhammad; comprising about 85 percent of all Muslims.

surah. One of the 114 chapters or sections of the *Qur'an*.

ta'a. Obedience.

tabshir. A negative word in Islam used to refer to Christian evangelism.

Tawrah. The first five books of Moses as accepted by Islam.

ummah. The community of all those who affirm Islam.

Zabur. The book of Psalms.

zakat. The "alms tax" a mandatory donation to charity, one of the essential duties of all Muslims.

zulm. Structures of oppression.

Bibliography

Abd al Atli, Hammudak. *Islam in Focus.* Beltsville, Maryland: Amana Publishers, 1998.

Abraham, Nabeel. *Arab Detroit: From Margin to Mainstream.* Detroit: Wayne State University Press, 2000.

Armour, Rollin. *Islam, Christianity, and the West: A Troubled History.* Maryknoll, N.Y.: Orbis Books, 2002.

Bacevich, A. J. *Books in Review: The Clash of Civilizations and the Remaking of World Order.* Available from http://www.firstthings.com/ftissues/ft9705/reviews/bacevich.html.

Badawi, Jamal. *Islamic Da'wah in the West.* Video lecture. London: Islamic Foundation, 1986.

Bagby, Ihsan, Paul M. Perl, and Bryan T. Froehle, "The Mosque in America: A National Portrait", http://www.cair-net.org/mosquereport/.

Barber, Benjamin R. *Jihad Versus McWorld.* New York: Ballantine Books, 1995.

Barnett, David, George T. Kurian, and Todd M. Johnson. *World Christian Encyclopedia.* Vol. 1. New York: Oxford University Press, 2001.

Bird, Christiane. *Neither East nor West.* New York: Washington Square Press, 2001.

Braswell, George W., Jr. *What You Need to Know About Islam and Muslims.* Nashville: Broadman and Holman, 2000.

————. *Islam: Its Prophets, Peoples, and Power.* Nashville: Broadman and Holman, 1996.

Brown, Stuart E. *Meeting in Faith.* Geneva: WCC Publications, 1989.

Buchanan, Patrick J. *The Death of the West.* New York: St. Martin's Press, 2002.

Emerson, Steven. *American Jihad.* New York: Free Press, 2002.

Esposito, John. *Unholy War: Terror in the Name of Islam.* New York: Oxford University Press, 2002.

Esposito, John, and John O. Voll. *Islam and Democracy.* New York: Oxford University Press, 1966.

Farah, Caesar E. *Islam.* Hauppauge, N.Y.: Barron's, 2000.

Flew, Antony. "Islam's War Against the West: Can It Abide a Secular State?" *Free Inquiry* 22 (spring 2002).

Frishman, Morton, et al. *The Mosque: History, Architectural Development, and Regional Diversity.* New York: Thames and Hudson, 1994.

George, Timothy. *Is the Father of Jesus the God of Muhammad?* Grand Rapids: Zondervan, 2002.

Haddad, Yvonne Yazbeck, and Jane Idleman Smith, eds. *Muslim Communities in North America.* Albany, N.Y.: State University of New York Press, 1994.

Haney, Marsha Snulligan. *Islam and Protestant African-American Churches: Responses Challenges to Religious Pluralism:* San Francisco: International Scholars Publications, 1999.

Hasan, Asma Gull. *American Muslims: The New Generation.* New York: Continuum, 2000.

Holden, David, and Richard Johns. *The House of Saud.* New York: Holt, Rinehart and Winston, 1981.

Hoogland, Eric, ed. *Twenty-Years of Islamic Revolution.* Syracuse: Syracuse University Press, 2002.

Huntington, Samuel P. *The Clash of Civilizations and the Remaking of World Order.* New York: Simon and Schuster, 1996.

Johnson, Patrick, and Jason Mandryk. *Operation World: Twenty-first Century.* London: Bethany House, 2001.

Kraft, Charles H. *Anthropology for Christian Witness.* Maryknoll, N.Y.: Orbis Books, 1998.

Kurth, James. "The American Way of Victory." *National Interest* (summer 2000).

Lacey, Robert. *The Kingdom: Arabia and The House of Sa'ud.* New York: Harcourt Brace Jovanovich, 1981.

Lippman, Thomas W. *Understanding Islam.* New York: Meridian, 1995.

Mernissi, Fatema. *Islam and Democracy: Fear of the Modern World.* Cambridge, Mass.: Perseus Publishing, 2002.

Meyers, Bryant L. *The New Context of World Missions.* Monrovia, Calif.: MARC, 1996.

Murad, Khurram. *Da'wah Among Non-Muslims in the West.* London: Islamic Foundation, 1986.

Murata, Sachiko, and William Chittich. *The Vision of Islam.* New York: Paragon House, 1994.

Nanji, Azim A., ed. *The Muslim Almanac.* New York: Gale Research, 1996.

Parfrey, Adam, ed. *Extreme Islam.* Los Angeles: Feral House, 2001.

Poston, Larry A. *The Changing Face of Islam in America.* Camp Hill, Pa.: Horizon Books, 2000.

Rashid, Ahmed. *Jihad: The Rise of Militant Islam in Central Asia.* New Haven: Yale University Books, 2002.

Ruthven, Malise. *Islam in the World.* London: Penguin Books, 2000.

Said, Edward W. *Covering Islam.* New York: Vintage Books, 1997.

Shahabuddin, Syed, and Theodore P. Wright. *India: Muslim Minority Politics and Society, Islam in Asia.* Ed. John L. Esposito. New York: Oxford University Press, 1987.

Siddiqui, Elisabeth. "A Brief History of Islam in the United States" at http://www.islamamerica.org/history.cfm.

Slack, James. Interview by author. Mill Valley, Calif., August 14, 2002.

Smith, Jane I. *Islam in America.* New York: Columbia University Press, 1999.

Voll, John Obert. *Islam: Continuity and Change in the Modern World.* 2d ed. Syracuse: Syracuse University Press, 1994.

Wagner, C. Peter. *Engaging the Enemy.* Ventura, Calif.: Regal Books, 1991.

Wilson, J. Christy. *Afghanistan: The Forbidden Harvest.* Elgin, Ill.: Cook, 1981.

Winters, Ralph D. *The Twenty-five Unbelievable Years, 1945–1969.* South Pasadena, Calif.: William Carey Library, 1970.